TATYASAHEB

TEJASWINI APTE-RAHM

TATYASAHEB

THE STORY OF A BOMBAY ENTREPRENEUR

WESTLAND
BUSINESS

WESTLAND
BUSINESS

Published by Westland Business, an imprint of Westland Books, a division of Nasadiya Technologies Private Limited, in 2025

No. 269/2B, First Floor, 'Irai Arul', Vimalraj Street, Nethaji Nagar, Alapakkam Main Road, Maduravoyal, Chennai 600095

Westland, the Westland logo, Westland Business and the Westland Business logo are the trademarks of Nasadiya Technologies Private Limited, or its affiliates.

ISBN: 9789371978194

10 9 8 7 6 5 4 3 2 1

Typeset by Jojy Philip

Printed at Manipal Technologies Limited, Manipal

For my father, Arvind Apte

Contents

Introduction xi

A Note on the Names Used in This Biography xix

1. The Early Years in Bombay: 1869–81 1
2. Tatya Returns to Bombay: 1892–1900 11
3. The Textile Years: 1900 Onwards 19
4. The Film Industry Years: 1917–32 54
5. The Phaltan Sugar Years: 1932–52 104
6. Oil, Paper, Cans, Land: Other Business Ventures 151
7. The Family 160
8. Tatya and Kaku 213

A Note on This Biography 230

Appendix 1: Annual Information About Kohinoor Mills 1933–51 235

Appendix 2: Filmography of the Hindustan Film Company 244

Appendix 3: Filmography of the Bharat Film Company 256

Notes 258

Bibliography 265

Family Tree of Shridhar Apte (Tatyasaheb's father)

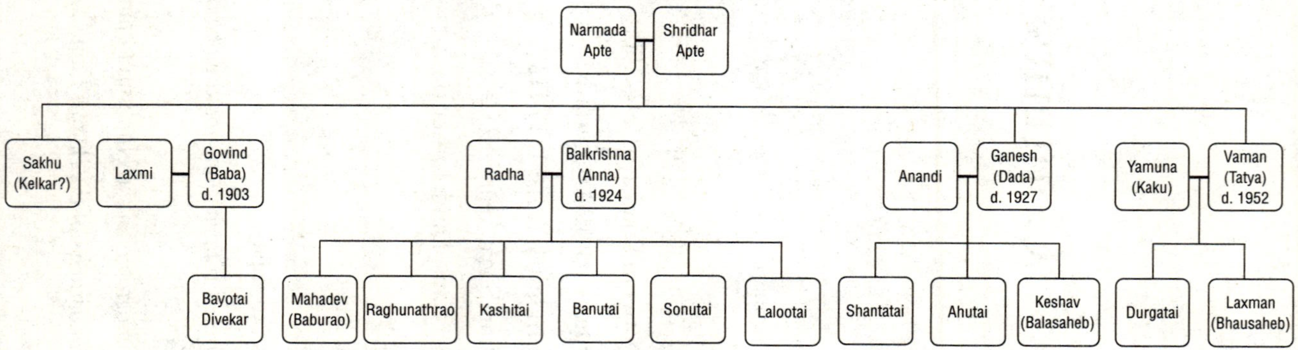

Family Tree of Vaman Shridhar Apte (Tatyasaheb)

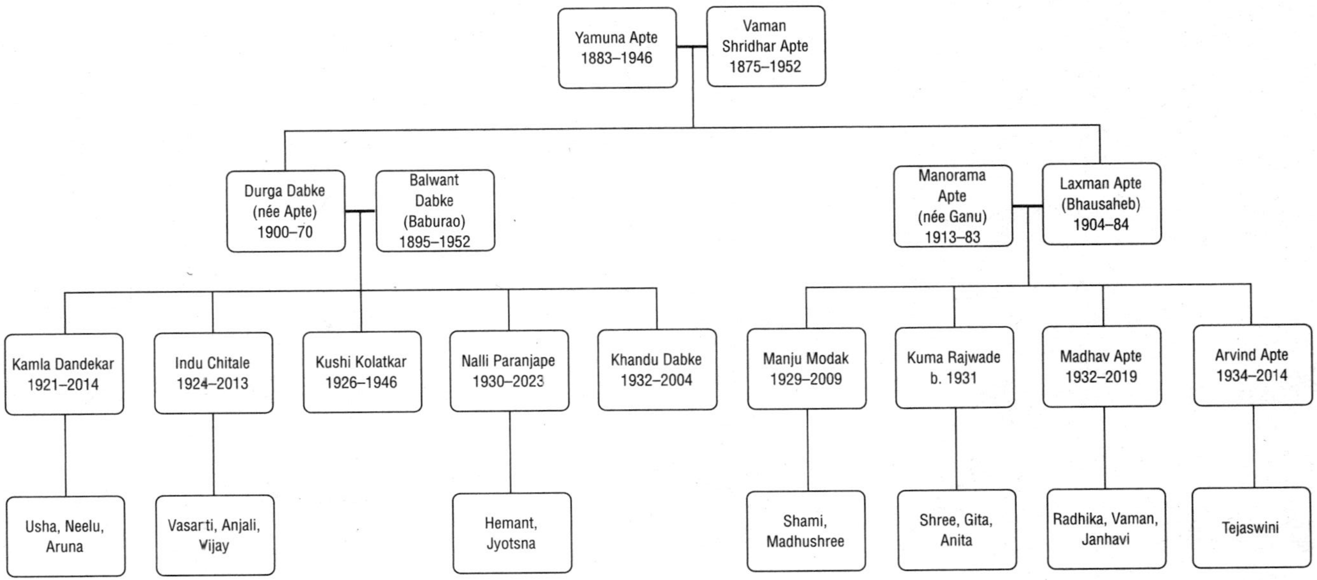

Introduction

ABOUT TWENTY-FIVE YEARS AGO, I LIVED FOR A FEW MONTHS IN the old family house on Prabhat Road in Pune, an elegant art deco structure full of polished dark wood and fading furnishings. I see it as if I were there right now: the dim rectangular living room is divided into two seating areas, two groups of chairs and sofas placed on fraying carpets. At one end is a wide, sunny opening into an enclosed courtyard, where clothes are often hung to dry. A small, quiet tortoise plods around the age-bleached stone flooring. It is still there years later. The light airiness disappears quite suddenly as one backs into the living room, and at the other end of this long room are a stillness and dustiness that remain peculiarly unshakeable in the face of dusting and sporadic family activity (no one lives permanently in this house). The windows at this quiet end look out onto an orchard of banana trees, planted close and thick, so that a green, leafy light filters into the room. On a wall, above a wood-framed door, are two small portraits. In one is an old man in a long grey-blue coat and red pagdi, seated on a low, wide-backed chair. His back is slightly stooped with age, but his body seems sturdy enough. He has not reached frailty yet. His gaze is steady through small, round-rimmed glasses, and his mouth obscured by a white moustache like a neat, thick brush.

He holds a walking cane in his hand. The other portrait is of his wife, a stern woman in a dark, red-bordered nine-yard sari that covers both her shoulders; she wears a large nose ring of pearls and precious stones. She looks middle-aged, not old, for her hair is still black and her bearing upright. Her eyes are stony. Her hair is pressed tightly against her scalp, combed into an invisible bun behind her head. She seems impatient and ill at ease with the whole business of portraiture, as if she would like to get back to her brisk domestic doings. The man is more temperate. He is aware that the portraits serve a purpose; indeed, there is a reason for commissioning them. Ordinary people don't commission portraits. It is the affluent and respected who do so; not just the affluent but more particularly those who are acutely aware that they leave behind a legacy, one that they take a natural pride in. A portrait says, look, here is a man who is wealthy, for he has the means to commission a portrait and the leisure to sit for it; who is cultured, because he appreciates the value of art, for what is a portrait but the transformation of one's own person into a thing of beauty and contemplation; who has foresight, because he leaves behind a reminder of what once was, and why it was, because a portrait is not simply a mimetic rendering on to canvas, but a signifier of wider proportions. Often it is an inspiration for generations to come, an object of admiration.

This uncomplicated faith in the forthcoming continuity of things and generations is a foreign and fascinating thing for me, for I have grown up in an age of unprecedented fragmentation and dispersal where entire families have been globalised, flung far and wide. Increasingly, we have seen ourselves as independent agents, free to do as we please, and only superficially part of a larger whole; superficial, because whether the larger whole is a family, a city or a country, we are free to exit and enter it as we please and to define conditional relationships with it. If we don't like it, we can leave. In this freedom lies the essential and thoroughly modern aloneness of the individual. Certainly there are ties that bind; but it is a much simpler affair to cut or modify those ties than ever before.

It is a world view that would have shocked and saddened the man and woman in those two portraits. They are my great-grandparents, Vaman Shridhar Apte and his wife Yamuna Apte, known to the family as Tatya and Kaku. But just as much as they would find my world incomprehensible, so I find theirs strange and mystifying, and I require a rather vigorous exercise of the imagination to comprehend their lives and motivations. I am reminded of *The Go-Between* and L.P. Hartley's declaration that 'the past is a foreign country: they do things differently there'. It is one of those phrases that has so often been repeated that it has lost its potency and is often simply used to glibly explain away the oddities of our ancestors. It is an extraordinary statement, though, pointing to the vast spatial and intellectual chasm between Now and Then; it combines a deep awareness of absence with a desire to regain old knowledge not only about factual events (the most easily accessible and perhaps the least interesting part of history), but about the texture and moods of another age.

Over the years, the thought occurred to me now and again that I would like to know more about my great-grandfather, find out about how he lived, what thoughts might have passed through his head, what he would have been like to sit down and *talk* to. I didn't know anything about him at all, other than the fact that he was a highly successful and respected gentleman, and that in business circles he was known as Vaman Seth or simply as V.S. Apte, and at home as Tatya or Tatyasaheb. He also featured in another portrait in the same house in Pune, a life-sized oil painting, cutting an impressive figure; I would sometimes stand before it gazing curiously at him.

For a while, as I started digging around for information and questioning family members about how it all used to be, I wafted along in a misty-eyed haze of nostalgia for large warm families and tree-lined avenues of Bombay, a time when quiet pursuits were the order of the day, a time when life was simpler. Then the nostalgia dimmed somewhat; it had to, because I also knew that all this took place in the shadow of shaven-headed widows, child marriages, excruciatingly complex notions of clean and unclean, pure and impure, not to mention a rather stiff formality between husband and wife, father and son, with age and seniority an iron-clad constraint to human relations within a family. Many of these were social mores that had existed in one form or another for hundreds of years and which dissolved within a single generation of the twentieth century.

And that is what finally brought me to the crux of my fascination with my great-grandfather's life: Vaman Shridhar Apte had lived through a period of time that was unprecedented in the rapidity and scope of global changes, political as well as social. In terms of family life, religious and social rituals and expectations from life, he, his parents and his ancestors would have had more similarities than differences across generations. But by the time he died, the young people of the country were getting ready to rock and roll. And he had lived but seventy-seven years.

Tatya was born in the nineteenth century, in 1875, at the height of empire—a time when 'the sun never set on the British Empire'. Just eighteen years earlier, the British had brutally suppressed the Indian Mutiny, resulting in the discrediting of the East India Company and the beginning of direct government control over India, ruled from London. When he was two years old, in 1877, Queen Victoria was proclaimed Empress of India. Eight years later, the Indian National Congress was formed in 1885. In 1911, the same year that Tatya got his big break in textiles with the British-managed Kohinoor Mills, George V was crowned King Emperor of India at a lavish Durbar in Delhi. In 1919, when Gandhi and the Congress began actively fighting for home rule, he had already invested in one of the few 'modern' industries of India, silent film production. Gandhi's civil disobedience campaign in the early 1930s coincided with the beginnings of the sugar industry in the Bombay Presidency, and with Tatya opening a sugar factory. His life spanned two world wars, the scourge of plague, the departure of the British, the partition of India, the assassination of Gandhi and the dawn of industrialisation and socialism.

Though he was a supporter of the Congress and the independence movement, there is no evidence that he took any active part in politics. It would probably be fair to conclude that his interest in politics remained at the level of reading the papers and discussing topical events with his friends. The backdrop may have been the morphing of the social and political landscape beyond recognition, but he was just one among millions determined to make it in what was even then the city of dreams and opportunities. Indeed, he had a hand quite literally in the weaving of dreams in his role as the managing partner in the Hindustan Film Company.

It is hard to say whether he possessed admirable foresight, or sheer luck, or simply a nose for instinctively smelling out sound business opportunities—most likely some combination of all these factors—for Vaman Shridhar Apte made a dizzying amount of money by hitching his fortunes to the three foremost industries in what would later become the state of Maharashtra, just as they were about to take off: textiles, cinema and sugar.

Of Vaman Seth, as he was known by his contemporaries in the textile business, one gets the impression of an energetic entrepreneur beavering away at his various activities, one bee in the vast honey-making beehive that was Bombay. He went to work, made immense amounts of money, upgraded from one room in a chawl to a sea-facing mansion and looked after his extended family. Babies were born and some years later duly married; festivals were celebrated and the age-old rituals of a Kokanastha Brahmin household were performed and protected. What we now think of as era-defining historical events would have begun life, as always, as a fragmented series of newspaper headlines and inside columns, read while the average member of the Apte family was thinking of the bills to be paid tomorrow, or the puzzling question of what to call the new baby, or why tea seemed to be late this afternoon. While those historical events were unfolding, entrepreneurs, cooks, office-goers, artists, sportsmen, school children, mothers and daughters were going about their daily lives, dreaming their dreams and nurturing their ambitions. Vaman Shridhar Apte was one such individual, the son of a small-time trade agent, who happened to find success in a rather spectacular fashion.

Though he was a successful entrepreneur and eminent in his community and professional circles, he was by no means famous. Certainly his would not be the only rags-to-riches story of that period. But history being made up primarily of the composite doings of ordinary folk, the story of this individual's life would, I felt, be a documentation of social history and would record at least partially a way of life that is lost forever.

But no less is it a personal journey in discovering why I am what I am. Every family has a certain flavour to it—and even though my lifestyle would doubtless be shocking and alien to my great-grandfather, I think that basic flavour would still be recognisable to him today.

As my research into Tatya's life and times progressed, it became increasingly clear to me that each generation or era has its own complexities, and no matter how distant they seem from where I stand, it would be superficial to just say 'life was simpler then', because I can also think of a hundred ways in which life is simpler and freer today. And yet, there is no denying that there is something seductive about those old black and white photographs, something about those faces—perhaps it is the quiet assurance of those days that life would always be more or less the same, that the quality of the sunlight would never change. The thing that is truly enviable about that generation is that perhaps it was the last one to believe, without excruciating doubts, that everything was going to be just fine.

A Note on the Names Used in This Biography

I REFER TO VAMAN SHRIDHAR APTE AS TATYA, AND HIS WIFE Yamuna Apte as Kaku, as this is how they were known to the family. Similarly, I have referred to Tatya's brothers as Baba, Anna and Dada.

I have referred to Tatya's son as Bhausaheb instead of Laxman, and his nephews as Raghunathrao (instead of Raghunath), Baburao (instead of Mahadev) and Balasaheb (instead of Keshav), again because this is how they were known in the family.

Apart from the above, I have taken the liberty of referring to people by their first names purely for the sake of clarity.

Chapter 1

The Early Years in Bombay 1869–81

THE ORIGINS OF THE APTE FAMILY LIE IN DEVACHE GOTHANE, A small village on the Konkan coast. Tatya's father Shridhar Apte lived in Rajapur, about 25 kilometres away, near the Arjuna river.

In Rajapur, Shridhar owned small cargo boats used for coastal trade, and worked as an agent or broker in sea trade where he shipped goods to be distributed and sold. Shortly before 1869, his boats drowned in a storm, and some of the fishermen who sailed those boats were lost at sea. Unable to bear the grief of the families whose men had drowned, afraid of facing the merchants (and perhaps creditors) he was dealing with, and no doubt feeling that he was somehow responsible for the disaster, he fled Rajapur. For a while his whereabouts were unknown. It appears that Shridhar and his wife Narmada were then looked after by Narmada's family in Mutat, a village about 20 kilometres away, before finally arriving in Bombay in 1869, to start life afresh. With them were their children—at this time it is likely that Baba, their eldest son, was around ten years old. Possibly one or two more children had also been born by then. Tatya, the youngest of four brothers, was born in Bombay a few years later, in 1875. Tatya spent the first six years of his life in the city's Girgaon locality.

Shridhar was not poor—but nor was he wealthy, for he had left his home in dire circumstances. He settled in Kandewadi, in Girgaon, and began working in a shop known as Siddhaga's Pedhi on a monthly salary of 15 rupees. He did what he knew best—he was an agent, or a middleman, for all kinds of goods. Not very much more is known about him, and it seems that he may have died about a decade after arriving in Bombay.

A Family of Seven

Shridhar and Narmada had a daughter, Sakhu, and four sons. The sons were Govind (the eldest, known as Baba), Balkrishna (known as Anna), Ganesh (known as Dada) and Vaman (the youngest, known as Tatya).

What was Bombay like when Shridhar Apte arrived in Girgaon in 1869? And what kind of city was it that Tatya grew up in till the age of six? In 1869, Bombay was clearly the place to be to try one's luck. Within a couple of decades, it had evolved from a sleepy island to a wealth-generating treasure of the British Empire. From that point of view, Shridhar's decision to move to Bombay was well timed. In 1875, the Prince of Wales* visited the city. A member of the Municipal Corporation described the riches of the city in a speech to the Prince, declaring that 'from a barren rock, whose only wealth consisted in coconuts and dried fish, whose scanty population of 10,000 souls paid a total of revenue to the state of not more than 6,000 pounds a year, whose trade was of

* The eldest son of Queen Victoria, later King Edward VII.

less value than that of Thana and Bassein and whose climate was so deadly to Europeans that two monsoons were said to be the age of a man, she has blossomed into a fair and wholesome city, with a population which makes her rank next to London among the cities of the British Empire, with a Municipal revenue amounting to 30,000 pounds sterling a year and with a foreign commerce worth 45 millions and yielding customs duties to the imperial treasury three millions a year'.[1]

It was now a city of about eight lakh people,[2] with railways, hotels, wide metalled roads, educational institutions, spinning and weaving mills, markets spilling over with an array of goods and a number of harbours and dockyards where everything from fish to cotton was loaded and traded. The city teemed with the activity of all variety of men from far-flung parts of the country.

In 1853, sixteen years prior to the arrival of the Apte family in the city, the Great Indian Peninsula Railway had inaugurated Bombay's first railway, from where trains could chug along 34 kilometres of rail tracks to Thana. The opening ceremony was performed by Lord Elphinstone in the heat of April. The first train, known locally as aag-gaadi ('a car that moves with fire'), was decorated with flags and departed from the railway station—no more than a small wooden structure—at Bori Bunder, with a celebratory band playing in one of the carriages. The day was declared a holiday and thousands of people stood along the tracks to look upon a scene that many considered to be some kind of harnessing of demonic powers. K.N. Kabraji, editor of the *Rast Gaftar* newspaper, wrote in his memoirs: 'Most of them would not believe at first, that this strange locomotive called the steam engine could be a product of human skill and science. They saw no horses or bullocks were employed to draw the train and were convinced that the white man … had employed some demons or other invisible powers to draw so swiftly and easily the enormous load of wagons and carriages. There was no other way to account for this wonder, and so they brought propitiatory offerings of coconuts to the unearthly power and were ready to worship it.'[3]

Just ten years later, in 1863, this was followed by a railway which ran over the Bhor Ghat to the Deccan, again viewed with incredulity by the locals, who perhaps saw it as an even greater feat for scaling the mountains. This was vital infrastructure that would contribute to the growth of Bombay as a city of commerce. On the heels of this, an agreement between the East India Company and the Bombay Baroda & Central India Railway resulted in a railway line from Surat reaching Bombay in 1864, the aim being to ensure that cotton grown in Gujarat would easily be transported in large quantities to the mills of Bombay. From then on, the number of trains and services kept increasing, and by the time Shridhar arrived at Kandewadi in 1869, it was to a city familiar with the railway and its ongoing expansion.

On the streets of Bombay, Shridhar and his family would have seen the bustling of different kinds of horse-drawn carriages like victorias, hansoms and landaus, as well as palanquins and bullock carts—the conventional modes of transport then. Added to these was the introduction of trams. In 1874, five years after the family moved to Bombay, the Tramway Company began services in the city. Nine hundred horses were stabled at Colaba and near Victoria Garden, and horse-drawn trams ran from Colaba to Parel on a straight route, with various branch lines along the way. A tram was pulled by six or eight horses, the animals wearing hoods to protect them from the sun. Each carriage held forty passengers, seated in rows of five.

Gas lamps had made a relatively recent public appearance in the city—on an October evening in 1865, just a few years earlier, crowds of people had followed the lamp lighter at Bhendi Bazaar, the Esplanade and Churchgate as he went about lighting the first lamps.[4]

Mumbaiche Varnan,[5] a book written by Govind Narayan in 1863, gives a contemporary account of the bustling life of the streets: he estimated that over one hundred hawkers shouting out their wares in various languages passed one's door from morning to night, including hawkers of sweet and salty neera who started as early as 4 a.m., and dozens of mango sellers in the hot season carrying baskets on their heads. The presence of the high and mighty was evident too: 'One can daily spot the camps of the Indian Badshahs, kings and other nobles. One day the king of Nepal, Jung Bahadur, will arrive; the Imam of Muscat on the next … the Raja of Satara, the Maharaja of Kolhapur … tomorrow a Nimbalkar, the day after a Raste, followed by a Patwardhan, a Jamkhandikar, and a Kurundwadkar … every day one can see these people on the street, accompanied by their entourage.'

Chowpatty had previously been a forested area, but by now was full of 'beautiful houses and gardens', while by the sea were seven or eight warehouses for storing wood. Further afield, there was rice cultivation in places like Mahalaxmi, Worli, Parel, Mahim and Matunga, including vegetable and fruit farms. In the creek between Mahalaxmi and Worli was the rocky platform of the Haji Ali tomb, which was transformed into an island during high tide. Byculla is described by Govind Narayan as being 'the choice place of residence for the rich', with the fashion being to build houses that resembled mini-forts, while Parel was also packed with wealthy residents. There were numerous docks handling all manner of goods from cotton and tobacco to grains, coal, fish, opium, vegetables, wood and much more. Nearby were various trading establishments that benefited from proximity to the docks; for example, at Arthur Bunder in Colaba there were two large cotton mills, warehouses for storing cotton and a wharf for unloading goods, while nearby was a factory that produced cannons and cannonballs.

Behind the Mumbadevi temple was a lengthy market where one could find Amritsari and Kashmiri shawls, precious stones, copperware, rows of coloured sweets on display, dried fruit from Muscat, as well as shops selling coconuts, oil, sugar and so on. Just near this market sat the opium traders, mainly Marwaris and Gujjars, who conducted their trade on the street itself. During the mango season the fruit market was 'so bright and pretty', writes Govind Narayan, that 'many people come here just to have a look at the mangoes ... One can easily see fifty different kinds of mangoes in as many colours.' He complains that while most fruit can be had in Bombay all round the year, 'the prices are outrageous', adding that 'the prices can be so steep that for a rupee one can get only two mangoes, or four pomegranates, or eight figs, or about ten bananas'.[6]

There is no knowing, of course, what Shridhar's interests were, or what he had the time and inclination to do. However, had he gone on a stroll around town he would have seen not only the colourful sights as described in Govind Narayan's memoir, but also a city dotted with grand colonial buildings, like Watson's Hotel on the Esplanade or the School of Art (later known as the J.J. School of Art) with its ground and first floors fronted by geometrical rows of arches. He would have seen the new metalled Queen's Road, a clean and wide road that ran straight down the sea front; it was flanked by a railway track and the sea front on one side, and by a row of coconut trees on the other. These tall, well-spaced trees marked the perimeter of the green expanse of the Oval Maidan, and their fronds would have rustled noisily in the salty breeze blowing in from the sea. From 1878 onwards, from Queen's Road he would have seen the 280-foot Rajabai Tower attached to the university library building, dominating the view beyond the Oval Maidan; perhaps, if he was an indulgent father, he might have taken the three year-old Vaman and his older brothers to look at the clock tower that sounded every quarter of an hour, and to hear its joybells, which could be heard many miles away, playing tunes like 'Blue Bells of Scotland'.[7] He may have taken his boys to the Band Stand where the Governor's Band played thrice a week at 5 p.m. to entertain the public. Or perhaps the family joined the hundreds of people who went along to see Empress Victoria's birthday celebrations, held on 24 May each year, with a drill, cannon fire and an English band playing.

He might have glimpsed the green trees and sloping brown tiled roofs of the Europeans-only Bombay Gymkhana, which opened its doors for the first time in the same year that Vaman, his youngest son, was born. There were theatres around the city too—by 1875 a theatre on Grant Road was regularly showing plays in Marathi, Hindi, Gujarati and Urdu.[8] Perhaps the Apte family ventured to have a look at the ice-factory in Girgaon where crowds of people went to see ice being manufactured—ice was still a novelty to the extent that just a few years earlier, in 1863, Govind Narayan wrote in all earnestness, 'It has to be stored very carefully because if it is exposed to air, it melts and becomes water ... It is very cold to touch.' He added, also, that 'hardly any Hindu consumes this product'.[9]

Of course, then, as now, there was a rather different side to Bombay, one outside the carefully planned areas of Colaba, Fort and the Esplanade. This was the world of the working classes, many of whom settled, like Shridhar, in Girgaon. There was a lively street life here, but living conditions were crowded and unsanitary, with a scarcity of services like water supply and sewerage.[10] Historian Chandavarkar's description of Bombay's congestion in the nineteenth and early twentieth century could easily pass off as a modern gripe: 'In the absence of any coherent or sustained urban planning, and sometimes because of its monumental incompetence, the prodigious growth of the city in the nineteenth century had been accompanied by the rather haphazard settlement of the island. Buildings were thus squeezed into every available space between municipal thoroughfares.' Quoting a government report of 1907, Chandavarkar writes that town planners in the early twentieth century were confronted with 'the extraordinary anomaly of rice being cultivated and buffaloes grazing within a few miles of land selling at Rs.150 per square yard, while the bulk of the population is herded together in the south and centre of the town'.[11] In 1871, the Bombay Health Officer wrote in his report about the scarcity of hygienic or sufficient water in the city and the 'pitiable sight … of men, women and children awaiting around a pipe eagerly and quarrelling for the miserable dribble from it'.[12]

Bombay, via Gujarat: 1881–92

By 1875, when Tatya was born, the family appears to have moved out of Kandewadi, as his birth took place in Damulji Mauji's Wadi (later known as Amrut Wadi), situated near Angryanchi Wadi in Girgaon. His primary education, till 1881, was done in a school conducted in the grounds of a temple near a place called Paach Deool (Five Temples). The school was run by a man called Dinkar Pantoji Date. Presumably Anna and Dada attended the same school.[13]

Strangely, though a good amount of information was to be found on all four brothers, there were no leads regarding their sister. Not one of the many family members I interviewed was even clear whether her name was Bhagu or Sakhu, though it is likely that her married surname was Kelkar. The four brothers were extremely close over the years. The bonds between them were so strong that not only did their grandchildren practically grow up together but even today many of their great-grandchildren are in close and affectionate contact with each other. Given this background, it is peculiar that no oral history, not even a stray anecdote, about their sister seems to have survived. Finally, when a search through an old box of papers revealed Baba's will, in which he had gifted some money to his sister, it became clear that her name was in fact Sakhu—and that's all that is known about her.

Baba, the eldest brother, had begun working in Bombay while his younger siblings were still at school—he completed his school education in Bombay and got a job with the customs department at a monthly salary of 45 rupees.[14] He also began earning 45 rupees a month for teaching one Vasudev Jagannath. It is not known how old his pupil was or what he was teaching him. Nevertheless, for Baba it was the beginning of a career in education.

In 1880, Baba passed his B.A. and in 1881 secured a job in Navsari, in present-day Gujarat, as headmaster of the Sir Cowasjee Jehangir High School. By this time Tatya was only six years old, and moved with his elder brother from Bombay to Navsari. The rest of the family also moved to Navsari around this time. The only exception was Dada, who stayed behind in Bombay as he was doing his matriculation. It may be that their father, Shridhar, passed away around this period. The family's story now appears to have centred around the fortunes of Baba, the eldest son.

Baba served as headmaster of the school from 1881 to 1886. In 1886, he entered the services of Baroda State, employed by the Maharaja of Baroda. His job was in the Department of Barkhali and Survey Settlement, for which the entire family moved from Navsari to Baroda.

In Baroda, the family lived in Anandpura, and initially stayed in the home of one Rambhau Gokhale. As a side job, Baba began tutoring one Laxman Jagannath, possibly a relation of his old pupil Vasudev Jagannath in Bombay. At the time of moving from Navsari to Baroda in 1886, Tatya was in the third standard of an English-medium school, and was eleven years old. Now in Baroda he joined the Baroda High School, while his elder brother Dada took up a job in 1887 at the same school as a teacher, where he remained for four years. Meanwhile, Anna matriculated in 1886 and joined Baroda College for further education.

In 1889, Baba once again moved, this time to Palsana, where he was posted as an official, still in the employ of Baroda State. He went alone this time, as his three brothers were studying or teaching in Baroda. However, it was soon time for Tatya to move again, this time because of Dada, who got a job in 1890 as a school teacher in Pattan. Tatya, now fourteen, moved to Pattan along with Dada and continued his education there. Later in the same year, Baba was posted from Palsana to Dwarka. Just a year after that, in 1891, Tatya moved from Pattan to Dwarka to join Baba there. He was sixteen and doing his matriculation at this time, and this was the fourth school he had attended within a span of six years.

It is not known whether Tatya followed his brothers out of choice or necessity. However, it is likely that the disruption to his education, created by these frequent moves, discouraged Tatya from the scholarly career paths of his brothers. Clearly the family greatly valued education, but Tatya was the only sibling who decided to try his luck in the world of business.

In Dwarka, Baba came into contact with a man called Vallabhdas Jairam. This acquaintance was to be of great consequence in the fortunes of Tatya, as well as the entire family—Vallabhdas happened to have a cloth business in Bombay's Mulji Jetha Market (also known as MJ Market). He agreed to take on Tatya as an unpaid trainee.

When Tatya left Dwarka for Bombay, the year was 1892 and Tatya was seventeen years old. He was hard-working, ambitious and fluent in Gujarati, Marathi and English—and at the end of the nineteenth century, Bombay was still the ideal city in which to try one's luck.

Chapter 2

Tatya Returns to Bombay
1892–1900

THE TEXTILE INDUSTRY WAS BOOMING IN BOMBAY. IN 1880, THERE had been forty-two spinning and weaving mills in the city. This number increased to sixty-eight mills in 1885 and ninety-four mills in 1890. By 1895, three years after Tatya began work at MJ Market, the number had gone up to 102. By 1900, there were no less than 136 spinning and weaving mills in Bombay,[1] an increase of more than 200 per cent in the span of twenty years.

By the late nineteenth century, Bombay was the largest cotton market in Asia and an important node in the cotton piece goods trade. Cotton textile was India's—and Bombay's—most important industry and determined the economy and social organisation of the city of Bombay. Indeed, the textile industry was the only large-scale employer of labour in the city. From the late nineteenth century onwards, the city's growth and prosperity, and its status as a leading commercial centre, were built on the foundations of this industry.[2] It was on the wave of this boom that

Tatya began working at MJ Market, the biggest wholesale textile market in the city.

Freshly arrived in Bombay in 1892, Tatya took up lodgings in Girgaon in Damulji's Chawl. He was back among his old childhood haunts now. Just a few months later, around 1892–93, he had bad news from Dwarka—Baba's wife, Laxmi, had passed away. Having lived with Baba as a young boy, Laxmibai must have been a mother figure to Tatya. Her death surely came as a blow, heightened by the fact that he was alone in the city and far from his loved ones. Despite this family tragedy, Tatya had to get down to working and settling into a new life. In Damulji's Chawl, Tatya shared his room with a man called Nana and ate his meals at Maameenchi Khanaval located in Samartha Chawl. Khanavals were eating houses catering to the working classes, particularly mill and dock workers, as well as middle-class office-goers who did not have access to cooking facilities in the small, often shared chawl rooms where they lived. The khanavals charged between one and four annas, and were often places where caste taboos had to necessarily be left at the door for there was an unavoidable intermingling of people of varied backgrounds within. Some of the khanavals provided accommodation as well.[3] Often it was a place run by a widow. Unlike at a restaurant, one paid the bill on a monthly basis. Govind Narayan, in *Mumbaiche Varnan*, writes: 'The prices are very low ... For an anna, one gets plain rice, buttermilk kadhi, a vegetable and just enough ghee to purify the food ... Those who pay two annas are provided with hot water for their bath, a room to sit and sleep, and a meal consisting of pulses, rice, a couple of vegetables, saar, curds, ghee, pickles and chapatis made of wheat. For four annas, one can get clothes laundered and meals are served with puris and a sweet.'[4]

Thus Tatya began his new routine of work and life at Vallabhdas Jairam's shop in MJ Market in 1892. As a trainee, he would have been expected to do a little bit of everything and must have learnt the ropes quite quickly because, just over a year later, he stopped working for Vallabhdas and in 1894 began a small business venture: he joined a man called Govindjee Karsandas as a four-anna partner (a 25 per cent partner since there were 16 annas in a rupee). Govindjee was a cloth retailer and had a shop in Bhajia Galli in MJ Market. From this venture, Tatya was paid 15 rupees every month for immediate expenses. Later in life, when narrating his memoirs to his nephew, Tatya called it 'pocket money'. But at the time, it must have been satisfying for this novice to earn some money from his own business. At nineteen years old, this was Tatya's first attempt at getting out of the grind of his traineeship and putting some of his own earnings into a business. However, he also decided to gain more experience by joining yet another shop as an apprentice, where he was assigned outdoor work—this shop belonged to Morarjee Veljee, who was the uncle of Govindjee, his new business partner. In another early attempt at business in the same year, Tatya formed a partnership with four other men to rent a room in Khatryachi Chawl in Girgaon for 6 rupees a month, most likely to run some kind of small textile business. Tatya may have also shifted his residence to Khatryachi Chawl around this time, very close to Khetwadi. These were years of hard work—there are reports of him having done manual work as well, such as carrying bundles of cloth on his back through the streets, possibly for Morarjee Veljee, and often working eighteen hours a day. Meanwhile, having become addicted to beedis, he sometimes used to walk from Khatryachi Chawl to MJ Market to save a few coins on transport, which he could then use as smoking money.

The year 1894 was a milestone for Tatya because of these first forays into small-scale business; it was also a new beginning in his personal life for in the same year, even before joining Govindjee as a partner, he had married. His bride was called Ganga Gokhale. While he was nineteen years old, she was about eleven or twelve, as per the customs of the time. On marrying Tatya, Ganga's name was changed to Yamuna. The newly married couple lived in Khatryachi Chawl after a wedding ceremony that was extremely modest—so modest in fact, that the varaat, or bridal procession, normally taken through the streets, was simply taken from one room to another as a kind of token procession.

Poor they may have been, but living in Khatryachi Chawl they were firmly in an area inhabited by the middle classes: Girgaon had become, by the mid-nineteenth century, a residential area for a 'respectable' Maharashtrian middle class, including those who were still rising in the world.[5]

Though Yamuna came from a well-to-do family, she proved to be a thrifty housewife. Both she and Tatya were inordinately fond of mangoes. In mango season, therefore, the daily menu was only aamras-poli (mango pulp and chapatti). It became a staple diet for them for about two months, saving on the family budget by cutting out other dishes. Another way she economised was to save on the oil used for lamps. They had two rooms at Khatryachi Chawl, and there was no electricity. So she would keep an oil lamp in the doorway between the two rooms so that only one was needed to light up both. Every bit of money counted, and she was careful with what they had.

Why did Yamuna, whose father was an engineer or surveyor in the government, get married to a young man who was living in a congested chawl and whose future was still a question mark? The answer is perhaps to be found in the fact that in those days, the background of the family mattered more than the material wealth of the bride or groom. The fact that Tatya's brothers were all well-educated would have gone in his favour. Moreover, Yamuna was not a beauty; she was short of height, a bit plump even, and by the time she was eleven years old, her parents were worried that she was getting a little too old to find a good husband. From Tatya's point of view, a plus point was that Yamuna was said to be paiguni, meaning that she was said to have good fortune in her feet, and that she would bring prosperity into their lives. All things taken into account, it must have appeared a suitable match. Tatya and Yamuna's marriage was a success. Neither did the couple remain in humble circumstances for long, nor did they experience marital discord.

In Khatryachi Chawl, Tatya had taken up rooms next to the Lele family—relations of his mother, whose maiden surname was Lele. The Joshi family also lived in Khatryachi Chawl, and the son of the family, later known as Joshi bua, used to come round to play cards with Tatya. These friendships were to last for many years to come. Even when Tatya had moved to his mansion on Pedder Road, every couple of weeks he would send a message to his old friends from Girgaon—Bhide, Joshi bua, Govindrao Abhyankar—inviting them for a card game of bezique.

In 1896, only two years after their marriage, Tatya and Yamuna had to flee from Bombay due to a severe outbreak of bubonic plague. The 1896 plague in the city was a disaster that had been waiting to happen. The British had been more concerned, over the years, with developing the commercial infrastructure of the city rather than investing in improving living conditions for the local population. Municipal money went into roads rather than sanitation. Selective improvement was undertaken, with facilities being improved primarily in the quarters where Europeans were more likely to venture. So it was that as early as 1848, the Girgaon and Kalbadevi roads had their drains covered since they were the two principal thoroughfares of what was called the Native Town, and were the roads most often used by Europeans. But even as late as 1925, when there were more sewers in Bombay than in any other city of the East, the poorer parts of Bombay had none at all. Much before the plague broke out, municipal health officials had been predicting some kind of health calamity due to the abysmal sanitary conditions and poor drainage system. In 1875, the annual report of the Health

Officer of Bombay stated that some terrible disease could well 'arise and sweep away the most effete of the population'. In 1892, the health officer wrote in his annual report: 'There will surely come a time when the population of each district will not be able to live in health.' All these progressively dire warnings crystallised in 1896, when the long-feared health catastrophe finally raised its head in the form of bubonic plague. The city emptied out, with about half its population running away. Street corners saw open bidding for labour as businesses found themselves without manpower; wages doubled and had to be paid on a daily basis.[6]

Tatya and Yamuna fled to Baroda to stay with family, though it is not clear which of his three brothers were in Baroda at this point. The following year, in 1897, Baroda was also struck by plague, and the entire family fled the city to a safer rural location at Ghayaj, not far from Baroda.

By 1898, two years after the initial outbreak of disease in Bombay, the danger of plague was over in Baroda, and the Apte family returned to Baroda. Meanwhile, the partnership that Tatya had begun in 1894 along with Govindjee in Bombay had started incurring losses—the instability caused by the plague was one of the major reasons for this. At the age of twenty-three, Tatya was fed up and disheartened by all the setbacks and unsettled existence of the past couple of years, and in April 1898 he decided to go to Bombay to wind up the business and settle in Baroda for good. But while in Bombay, before leaving for Baroda, he went to meet Vallabhdas Jairam, who had been his first employer in MJ Market six years earlier. Vallabhdas advised Tatya to remain in Bombay and not give up. Set up an independent shop and try again, was his advice to the demoralised young man. Vallabhdas happened to be a cloth selling agent of the New Great Eastern Mills in Bombay, and he assured Tatya that he would use his position and knowledge to help Tatya as much as possible. When

Tatya related all this to Baba, his elder brother advised him to do as Vallabhdas had said.

So it was that instead of winding up things, Tatya set about preparing to open his own shop.

On 1 July 1898 Tatya opened his own, independent shop in 6th Lane, Chandra Chowk, in MJ Market. The shops in MJ Market were known as pedhis. Tatya's shop remained with him till the end of his life. Being situated in MJ Market, and having followed the advice of Vallabhdas, who was a selling agent, Tatya's business too was a selling agency. Though Tatya owned the shop, he had no capital with which to buy goods; so Vallabhdas, true to his word, helped him out by supplying him goods on credit. The arrangement probably was that Vallabhdas supplied Tatya with cloth from the New Great Eastern Mills, with Tatya paying him only after he had sold the cloth himself from his new shop.

In the very first year, Tatya made a profit of 300 rupees. It was a good start. From then on, there was no looking back. Tatya had chanced upon a business he was good at, and which turned out to be lucky for him. It turned out to be a time of other good news as well—in June 1898, his brother Anna had a son, a cause for celebration, being the first male child among the four brothers. In November, Tatya and Yamuna too had a son—they named their first child Shankar. At this time Tatya was twenty-three and Yamuna was sixteen years old. Their happiness was short-lived, however—while Tatya's business was doing even better a year later in 1899, with a profit of 1,100 rupees, tragedy struck with his son Shankar passing away—the child would have been less than a year old.

Yamuna was soon pregnant again and gave birth to a baby girl on 8 October 1900, about a year after the death of their son. They named their daughter Durga. To their shock, she had been born with a deformed arm which was partially paralysed. Yamuna's mother, known as Rahtyachi Aai, could not understand why

Tatya and Yamuna loved their daughter so dearly. Leave her be, Yamuna's mother would say, why are you looking after her? This view certainly reflected the prejudices of the time—a girl child, and that too a 'deformed' one, could only be a burden on the family. But Tatya refused to listen to his mother-in-law. She is my dear child, he would say, and she has brought me great luck—for it was in this year that Tatya made an impossibly large profit of approximately 12,000 rupees.

Chapter 3

The Textile Years
1900 Onwards

The Early Years in Textiles: 1900–11

FROM 1900 ONWARDS, TATYA ENTERED A PERIOD OF GREAT success in the textile business. The grand profits of 1900 were a remarkable turnaround in the career of the twenty-five-year-old. At this time, he was perhaps becoming known in textile circles as an up-and-coming businessman, and was known to his business colleagues as 'Vaman Seth'. The first year of the new century, however, was not a good one. In 1901, he set up another shop in MJ Market, opposite his initial shop. The new shop was set up in the name of Mahadev Govind (Mahadev was Anna's son, and Govind was his eldest brother Baba's real name). However, from the beginning, nothing went right. Within a week of opening this shop, Tatya fell ill with Guinea worm disease and was bedridden for six weeks. Meanwhile it turned out that the man hired to look after the shop was dishonest. Within four months, Tatya decided to close this shop and move on.

In 1900, due to the great famine that overtook western India, there was a severe scarcity of cotton, with many of the mills in Bombay and Ahmedabad having to close down for long periods. For the next four years, the textile industry hit a bad patch, and some of the weaker concerns were sold off at highly depressed prices.[1] Despite the low fortunes of the textile industry, Tatya appears to have pulled through fairly well during this period.

In 1902, he acquired the selling agency of the New Islam Mills belonging to Haji Ali Mohammed Haji Kasam, whose mills were located on Suparibaug Road in Parel. It was a relatively small mill, but as its selling agent, Tatya had the opportunity to build up a good reputation.

During this period of early success, Tatya's eldest brother, Baba, passed away in 1903. He was no more than about forty-four years old, and left behind a daughter, Bayotai. She was his only child. He also left behind his second wife. After his first wife died around 1892–93, Baba had remarried—his second wife was Laxmi Sahasrabuddhe, but they had no children together. While Tatya had been finding his way in Bombay, Baba had been posted to various places such as Dehegaon, Kamrej, Siddhapur and finally Amreli, in the service of Baroda State. He had been a father figure to Tatya—there was a gap of about sixteen years between them—and his early death must have come as a great blow.

An interesting memento belonging to Baba has survived up to the present day: a pocket-sized notebook with a thin red leather cover, in fairly good condition save for one ripped-off corner. It provides an intriguing insight into the family life and allegiances within Tatya's joint family. Only a few pages have been used. It begins with three pages titled 'My Assets', dated 1902, written with a thick-nibbed pen and black ink, in hard-to-decipher cursive writing. These three pages include a list of postal savings bank accounts and amounts in the names of various family members. Then come three pages entitled 'My Wishes', in which he has written out a kind of last will, dated December 1902 and written in Dwarka. Since Baba passed away in 1903, he must have known in 1902 that he probably did not have long to live, perhaps due to illness. It is likely that these pages were a draft for a more formal will, because even though he has added his signature at the bottom, the notebook is also a sort of domestic scribble book (roughly written in pencil on another page is a list in Modi script which, if deciphered, would likely show something like a list of household provisions, followed by somebody's measurements probably to be given to a tailor, both lists dated 1900.)

The informal will makes for interesting reading:

My *wishes.*

My assets in all are more than 50,000 Rs—Out of this sum Bhaga claims Rs 1200, Ganu's I can't exactly state but say Rs 7,000 at the most, Waman's† say Rs 10,000 giving him the credit for all the profit he made in the shop.*

The balance at my credit Rs 31,800. Deducting however Rs 1,800 for any error, Rs 30,000. Yet deducting Rs 5,000 more for any discrepancy I take the balance at Rs 25,000. Which may be distributed as under.

- *Sakhu my sister Rs 750—in addition to what stands in her name in the shop.*
- *Bayo‡ or rather her son Rs 4,000.*
- *My wife—Rs 6,000—out of the interest she to defray her expenses in a style befitting my position. My dear brothers would not object to it. She not [sic] to touch the capital. However if any urgent need be she may touch it say to the extent of Rs 200 for pilgrimage. On her demise the capital to go to Babu.§ I wish she should not touch capital because her tendencies are on her brother's side. I don't wish my money should go there unless it be for education.*

* Ganesh, his brother, also known as Dada.

† Tatya.

‡ Baba's daughter, an only child.

§ Baba's nephew, i.e. Anna's son, known as Baburao.

Education to be understood to be—given to a Brahmin student and not as brother to my wife.

- *Charity*

  Education Rs 5,000—from interest
  Water (well) Rs 400—to be built up to Rs 250 + 150 for maintenance
  Clothing Rs 600—from interest
  Food Rs 1,500—from interest

  7500

- *Children*

  Kashi Rs 800 - marriage dowry*
  Awdi† Rs 750 - marriage dowry
  Dwarki Rs 700 - marriage dowry
  Durgi‡ Rs 700 - marriage dowry
  Babu§ Rs 1,800

  3,750

  Rs 22,000

I want to dispose of as stated above and my younger brothers will, I am sure, respect my wishes. I have given them education and that is sufficient. I have made my youngest brother stand on his legs. As for education sum, they are at liberty to deposit it in the name of my dear mother Narmada bai to whose kindness I owe everything and through me my brothers.

—Govind Shridhar Apte.

In this extremely personal document, the following points are worth noting: there is a particular mention of Tatya—he is singled out for the largest share of assets, 10,000 rupees, due to his

* Anna's daughter.
† The pet name of Ahu, daughter of Dada.
‡ Durga, daughter of Tatya.
§ Anna's son, Baburao.

contribution to the family arising from the success of his shop. In addition, Baba seems to be particularly proud of the fact that his youngest brother, Tatya, is now independent and doing well, and rightly takes some of the credit for guiding and supporting him to 'stand on his legs'. We get confirmation of the fact that their mother was named Narmada and their sister was named Sakhu, and further that Tatya had also made some provision for his sister by adding her as a beneficiary of his shop. The fact that Baba chose to write his will in English rather than in Marathi shows us his fluency and comfort with the language. The will also shows us that Baba was an extremely cautious man—he states that his cash balance is 31,800 rupees. He rounds this down to 30,000 rupees in case of any error in calculation. And then he deducts a further 5,000 rupees 'for any discrepancy', and ends up with a cautiously underestimated figure of 25,000 rupees to be distributed among his family. He ends up distributing only 23,000 rupees (Rs 22,000 noted by him, but it adds up to Rs 23,000), which leaves a balance of a couple of thousand (probably more, since he has begun with an underestimated figure)—apparently to be distributed as his brothers thought fit. This fluidity of finances within a joint family of that time is interesting to note, also seen in his very rough estimate of the share his brothers have in his assets (e.g. 'Ganu's I can't exactly state but say Rs.7,000 at the most …').

Finally, the question of the women—only Baba's wife and sister are honoured with any money to their names. While his wife gets the fairly large sum of 6,000 rupees, she is instructed to spend only the interest on this sum, and to not touch the capital unless she would like to use about 200 rupees from it for a pilgrimage. (There is also a rather personal aside about his wife's partiality to her brother, and a warning that he does not wish his money to end up benefiting his brother-in-law.) Following his wife's demise, Baba decrees that the money bequeathed to her ought to go, not to his daughter Bayo, but to his nephew Babu (Anna's son). Meanwhile, though he leaves 4,000 rupees to his daughter Bayo, he casually mentions that the money is not really for her, but for her son. Meanwhile his nieces get money not for themselves, but to be used specifically for their marriage dowries. These financial arrangements in no way indicate any lack of affection on Baba's part for these women, but they do show in compelling detail how money, in that era, for the most part simply did not reach female hands, or if it did, there were strict instructions as to how it was to be used.

About a year after the sadness of Baba's death, good news followed—a son was born to Tatya and Yamuna in 1904. They named him Laxman. In the same year, Tatya acquired the selling agency of Swann Mills in Sewree, which was managed by agents Messrs James Finlay and Co. who had their offices in the Chartered Bank Buildings in Fort. But by now, Tatya had his eye on a big catch: he wanted the selling agency of the prestigious Kohinoor Mills and started thinking about ways and means to get it. It is likely that he tried to talk to various people to get himself an introduction at Kohinoor, an effort which was to pay off only several years later.

Meanwhile, he had other irons in the fire. In 1906, he started a shop in Baroda under the name of 'Apte and Nerurkar'. No information is available as to who Nerurkar was or how Tatya came into contact with him. In 1907, he began a ginning factory—where cotton seed is separated from the cotton fibre—in Yavatmal. It was a textile-related business, albeit at the other end of the production process: whereas Tatya's experience thus far was as a seller of finished cloth, the ginning factory worked at the beginning of the process, dealing with the raw materials that went into making textiles. In the early years, Tatya had also been involved in miscellaneous sales of cloth, but now he decided to discontinue dealing in miscellaneous sales.

The year 1907 proved to be disastrous—his business partner in the ginning factory turned out to be crooked, and the factory closed down; he lost the Swann Mills agency after only two years, apparently due to some mischief played by one Rattansey (it is not clear what exactly happened, but this is how Tatya mentions it in his brief memoir, narrated to and written down by his nephew Baburao Apte); and to top it all off, the New Islam Mills burnt down and he lost that selling agency as well. However, Tatya did have some other selling agencies in hand and managed to stay afloat.

In 1908, he won the selling agency—for Bombay only—of seven mills in Ahmedabad belonging to Manikbhai Bhagubhai. He worked hard on this job for the next two years, often from 7 a.m. till midnight, no doubt to compensate for the losses of 1907. He acquired substantial experience of the mills' working during this time. Two years later, though, in 1910, he gave up the selling agency of Manikbhai's mills as the work proved to be an overburden. He also closed the four-year-old 'Apte and Nerurkar' shop in Baroda as it was incurring losses.

And then we come to 1911, which was the most significant turning point in Tatya's life and fortunes.

Kohinoor Mills

In 1911, Tatya was already well-acquainted with a man called Seth Nahalchand Laloochand who, like Tatya, also owned a pedhi. Seth Nahalchand was the yarn selling agent for Kohinoor Mills. He had developed good business relations with the British managing agents of Kohinoor Mills, a firm called Killick Nixon & Co. However, he did not speak a word of English. Tatya, on the other hand, was fluent in English—he had studied up to matriculation and had excellent reading habits. One day, Seth Nahalchand took Tatya along to the Killick Nixon office to act as an interpreter, to strike a deal regarding the purchase of yarn. Kohinoor Mills had a large stock of unsold yarn that they wanted to get rid of. During discussions, the Englishman representing Killock Nixon quoted a price for the yarn that Nahalchand felt was ridiculously high. They began haggling but the Killick Nixon officer would not budge. Nahalchand lost his temper. Turning to Tatya he fumed, 'This red-faced monkey, what does he know of business, how can he ask for this price?' The Englishman turned to Tatya and asked, 'What is he saying?' Thinking on his feet, Tatya said, 'He is saying what a handsome man you are, like a lord.' And thus the deal concluded amicably.

After this comic scenario of colonial-era crossed wires, a pleased Nahalchand informed Tatya that Kohinoor Mills was setting up new loom sheds, and that a new selling agency might be on the cards. He set up a meeting for Tatya with the chairman of Killick Nixon, the Hon. Thomas Birkett. The meeting would almost certainly have taken place at the Killick Nixon offices in Forbes Building on Home Street, Fort. The mills themselves were situated on Naigaum Cross Road, Dadar. There were two mills initially, known as Kohinoor No. 1 and 2. Both produced cotton textiles. (A third mill, Kohinoor No. 3, was added several years later.)

The Kohinoor Mills Company Ltd had been formed in July 1896. By 1911, Kohinoor was a spinning and weaving mill, meaning that apart from producing cloth, it spun its own yarn, which was used to weave the cloth and was also sold separately. This was called the 'Manchester pattern', meaning that everything, from buying and spinning the cotton to bleaching and dyeing the final cloth, was done in-house.

Initially, however, Kohinoor had been only a cotton spinning mill, with about 30,000 spindles producing yarn. In 1907, the directors had decided to begin weaving cloth as well and constructed a weaving shed with a preliminary 750 looms. The first loom started in January 1910, and in May 1913 an additional 250 looms were installed. In 1909, the directors spent 4 lakh rupees to buy property at Naigaum where an existing mill had been partially destroyed by fire. They reconstructed the mill by 1912, when 484 looms and 18,000 ring spindles were installed. This mill began operations in 1915, running on electric power from the Tata Electric Power Supply Company.[2] It was in the midst of this expansion of Kohinoor Mills that Tatya met the Hon. Thomas Birkett in 1911; the meeting was a success and Tatya became the sole selling agent for the mills. Tatya's company, through which he conducted his selling agency business, was called V.S. Apte & Son. While Tatya was the sole selling agent of Kohinoor cloth, Nahalchand Laloochand, who had set up Tatya's initial meeting with the Kohinoor Mills management, was the selling agent of Kohinoor yarn.

Killick Nixon & Co., the managing agency of Kohinoor Mills, was a well-established business. It had been founded in 1857 by Charles Killick and Robert Preston Nixon for the purpose of doing business as 'General Merchants and Commission Agents'.[3] Its interests included various businesses such as railways, textiles and electricity. The managing agency system played a dominant role in Indian industry till it was abolished in 1967. Managing agencies performed three main functions: first, they acted as prospectors and pioneers of new enterprises; second, they provided the finances required for fixed and working capital; and third, they looked after the day- to-day management of the concerned industry. For servicing the client industry, the managing agency was paid a commission as well as an office allowance. In Bombay, commission was usually calculated on gross profits, before providing for depreciation. Often the managing agency itself owned substantial shares in the industry that they were managing. Killick Nixon, for instance, owned substantial shares in Kohinoor Mills. The managing agency system was handed bouquets and brickbats almost since its inception.[4] This is not the place to go into the pros and cons of the system. Suffice to say that as far as

Tatya's association with Kohinoor Mills and Killick Nixon was concerned, it was a mutually profitable relationship that lasted for decades. (The sole selling agency of V.S. Apte & Son eventually came to an end in 1962, about ten years after Tatya's death.)

In 1911, there were several contenders angling for the lucrative selling agency of Kohinoor Mills—but on Tatya's side was an excellent personal reputation he had built up over more than a decade, and he was known for his honesty and business skills. His years of hard work and accumulated experience now paid off. Also on his side was—as he himself put it in a magazine interview many years later—the fate written on the lines of his forehead. But his wasn't a blind faith in destiny; he also believed in putting in the hard work, so that when fate was ready to smile on him, he was ready to take the catch. He gave the interview to journalist T.V. Parvate for *Kirloskar* magazine around 1947; either it was the only interview that Tatya ever gave or it is the only one that has survived. During this interview he reflected on the effort and learning that was needed to succeed in a new venture. It is a rare insight into his mind in which he outlines his work ethic in a lucid manner:

> If one wants to succeed in any new field, then one must not feel that any job in that field is beneath him. One must with all humility get a full understanding of all the obstacles in that field, an understanding of where one might stumble and fall, and one must do so without getting bored or weary of the smallest details. One must have courage. One must take for granted that there will be problems and must be ready to face them. You have to be able to face adversity when necessary. However, having said all that, there is such a thing as luck—the fate written in the lines of your forehead. If these lines are unfavourable then all your efforts are useless. It will never do for a person to think that he knows and understands everything. However much you know, there will always be a gap in your understanding; and there is no way of

> telling where and when that gap in understanding will betray you, trip you up. Therefore I cannot claim in all honesty that my well-being is entirely due to my efforts ... there are so many others like me who have tried and who are cleverer than me. But there is no doubt that I had luck on my side. There are men who have a certain quality in their hands. Even if they pick up mud, it turns to gold. To a large extent, that is what has happened with me.[5]

Kohinoor Mills certainly was a prize catch, one that Tatya had been eyeing since 1904. Now, finally, at the age of thirty-six, he was contracted as the sole selling agent of the mills for two years. From then on, he was retained as the sole agent year after year. This meant that all the cloth produced by Kohinoor Mills would be sold exclusively through him, and that he would get a commission on every piece of Kohinoor cloth sold. This was a major breakthrough indeed: Kohinoor Mills was among the most prominent mills of the time, and continued to prosper for years. In 1950, *The Indian Cotton Textile Industry Centenary Volume (1851–1950)* described the major mills: 'When a consideration of the working of the Textile Industry is taken up, the names that occur to every mind at first thought are those of Bombay Dyeing, Kohinoor, Buckingham Carnatic, Madura Mills, etc.'[6] Shambhu Kumar Kasliwal, founder of S. Kumar's textiles, describes Kohinoor as one of the 'very top mills' of the time.[7]

Most mills were known for a certain speciality. In Bombay, most of the mills produced plain cloth, while mills in Ahmedabad were better known for producing fancy cloths like shirtings. Kohinoor Mills mainly produced sheetings (plain cotton cloth, for bedsheets, for example) and long cloths (plain cotton cloth for clothes like kurta pyjamas). While Kohinoor produced a small quantity of fancy cloth, especially with its silk production in later years, it was known primarily for its high quality long cloth and cambric (a lightweight, closely woven, plain cotton cloth).

Tatya happened to be in the right industry at the right time. At the turn of the century, the city of Bombay was the most prominent textile centre in the country, and continued to be so for decades. The city's mills comprised 50 per cent of the total spinning and weaving capacity of all the mills located in India and generated a great deal of wealth.[8]

The First World War

During the early years of textile trading, Tatya did some business in ship breaking, and the buying and selling of used steel, as a brief side venture. Any good opportunity to make money seemed to act like a magnet for him.

Before the beginning of the First World War, he also ran an iron and steel factory in Bombay called 'Climax' (likely connected to his brief venture into ship breaking). This factory continued operating through the war and is described in the *Kirloskar* magazine interview where Tatya's interviewer writes:

> He earned good money on that [factory] during the tumult of the war. But in 1918 when it looked as if there would be a cessation of hostilities, he sold the factory to a European businessman from Calcutta about four–five months before the Armistice, for a sum of Rs. 3 lakh to 3.5 lakh more than its initial cost. Apte told me that after the war that factory did not run profitably and had to be closed down. However, while the war lasted, the buyer of the factory made large profits.[9]

While the iron and steel factory had brought in an enormous profit for Tatya during the war, the textile industry had also been booming.

When the First World War began in 1914, the initial panic of the market led to the prices of cotton, yarn and cloth slumping to record low levels regardless of the actual supply and demand.

Bankers became jittery and began calling in loans, even those that had been considered safe and secure. The industry survived this initial shock however, only to emerge into a booming war economy. Cloth shipments from foreign countries began to decrease as the transport system was diverted towards the war. This led to a growing scarcity of cloth in the market, and local prices rose substantially. *The Indian Cotton Textile Industry Centenary Volume (1851–1950)* describes the wartime price rise for cloth and yarn: 'Ordinary long cloth which was sold as low as 6 annas to 7 annas a pound, reached the top figure of Rs. 3 per pound and coarse yarns from 4 annas to over a rupee. Cotton prices assumed a firmer tone as foreign mills were on intensive war work for supplying materials to the Defence Forces. India's contribution in this direction was also considerable.'[10]

Prices were further pushed up due to speculative hoarding by mills as well as dealers. It was known, however, that Tatya was among the few who refused to hoard goods during the First World War as well as the Second World War—his reputation was built on his above-the-board practices (though his trade would certainly have benefitted from the general increase in prices). In 1917, the annual report of the Bombay Mill Owners' Association noted that the mill industry had 'beaten all records in the matter of the prosperity of the Cotton Mill Industry in India'. Even when peace broke out in 1918, there was no stopping the rocketing profits. In 1920, the Bombay Mill Owners' Association was reporting 'unprecedented and unparalleled prosperity' for the Bombay mills, with profits estimated at 16 crore rupees. Even after the war, the disruption to international trade still meant that cloth imports were limited, while the Swadeshi movement to boycott foreign goods created a severe setback for imports in 1921–22 and increased demand for cloth made in India.[11]

These profits and prosperity were despite the British government forcing upon Indian mills an excise duty of 3.5 per cent on all cloth made by them, to protect the Lancashire mills. The Lancashire mills were, at the turn of the century, the principal source of cloth for the Indian market, supplying around 3,000 million yards every year. But as Indian mills began displacing them, the Lancashire mills found it hard to compete with Indian prices—hence the excise duty on Indian mills to balance costs in favour of imported Lancashire cloth. Politically this created much ill will and led to regular boycotts as well as bonfires of Lancashire goods. The excise duty remained in place long after the First World War.[12]

In 1916, in the midst of the war-time boom, Tatya formed a syndicate comprising of five partners. This is narrated by Tatya in his memoirs but there are no details about the workings of this syndicate, though it would certainly have involved the buying and selling of cloth. A syndicate may be created in a situation where those who have liquidity take up an opportunity to buy goods and make a profit. When a stock of goods is available in bulk, and the seller wants to get rid of it in a hurry, perhaps as a distress sale, the seller would likely offer a substantial discount; as the risk of buying the lot might be too great for an individual to bear, a group of persons may come together to form a syndicate and jointly buy the stock of goods and later sell it at market rates, making a good profit. Within eight months, Tatya and his partners had wound up the syndicate, having made a profit of 4.5 lakh rupees. Assuming that it was an equal partnership, Tatya would have made a princely sum of 90,000 rupees from this venture.

It was only in 1922 that it became clear that the boom of the war years was finally over, and in December that year the Bombay Mill Owners' Association declared the end of 'the cycle of prosperity'.[13] However, textile production remained an important industry for decades—cotton textiles was India's largest industry, and its epicentre was Bombay. Historian Chandavarkar writes, 'despite the expansion of the industry at a number of up-country centres in the early twentieth century, it was still reported in the mid-1920s that the industry in Bombay "not only exceeds the combined output of the 126 factories in other parts of Bombay Presidency, but also exceeds the total production of the 125 factories working ... in all other parts of the country".'[14]

Around 1927, Tatya became the selling agent for Standard Mills. When Tatya started his business in 1898, he had met a man called Mafatlal Gagalbhai who had come to Bombay from Ahmedabad, and who was also about to start his own textile business. The two met in MJ Market and became friends. Mafatlal Gagalbhai began as a trader, but he shortly acquired his own mill, Standard Mills, and offered the selling agency to Tatya around 1927. After three years, Tatya gave up the selling agency because he felt that he would not like to mix business with friendship. The two remained very close friends. Indeed, the bond proved to be strong enough for Tatya to reverse his decision about not doing business with friends, because they became business partners in the 1930s when they started the Phaltan Sugar Works together. Mafatlal Gagalbhai, of course, went on to build the Mafatlal textile empire.

Between the Wars: A Pedhi in Calcutta

In the 1920s and 1930s, Bombay became a centre of working-class political action. Until the First World War, strikes had affected only individual mills, or even just departments within a mill; occasionally they affected groups of mills. However, after the First World War ended in 1918, strikes became increasingly coordinated across the textile industry. There were eight general strikes between 1919 and 1940, all lasting at least a month, some longer.[15]

In 1931, business from Kohinoor Mills had declined since, being British owned, it faced boycotts and pickets from the public as well as the Congress during the Swadeshi movement. In order to counter this decline in his business, Tatya decided to open a textile shop in Calcutta's Cotton Bazaar, renting it for 65 rupees a month, to sell cloth from Kohinoor as well as from other mills for which he was selling agent. He also rented a pedhi and accommodation in Pollock Street for 175 rupees per month, a fifteen-minute walk from the shop. Tatya sent a relation, Appa Khidkikar, to set up this basic structure in Calcutta.

Meanwhile, Tatya's nephew Balasaheb (Tatya's brother Dada's son) was completing an apprenticeship in Andhra with a construction contractor. Tatya's intention was for Balasaheb to move to Calcutta to look after the new textile business there. He initially took Balasaheb to Calcutta for a week and left the choice to him as to whether he would shift there, at the same time impressing on him the need to do so for the larger benefit of the family. Tatya took him to meet around twenty-five dealers, retailers and shop-owners, and Balasaheb later recounted his amazement at how well-networked Tatya was in Calcutta, despite hardly ever visiting the city. So it was that Khidkikar returned to Bombay, and Balasaheb, newly married, shifted to Calcutta with his wife Saraswati.

Balasaheb's work included going to the docks to supervise the unloading of goods that came by sea, since most of the cloth from Bombay came on steamers. Only if the delivery was urgent did it come by railway. He hired go-downs to store the bales of cloth. All transactions at the shop were in cash, so every day he took bags of notes and coins to deposit in the Chartered Bank of India, and he employed a permanent staff of three men at the shop to keep the cash secure. Balasaheb also established a credit society to lend money. Between 1931 and 1934, Tatya visited Calcutta a few times, and by May 1934 decided to close the Calcutta operations, instructing Balasaheb to return to Bombay. The pressure from the boycotts on Kohinoor had lessened, and with his Calcutta trade networks well established, it made better sense for the cloth destined for Calcutta to simply be sold and delivered directly from Bombay.[16]

The Second World War

By 1939, at the beginning of the Second World War, India was the second largest textile producer in the world, the first being the United States.[17]

In 1944, Kohinoor Mills opened a third mill, known as Kohinoor Mill No. 3, on Lady Jamshedji Road, Dadar, near Shivaji Park, standing on an area of 4.9 acres.[18] This mill produced pure silk as well as art silk (synthetic silk).* Unlike Mills No. 1 and 2, Kohinoor Mill No. 3 was not a spinning mill, but a weaving and processing mill. The silk yarn was not produced in-house, but bought, since silk spinning was a more specialised process. The yarn for synthetic or cellulose silk was also bought and then woven and processed in Mill No. 3.

During the Second World War, Kohinoor Mill No. 3 started supplying silk to the air force for the manufacture of parachutes, which needed to be made with pure silk and had to be of perfect quality since even a small hole could be disastrous. Tatya's son, Laxman, known as Bhausaheb, was mainly in charge of this, and did it very successfully. Whenever there was any weaving or finishing defect, the silk would be rejected for parachute use. It was then either sold on the market for other uses, or simply sent home, which meant that, rather incongruously for wartime, boys and men in the Apte household often wore pure silk shirts during the war years, made of the rejected material.

---

* The Kohinoor Mills had earlier acquired the Courtaulds Artificial Silk Mills, and it used the acquired art silk processing machinery and 282 looms in Kohinoor Mill No. 3 (Singhania et al., 1948, p. 248).

Kohinoor Mills: Expansion and Success

Since commencing operations in 1896 as a cotton spinning mill, Kohinoor Mills had expanded over about fifteen years and was one of the most prestigious spinning and weaving mills by 1911.[19] By 1928, both Mills No. 1 and 2 together had 68,840 spindles and 1,430 looms.[20] The Annual Reports of the Mill Owners' Association of Bombay illustrate the expansion of Kohinoor Mills production over the years. Though Tatya took over the sole selling agency of Kohinoor Mills in 1911 and held it till his death in 1952, the figures I found reflect only the latter half of this period, from 1933 to 1951. Nevertheless, they are indicative of the fact that production and sales were continuously increasing. The table below presents an abbreviated set of figures for a few key years. The full set of figures for 1933 to 1951 is included in Appendix 1.

Expansion of Kohinoor Mills 1933–51[21]

	Kohinoor Mills No. 1 and No. 2			***Kohinoor Mills No. 1, No. 2 and No. 3***	
	1933	**1939**	**1943**	**1944**	**1951**
Hands employed daily	3,162	4,144	4,187	5,365	5,439
Spindles at work daily	59,433	84,703	94,569	95,541	1,06,531
Looms at work daily	1,338	1,549	1,552	1,834	1,817
Quantity of cotton consumed annually in candies of 784 lbs.	9,163	18,793	26,265	24,868	20,767

Noteworthy in the above table is that in 1933, Kohinoor Mills No. 1 and No. 2 employed over 3,000 workers daily, which rose by about a thousand workers a decade later, in 1943. In 1944, when Kohinoor Mill No. 3 was acquired, the number of daily workers rose to over 5,000. The number of spindles at work daily was more than 59,000 in 1933, a figure that had almost doubled by 1951. The quantity of cotton consumed annually doubled between 1933 and 1939, and peaked in 1943, in the middle of the Second World War. Similarly, the number of looms at work daily rose between 1933 and 1951; from 1944 onwards, this figure includes 285 additional looms in the new Kohinoor Mill No. 3. (The acquisition of Kohinoor Mill No. 3 does not affect the cotton figures since it did not use cotton, and only produced silk and art silk. Mill No. 3 also does not affect the spindle figures since it did not produce its own yarn.) These figures illustrate the increasing production and prosperity of Kohinoor Mills, reflecting the success of the mill management as well as the success of Tatya's selling agency.

Tatya's Role as a Selling Agent

One of those rare and delightful bits of information that reveal the texture of the time is that the cotton mills of Bombay had nicknames invented by their mill hands, and these nicknames bore not the remotest resemblance to the real names:

> … the Star of India Mill whose machinery was old and noisy was known as Khatara mill [clunky old mill]; the Union Mill as Bin Chimnichi Giran (chimneyless mill); the Hong Kong and later the Apollo Mill as Tabelyachi Giran [stable mill], because they were located near the municipal stables; the Jam Mills as Patryachi Giran [metal sheeting mill], since its roof was made of iron sheeting which probably made working conditions extremely hot; the India Mill was known as Mulmulchi Giran after the

> type of cloth whose production it instituted, the Khatau Mills as Sakli Talayachi Giran, the lock and chain mill. Some mills were identified by their location; others by proper names, perhaps of former owners, managers or jobbers, such as Narayan (Meyer Sassoon), Trikamdas (Edward Sassoon), Kapidas (Elphinstone) and Bania Mill (Swann).[22]

Tatya would surely have been conversant with this lingo, and known that he had held the selling agency of Bania Mill (Swann Mills); and Kohinoor Mills would almost certainly have been christened with a nickname too.

Tatya being the sole selling agent for Kohinoor Mills meant that every piece of cloth produced by Kohinoor was sold exclusively through him. However, where Tatya did not have the sole selling agency for a mill, this meant that he was responsible for selling only certain brands or types of cloth produced by the mill, while other types of cloth would have been handled for the mill by a different selling agent.

What was Tatya's role at Kohinoor Mills, as the sole selling agent? First of all, he was not an employee of the mill. He was his own boss, and had his own pedhi at MJ Market. He did not buy cloth from Kohinoor Mills—he simply sold it for them. He was respected by the Kohinoor management for his honesty and business skills, and when he visited the British managers at the Killick Nixon office in Fort, he met them on almost equal terms. At Kohinoor Mills, Tatya would have interacted with the on-site British bosses almost every day. The manager of the mills was British, and so was the spinning master and weaving master, while the processing master was traditionally an Indian.

MJ Market was among Asia's largest textile markets under one roof. At the beginning of the twentieth century, almost every textile mill in India was represented at this market, either directly or through their selling agents. While the textile industry was concentrated in Bombay and Ahmedabad, the major trading of textiles happened mainly in Bombay. There were other textile markets in Bombay known for cotton piece goods trade, namely the Laxmidas Khimji market on Sheikh Memon Street and the Morarji Goculdas market on Kalbadevi Road.[23] But it was MJ Market that was the hub for wholesale trading. Being a wholesale market meant that a buyer would not have been able to purchase a piece of cloth there—he would only be able to see samples of cloth that could be ordered wholesale. A pedhi, such as the one Tatya owned in Chandra Chowk in MJ Market, was a shop where cloth samples were stored and transactions took place with wholesalers. An up-country buyer, for example, would send his agent (known as an adatiyaa in Gujarati) who would book business on his behalf. The adatiyaa had to feel the cloth, look at the rates and then book it; the up-country buyer only saw the goods when the cloth was actually delivered to him. Many of these cloths were sold by brand names, and the sale was concluded based on the reputation of the mill as well as the reputation of the selling agent, for if there was a problem with the quality of the cloth at any point, it would be resolved through the selling agent. For instance, if there was a problem with a shipment of cloth, Tatya, as selling agent, might ask the buyer to return the goods, or simply offer a hefty discount for the buyer to keep the cloth. The discount would then be borne by the mill management.

MJ Market was open every day of the week except Sunday. It usually opened for business around 11 a.m., while many of the bosses would arrive at their pedhis by 1 p.m. The market closed by about 7 p.m. Tatya would visit the mills in the morning and the pedhi in the afternoon. He would head out to work wearing a dagla (a long coat) and a dhoti, with a pagdi on his head. (Apropos the pagdi: one of the hazards of MJ Market was its large population of monkeys; one day Tatya lost his pagdi to a monkey, which scampered off with it, though it was retrieved later.) Eventually Tatya employed about seven or eight people to work for him at the pedhi. A fixture since these very early days was Gotu Mule, who became Tatya's right-hand man, trusted to look after keys, accounts and money. If any spending money was needed by Tatya's family, it came from him. He remained with Tatya for decades.

The pedhi itself was a small room. Above this room was a mezzanine level. The entire front of the room was open to the market lane where it was situated. When one entered the pedhi, there were gaadis (mattresses for sitting) laid out on either side of the room, on the floor. A person would remove his shoes and put them on a shoe rack, and then step up into the pedhi. Tatya would conduct his business by sitting in this open-fronted room and talking to his dealers, who would gather every day in the pedhi. The gumastas sat in a closed-off area inside, or up on the mezzanine level, with their books of accounts. The mezzanine floor in Tatya's pedhi was accessed by climbing a wooden ladder with a rope dangling by its side for support. Not far off was a warehouse where stock was kept. Like in most other pedhis, there was a steel safe. There was also an earthen pot with a ladle for drinking water, replenished every day from nearby wells by water carriers. Just outside Tatya's pedhi a paanwala had set up his shop. Visitors to Tatya's pedhi were free to order a paan from the paanwala, with Tatya paying him at the end of the day. In fact, so popular was the habit of chewing paan that most pedhis kept a tray of paan-supari for their visitors.

Business was conducted in Gujarati—MJ Market was a Gujarati bastion. There were some Marwaris and Sindhis too, but Tatya was the sole Maharashtrian conducting business there. Having been brought up in Navsari and Baroda, he spoke Gujarati fluently and managed to hold his own among the Gujarati traders. He was also fluent in Marwari, the other language of commerce. There is no doubt that his fluency in Gujarati contributed greatly to the success of his pedhi—later his son Bhausaheb too was fluent in the language. Even Tatya's accounts, written in red-covered hand-stitched books called 'chopdya', were kept in Gujarati, rather than in Marathi, and both his accountants were Gujarati too. Reed pens were used with thick black ink in ink wells. To prevent the ink from smudging, grey sand was sprinkled on the writing, and ink blotters of the wooden rocking style were used as well.[24]

In those days, it was extremely unusual for a Maharashtrian Brahmin to be a businessman, and that too a successful one. A man from Tatya's background was more likely to take up a job, say as a government official or a teacher (which is what all three of his brothers did). This was true even decades later, when he gave the interview to *Kirloskar* magazine, in which he urged Marathi youngsters to venture into business.

What skills would have been necessary for Tatya to have succeeded as a selling agent?

Though he was essentially an introvert, he was a good communicator and people manager, keeping up good relations with diverse merchants and wholesalers, deciding what volume of cloth to give to which merchant, setting up long-term contracts with merchants for, say, three or six months, managing the logistics of ensuring that goods were delivered on time from the mills to the merchants, choosing the right merchants to deal with, and ensuring that payments were received on time and passed on to the mills in time. And, of course, he had a head for numbers, which was essential to strike good deals. These were skills acquired purely through hands-on experience.

As a selling agent, he had to have detailed knowledge about cloth—the broad categories of cloth (long cloth, voile, etc.), its construction (e.g. fine or super fine), the processes by which it was made such as bleaching, dyeing or printing, and also the feel and finish of the cloth (whether it was smooth, glossy, stiff, etc.), for while the basic cloth made by different mills might be the same, the finishing of the cloth could make a world of difference. Of course as a selling agent he also had to know the market for various kinds of cloth. He had to be aware of which products were being sold by other mills, and at what price. As market environments changed over the years, he had to be able to adapt to changing conditions too. In short, he had to know his product inside-out, from process to finishing to sales. Though Tatya was very knowledgeable about cloth production, his son Bhausaheb became much more involved in the technical aspects of cloth manufacture from spinning to finishing, while Tatya's strongest point was his knowledge of textile trading.

Tatya's ultimate responsibility, as a selling agent, was first to make sure that he fixed the best possible price for the cloth, based on the costing of the mill, and second, to make sure that the payment for the goods was made to the mills. Whether or not the buyer paid him, he was responsible for making the payment to the mills. If someone defaulted, Tatya would have to pay for it. A key part of his business acumen was to choose his wholesale buyers carefully—much of his success can be attributed to the fact that he managed to choose and cultivate trustworthy merchants who did not default on payments.

Unlike many selling agents, Tatya developed a very close relationship with Kohinoor Mills—he carved out a niche for himself whereby he wasn't just an agent who sold cloth. Though he was not a part of the management, slowly all management decisions regarding production, what to make and what to sell, started being taken with his involvement. It was a hand-in-glove relationship, where Tatya became a key cog in the bottom-up movement of information. He knew the market and he knew what would sell, and would advise the mill management to produce cloth as per his knowledge of the market. He also had a role in the costing of the cloth, which was an important part of the production process, as the costing would determine whether or not it was worthwhile to produce a particular kind of cloth. This involved determining the costs of the yarn, the sizing (i.e., the strengthening of the yarn by starching it), the weaving, the packing, and so on, in relation to the price the finished cloth could fetch on the market. This close association between selling agent and mill was unusual—often, for example, mill managements hid their production costs from their selling agents if mutual trust did not exist.

Another interesting aspect of Tatya's involvement in the production process was that if a wholesaler wanted any new product, he would come to Tatya with a sample of cloth—perhaps imported—and enquire whether Kohinoor Mills would be interested in producing it. Tatya, with his knowledge of the manufacturing process, would then be able to say whether or not it might be possible—if it seemed likely, he would take the sample to the technicians at the mills, such as the spinning master, the weaving master and the finishing master—and try to replicate the sample. If the production turned out right, and if the price was right, then the cloth could be made for the wholesaler.

Once the sales money was passed on by Tatya to the mills, he would get a commission on the cloth he had sold. Superfine cloth (e.g., mulmuls and saris) and fine cloth (e.g., pure combed cotton) would earn him a commission of 4–4.5 per cent. Medium cloth, of lower quality, earned him about 3.5 per cent. Coarse cloth, also known as 'maanzar paat', which was cheap, uncombed cotton cloth used for sheets and curtains, got him a commission of about 2.5 per cent.

It is worth pointing out here that though Tatya was a selling agent, his role was not really that of a salesman—which is to say, there was no marketing or advertising involved, no real need to make great efforts to persuade people to buy his cloth. The cloth was sold on the strength of the reputation of the mill and its brand, as well as the reputation of the selling agent, and this reputation was built up over time, by word of mouth (as opposed to marketing and advertising). In Tatya's case, he built up a select group of about twenty-five or thirty trusted wholesale merchants who would buy from him. He was among the very first agents to set up this kind of restricted or vetted system of dealers. This eventually meant that to be a Kohinoor dealer was something of great repute. It was not possible for just anyone to present a cheque and buy the cloth; merchants were appointed carefully, because the cloth was sold not as a commodity, but as a brand. Prior to this sort of system, cloth tended to be sold as a commodity, with preferences given to dealers who wanted the most cloth on a given day. However, Kohinoor Mills was able to sell cloth at a premium, first because of the good quality of the cloth, and second because it had built up a brand through Tatya's sale system. It is also worth pointing out that during both the world wars, it was a seller's market—all the cloth that was produced was sold, due to rationing of cloth and diverting of cloth supplies to the war effort, which meant that during these periods it was relatively easy to sell whatever was produced.

The cloth went from mill to shoppers, through the following chain:

Mills → Selling Agent (Tatya) → Wholesaler → Semi-wholesaler → Retailer → Customers in a shop

So Tatya would sell the mill cloth to wholesalers, many of whom also had their shops in MJ Market. The wholesalers who bought from Tatya were not exclusive to him—they would get their cloth from several mills, of which Kohinoor was one. The wholesalers often tended to specialise, so that there were some who dealt only in high value, fine and super fine cloths, while others dealt in cloth at the lower end of pricing. The wholesaler would buy the cloth from Tatya in bales. A bale might, for example, comprise 1,000 yards. The wholesaler would make a contract with Tatya for, say, fifty bales, to be delivered within a certain timeframe. Having gotten his delivery, the wholesaler would sell the bales to various semi-wholesalers. A semi-wholesaler would, in turn, open up the different bales that he had acquired from different wholesalers, and supply a variety of cloth to retailers and shopkeepers. A shopkeeper always needed a range of cloth to display to shoppers, in different colours, varieties and prints, and would buy a little of each from the semi-wholesaler, say five pieces of long cloth, ten pieces of mulmul, a dozen pieces of voile. To describe the chain in other words, each link of the chain held the cloth stock and provided credit to the person in the link below him: credit to the retailer was provided by the semi-wholesaler; credit to the semi-wholesaler was provided by the wholesaler; and credit to the wholesaler was provided by Tatya. And Tatya had to make sure that whether or not his wholesaler paid up, Kohinoor Mills would receive the money for their cloth. It was not, however, a very long period of credit provided by Tatya—in Bombay, the system of credit was known as 'dhaaraa', where money was paid by the traders within five days, usually by cheque, though some paid in cash. Tatya's wholesale merchants came to meet him every day at the pedhi, at least for 10–15 minutes, to keep him updated on business and to check for their delivery of cloth, usually between 2 p.m. and 4.30 p.m. There was one merchant in particular who took much more initiative than the others and made it a point to visit the mills himself, which was highly unusual. He was a wholesaler appointed by Tatya's son, Bhausaheb, as a Kohinoor dealer, and most of the cloth he dealt in was produced at Kohinoor Mill No. 3. Almost every day he would go along with Bhausaheb to Kohinoor Mill No. 3 to learn about textile manufacturing and to see the finishes and shades of the cloth, and to check whether all the looms were working, especially when he was short of goods. This dynamic dealer was Shambhu Kumar Kasliwal, who went on to found the S. Kumar's textile empire.

Though Tatya was not involved in the nitty-gritty of cloth production, he would certainly have become familiar with the way it was produced in Kohinoor Mills—he would have seen the cleaned, ginned cotton arriving at the mill in bales. The bales were enormous bundles of tightly compressed cotton weighing 300 kilos or 500 kilos, put into gunny sack covers and tied with iron hoops. The cotton came in different varieties, where the length of the fibre, also known as the 'staple' of the fibre, determined whether the cotton was classified as 'short staple', 'medium staple' or 'long staple', and also determined the fineness or coarseness of the cloth that could be produced from it. At the mills, he would have seen the cotton being removed from the bales and once again being cleaned, a process of removing dirt and very short fibre lengths, called carding. Having been carded, the cotton would go through a process that reduced it to a sliver. If the cotton was of a superior variety to be used, say, for superior shirt material, it would be combed, a process that removed the short fibre from the cotton and made it smoother and softer, without any specks. If the cotton was of a lower quality, to be used for, say, tarpaulins, it was not combed. This combed or uncombed cotton was in turn sent to the spinning department to be converted into yarn, a process of reducing the thick rope-like cotton into fine yarn by using a spindle, minded by spinners. Tatya would have seen yarn being covered in starch to strengthen it, a process known as sizing, where about 10,000 yarn strings at a time passed through semi-liquid starch, arranged in a way that all those separate yarn strings looked as if they formed one giant sheet. In fact, the costing of the cloth would begin in the sizing department, which functioned as a cost centre, with discussions with the sizing master about what it might cost to go from the sizing all the way to the packing of the finished cloth. Tatya, being involved in costing, would have likely spent some time in the sizing department.

And once the yarn had been starched, he would most certainly have seen it going onto the looms to be woven into cloth, would have seen workers knotting broken threads to keep the looms going—usually two looms to a worker—and would have watched the shuttle shooting back and forth, clattering noisily, to create the weft of the cloth, while the warp went up and down in a pattern determined by the weave being created. Different weaving patterns would create different cloth surfaces, producing different kinds of cloth such as drill, sateen, cambric and so on. The woven material was now passed through a boiler to remove the starch on the yarn, and emerged as a grey-coloured cloth. At this stage, the cloth was called maanzar paat in Marathi, and could be used for cheap sheets or curtains. But if it was a better-quality cloth, it would be bleached white, and then might go through an additional finishing process, for example to add lustre, for which it would go through more chemical vats. The cloth was then stretched to the required width on a machine called a stenter, and finally was taken to the holding department, where all the finished cloth came for folding and packing.

Tatya would certainly have spent time in the holding department, for here the cloth was also checked for faults, and it was important to see the cloth here, feel it, check if the bleaching was good, whether the dyeing had been done well and whether there were any defects. At the folding machines, the operator cut the cloth to the required length—he might, for example, cut it every 20 metres—and then it was stamped with the Kohinoor Mills brand by a worker using a manual screen and ink. Finally, the cloth was ready for weighing and packing into bales, where a bale was made up of several packets of folded cloth of a single variety. These were the bales that Tatya sold to his select group of wholesale dealers.

Though the managing agents, Killick Nixon & Co, were responsible for the mill's policy and administration, day-to-day operations at the mill were supervised by a technical cadre—a manager ran the daily operations, while the various departments were under the direction of the carding master, spinning master, weaving master and their assistants. Next in the hierarchy were the jobbers, who were the supervisors of the workers in each department. In the earliest years of the textile industry in India, the administrative as well as the technical staff came from England, but Indians started to take over as masters and managers very soon—as early as 1895 more than half of staff positions in the Bombay mills were held by Indians.[25]

Inside Kohinoor Mills

What was Kohinoor Mills like as a place of work? When I visited Kohinoor Mill No. 1 briefly in 2009, it was a dilapidated structure with broken windows, and I was not allowed to go more than a few steps through the gate. However, just inside the gate was a small building, probably with no more than one or two rooms inside, where Tatya used to sit for his work when visiting the mills.

Many of the old textile mills in Bombay had their own water tanks that had existed for more than a century. Kohinoor was no exception, and all three of its mills had old water tanks. By 2002, when Kohinoor No. 3 employed just 'a handful of workers paid for doing nothing', the water tank was the only feature that was active: '… the unit swung into operation sporadically during the day when the watchmen opened the gates for the tankers which would trundle in to draw water from the tank to sell to the public. That was the only source of revenue for the unit.'[26]

A study of Kohinoor's dilapidated buildings in 1995 noted that

> … there are multi-storey buildings as well as single-storey ones. The single storey structures have magnificent north-facing glazed roofs, designed to provide even daylighting in an era before

> electricity … The structure of the overall built form that evolved incrementally is almost a microcosm of a city with spaces within that suggest streets and squares … Most of the buildings still have their machinery within, while many of the open areas are also littered with junk, scrap and defunct machinery. [There are] vast warehouses and shed spaces …[27]

Inside Kohinoor Mills, the daily life of a cotton mill worker would have been very similar to this graphic description about cotton mill workers in Bombay between 1890 and 1919:

> A cotton millworker had to get up very early in the morning at about 4 or 4.30 a.m. After making his ablutions, he cooked his meals if he was alone. If he had a family or ate at the khanavali, he either took a quick meal or simply started for work and had his meals brought to the workplace later in the day. He could not afford to be late because fines would be imposed otherwise. In his worry not to be late, if he arrived at the factory a bit too soon he lay down on the pavement besides it and took a short rest till the factory gates opened. Then he had to insert his 'chappa' or the 'ticket of presence' into its proper slit in the box kept for the purpose. After this, he was allowed in. By now the machinery had already started moving; the temperature and humidity inside the mill kept increasing partly because certain levels were required for the purpose of manufacture, and partly because so many people were crammed in an ill-ventilated space. If the worker was new to the city and the work, the sight of these 'vast, dim, cavernous places, with their bewildering vistas of rotating wheels and belts and shaftings' must have filled him with awe. Even if he was an old hand, running to-and-fro among the ceaselessly moving intricate machinery demanded a kind of attention which would soon exhaust him.[28]

The textile mill strikes that had increased in frequency and organisation between the two world wars also indicate that working conditions and salaries were less than ideal. Without going into the details of working conditions, it is clear that the life of a textile mill worker was a gruelling one.

Diverse Selling Agencies and Investments

In 1943, in the midst of the Second World War, it emerged that the Sassoon United Mills, comprising of five textile mills, was up for sale. The Sassoons, a Jewish family, were among the richest Indians at the time. They wanted to exit from the textile industry entirely and wanted to sell their mills. Tatya, along with other investors, decided to buy them. The deal was structured by one of Tatya's close Marwari friends, Tansukhrai Karundia, who was connected with a firm called Ganesh Narayan Omkar. Karundia was reputed to be a financial wizard. He created a deal whereby the Sassoon Mills would be bought by a group of businessmen for about 4 crores.*

At this time, Tatya had a stake in the Morarjee Gokuldas Spinning and Weaving Mills (known as Morarjee Mills) located on Suparibaug Road, Parel. Morarjee Mills was the oldest textile company in India, established in 1871. It was acquired by the Piramal family in 1935, and was well known for producing khaki cloth for soldiers' uniforms during the Second World War, earning a gold medal from the Viceroy of India for this contribution.[29] Tatya had bought a stake in Morarjee Mills when the owners, the Piramals, needed his help after suffering losses on the stock market. Tatya was the chairman of Morarjee Mills, while his son-in-law, Baburao Dabke, was given the role of purchase manager. In August 1941, Tatya had also received the Viceroy and Governor General of India, the Marquess of Linlithgow, on a tour of the mills.

---

* After India became independent, the name of the Sassoon Mills was changed to India United, but was often referred to as 'Indu Mills'.

When the Piramals recovered from their losses, they offered to buy back Tatya's stake in the Morarjee Mills. So it was that Tatya exited from his investment, instead taking a '2-anna stake' (a 12.5 per cent stake) in buying the Sassoon Mills, which meant an investment of about 50 lakh rupees. The other investors were various Marwari business families. Due to Tatya's experience as a selling agent, the group of investors decided to hand over the selling agency to Tatya. Tatya put his nephew, Raghunathrao (Anna's son), in charge of this agency.

Within six months, it became clear to some of the other investors that Tatya, as per his reputation, had no intention of dealing in any black money as the selling agent for the Sassoon Mills. During and after both world wars, when cloth was scarce, many selling agents made vast amounts of money by receiving the cloth from the mills at a fixed price and selling it for three times the price. But Tatya had not profited from black money in the First World War, and was not about to do so during the Second World War either. Due to this mismatch in chemistry with some of the other investors, Tatya decided to exit from the investment and sold his stake.

The above is just one example illustrating why Tatya was widely respected, and known for his insistence on honesty and integrity in his business dealings. He was a prominent member of the textile community, and in the 1930s also served as an arbitrator and an umpire on the Piecegoods Merchants' Panel appointed by the Millowners' Association to settle disputes.[30]

Other selling agencies acquired by Tatya over the years were the selling agency of W.H. Brady & Co.'s City Mills, located on Albert Road in Chinchpokhli, of which his nephew Raghunathrao was given independent control, and the sole selling agency for two mills belonging to the Nizam of Hyderabad. In 1939, seeing the success of City Mills and Morarjee Mills, the Industrial Nizam Trust had sent an invitation to Raghunathrao and Tatya to take over the selling agency of the Osmanshahi Mill in Nanded and the Azamshahi Mill in Warangal. Both mills produced Maratha-style dhotis made of coarse, thick material, and both were running at a loss. About 22,000 bales of dhoti cloth were lying unsold. Tatya asked Raghunathrao to look after the selling agencies of both these mills through two firms formed for the purpose: 'Madhav Surendra' and 'Arvind Surendra' (named after Raghunathrao's son Surendra, and Tatya's grandsons Madhav and Arvind). Within three years, Raghunathrao and Tatya's son Bhausaheb, with guidance from Tatya, had managed to dispose of the unsold bales at various markets around India, and turned both Osmanshahi and Azamshahi into profitable mills. Both soon began giving annual profits of 30–50 lakh rupees.[31]

It was due to Tatya's reputation and his knowledge of the business that he was able to acquire and successfully handle the selling agencies of multiple textile mills simultaneously. Shambhu Kumar Kasliwal of S. Kumar's textiles, and a close friend of Tatya's son Bhausaheb, points to the importance of ethics in Tatya's success:

> Every dealer in cloth would [in those days] prefer to be a Kohinoor dealer than [being] with any other mill .... I would say following ethics fully was their [Kohinoor's] biggest plus point, rather than superiority in fabrics. Because fabric was produced by many mills. I would rather say that 60% of the credit goes to Tatyasaheb's sale policy or sale system, and 40% to the management for maintaining the quality [of the textiles]. The management was also ethical .... So that was a very great point of Tatyasaheb—ethics—that is the point of what made him what he was. Ethics do not stop at honesty—it is also about how you carry out so many other things.[32]

An Unexpected Direction

Textile trading remained at the core of Tatya's wealth till the end of his life in 1952. It was not, however, his only business. Towards the end of the First World War, he branched out into an entirely different industry.

By 1918, through the run-up to war as well as during the boom-time of the First World War, Tatya had established himself as a premier businessman. His fortunes had risen to incredible heights. In 1911 or 1912, shortly after gaining the sole selling agency of Kohinoor Mills, he had moved his family from the cramped rooms of Khatryachi Chawl to spacious apartments in a building called Peerbhoy Mansion on Sandhurst Road (now Sardar Vallabhbhai Patel Road), just a couple of minutes' walk from Khatryachi Chawl. It must have seemed that as fast as Kohinoor was spinning yarn, Vaman Seth was spinning gold. Even beyond the end of the war in 1918, boom conditions prevailed, with Indian mills making record profits between 1918 and 1921, and the scrips of mills being quoted on the stock exchange at six or seven times over the par value.[33] It was said that the triangle formed by the Esplanade Cross Road, Kalbadevi Road and Sheikh Memon Street 'contained the greater part of the accumulated riches of Bombay'.[34] MJ Market was located in the middle of this triangle, and Tatya was very much a part of this story of the rapid accumulation of wealth.

By the end of the First World War, we see the emergence of an entrepreneur who was extremely ambitious and not afraid to diversify into new territory. He was not content with linking his fortunes to textiles. While the textile industry was among the first indigenous, modern industries in the country, another thoroughly modern enterprise was about to take hold in India—the film industry. The next opportunity to come Tatya's way was motion pictures.

Chapter 4

The Film Industry Years 1917–32

IN 1917, TATYA ENTERED A BUSINESS THAT WAS A STARTLING contrast to his background. He became a silent film producer and financier, running the Hindustan Film Company from 1917 to 1932. In the *Kirloskar* magazine interview, almost thirty years after entering the film business, he recounted that Dadasaheb Phalke, who is now known as the father of Indian cinema, had come to him with a request for financial assistance in making films; Tatya agreed to help him out, but Phalke insisted on his further involvement: 'Dhundiraj Phalke was my friend. I have great respect for those starting new ventures. I simply wanted to help Phalke a little in his film business, but then he just wouldn't let go of me!'[1]

However, the apparent reluctance with which Tatya embarked on this project is completely at odds with his involvement in setting up the Hindustan Film Company in Nasik and running it successfully for a full sixteen years. Not only did he continue to run it following Phalke's exit, but he also set up a second production house called the Bharat Film Company in Pune. Therefore, I am inclined to take Tatya's declaration of reluctance with a pinch of salt. Perhaps he was not all that reluctant to get involved. Or perhaps it could be that he was indeed a man who did not believe in half measures and, having found himself embarked upon the film business, decided to go at it with gusto and make sure he spun money out of it. By the time the Hindustan Film Company wound up in 1932, it had produced around ninety-seven feature films and twenty-six short documentaries,[2] while the Bharat Film Company had produced ten feature films.[3] All were silent films.

When Tatya began financing Dadasaheb Phalke in 1917, these were the pioneering years of Indian cinema. Only five years earlier, in 1912, India's first feature film had released. Nobody could have predicted at the time that the film industry would turn out to have such a grip on the nation. A look further back to the end of the previous century provides an overview of the context in which moving pictures, and the Hindustan Film Company, emerged.

The Emergence of Moving Pictures

In 1892, the same year that Tatya had arrived in Bombay as a seventeen-year-old trainee in MJ Market, the first magic lantern show (also known as shambarik kharolika) took place in Bombay, put on by a family called the Patwardhans.

The magic lantern was essentially a slide projector. It produced a cinema-like show by utilising hand-painted, four-inch-wide glass plates and slides. It was a device that had been used by showmen in Europe since the end of the seventeenth century, and it remained among the most popular forms of entertainment till the advent of cinema.[4]

The Patwardhans screened their first show in 1892 on Lord Krishna's life, following it up with a new show depicting circus animals. Its popularity was such that they were able to begin selling tickets for regular shows at a theatre. Most of their stories were mythological. The technique for making the pictures 'move' was to paint one main scene on a slide and then paint another slide to overlay the first one. The second slide could be rapidly moved over the first slide to make certain elements in the scene appear to be in motion. In 1894, the Patwardhan family devised a way to make their moving pictures more realistic by using three magic lanterns simultaneously. Two were used to show the action while the third one was used to project the setting of the action, such as forests or palaces. By 1902, the Patwardhans had about a thousand picture slides and evolved their technique further by getting running commentaries written for each show; music was composed too and dialogues written, all to be performed live while the magic lantern pictures moved. The shows continued till 1918, long after silent films had become popular; in fact, silent films utilised techniques similar to the magic lantern shows, such as live commentaries and music during screenings.[5]

Just four years after the Patwardhans' first magic lantern show, the first Indian screening of a film took place in Bombay's Watson Hotel. It was 1896, only six months after the French brothers Auguste and Louis Lumière had held the first ever film screening in Paris; the Lumière brothers had then sent out touring agents to India to screen their film. It took place in Bombay on the same July day as a special film screening held for the Czar of Russia in St Petersburg. It was advertised as 'The marvel of the century, the wonder of the world. Living photographic pictures in life-sized reproductions'. The title of the show was simply 'Cinematographe' and comprised a series of scenes such as the arrival of a train, or workers leaving a factory. The elite of Bombay, both Indian and European, eagerly attended the first shows. A week later, the screenings shifted to a regular theatre charging a range of admission prices for different classes of seating. Within a few months, other showmen arrived in India with films described as diversely as 'Vitagraph', 'Moto-Photoscope' and 'Andersonoscopograph'. Eventually, silent films became popularly known as 'Bioscope' shows in India, until the arrival of talkies. (Incidentally, while we now call them silent films, we do so only as a way of distinguishing them from talkie films. But in an era when film sound was unheard of, there was no need to describe them as 'silent'.) Soon, foreign film-makers were shooting Indian scenes such as bazaars and religious processions, and popular Western short films like *Gulliver's Travels* (1902) and *Uncle Tom's Cabin* (1903) began screening in India. The first Indian film-maker was Harishchandra Bhatavdekar, a photographer and photo-equipment dealer, who made what was probably India's first newsreel in 1901.[6] Another pioneer, Hiralal Sen, began filming stage plays performed in Calcutta.

The grandeur of the Delhi Durbar in 1911 as well as the British royal family's visits to Bombay and Calcutta were filmed by Hiralal Sen, S.N. Patankar, Madan Theatres as well as several foreign cameramen.[7] However, no Indian had so far ventured into making feature films, i.e. dramatic stories designed and performed specifically for the camera, as opposed to merely stage-plays captured on film.

Enter the first Indian feature film, which was not Phalke's *Raja Harishchandra*, as is popularly assumed, but a film called *Pundalik* released in 1912, based on a Marathi play about a saint. It was made by three partners called Torney, Chitre and Tipnis. Film historian Suresh Chabria notes, 'Though the press praised the film it seems to have been rather crudely acted and made—a fact that has somewhat obscured its pioneer status.' The second Indian feature film attempted was called *Savitri* and made by S.N. Patankar, V.P. Divekar and A.P. Karandikar, who later formed Patankar Friends and Co., one of the earliest film companies. But they discovered that the developing of their film was defective. Despite having already advertised the film, it could not be released.[8]

So it was that Phalke's *Raja Harishchandra*, released in 1913, was the first Indian feature film to earn widespread acclaim.

The Formation of the Hindustan Film Company

It was in 1917, four years after the release of *Raja Harishchandra*, that Tatya, along with four other partners, agreed to finance Dadasaheb Phalke in his film-making ventures. A firm called Hindustan Film Company was set up towards the end of 1917, with five financiers—V.S. Apte (Tatya), Mayashankar Bhatt, Gokuldas Damodar, Madhavji Jesing and L.B. Phatak. Like Tatya, all of these gentlemen were involved in the textile industry, with the exception of L.B. Phatak, who was a well-known civil contractor. Tatya became the managing partner in the Hindustan Film Company, while Phalke was named as the working partner.[9]

Dadasaheb Phalke had, by then, already produced four successful silent films under his own production company known as Phalke Films, including *Lanka Dahan* in 1917, which has been described as India's first box office hit. He had also made several short documentary films. Why, then, did a successful film-maker like Phalke need financial assistance, and how did he end up working with financiers from the textile industry who had not the slightest background in films?

Phalke had, in fact, gone through a number of ups and downs in his film-making ventures, all of which throw light on the turbulence that was to characterise the working relationship between Phalke and the Hindustan Film Company under Tatya's management.

Phalke was born near Nasik in 1870 (and was therefore five years older than Tatya). As a young man, he studied art and architecture in Bombay and Baroda. He conducted photographic experiments in the photo studio in Baroda's Kalabhavan. He also participated in stage dramas and learnt to perform magic. All these skills, not to mention his boyhood knowledge of Hindu texts like the Puranas, Ramayana and Mahabharata, came in handy later in life when he made his mythological films.

The story of the beginning of Phalke's film career has by now assumed the stature of legend among cinema buffs and historians—his viewing of a film called *Life of Christ* in 1910 in a cinema on Sandhurst Road in Bombay led to a eureka moment for him, when he asked himself the question, if the life of Christ could be depicted on film, then why not the lives of Ram, Krishna and, for that matter, the entire pantheon of Hindu gods and goddesses? He embarked on a year-long series of filmic experiments, convinced that the time had come to introduce cinema as the new Swadeshi industry—Swadeshi being an idea full of patriotic fervour at the time.

In 1912, he travelled to England to acquaint himself with the latest in film-production techniques. On his return to India, he began what appears to have been an almost life-long struggle with finance, mortgaging his wife's jewellery to make his first film in 1912, *Raja Harishchandra*. All the roles, including the female ones, were played by male actors—a custom which endured several years into India's silent film era.

In May 1913, the film began screening at Bombay's Coronation Cinema. For the first few days, he had to arrange for a dance programme performed by a Miss Irene Delmar, as well as a juggling and comic act, to generate publicity and attract viewers.[10] The film got rave reviews in the press—the *Bombay Chronicle* called it 'a remarkable triumph'. One of Phalke's trump cards was his imaginative use of trick photography to create illusions such as the miraculous appearance of divine beings. Audiences found this as captivating and entertaining as the arrival on film of well-known and well-loved characters from Hindu mythology. The film ran for twenty-three days, which was an exceptional achievement at a time when films ran for barely four days. It was successfully released in other theatres too.[11]

Phalke then made two more mythological films, both in 1914: *Mohini Bhasmasur* (which featured the first Indian film actress, Kamlabai Gokhale)* and *Savitri Satyavan*. Wrote Phalke in the newspaper *Navyug* in 1917, 'One print each of the three films brought in more money than the total debt I had incurred.'[12]

Such was the demand for his films, which even became known abroad, that Phalke decided to travel to England once again to invest in new film equipment and screen his films there too. But just as he arrived in England in 1914, the First World War broke out. Panic ensued in India and his financier pulled out. Unable to make another film without an investor, Phalke began approaching princely families and businessmen, and even launched a public appeal for funds, but people were simply not willing to take any risks with their money during wartime. Phalke finally secured a loan of 5,000 rupees from the princess of the state of Indore and 1,000 rupees from the ruler of Aundh. With some additional loans from friends, he had a total of 8,000 rupees. On this amount, he managed to make a new film called *Lanka Dahan*, as well as a new version of *Raja Harishchandra*. *Lanka Dahan* was hugely successful. When it released at Bombay's West End cinema in 1917, surging crowds continuously surrounded the theatre. The road was filled with bullock carts in which religious devotees from small towns and villages had travelled for a darshan of Ram and Hanuman on screen. The demand was so great that the theatre had to abandon its normal schedule and screened shows continuously till late at night.[13]

---

* Kamlabai was the grandmother of the well-known actor Vikram Gokhale who passed away in 2022.

Phalke wrote about the film, '*Lanka Dahan* was a tremendous box-office draw. It collected Rs. 32,000 at West End, Bombay, in the first ten days alone. The Aryan Cinema, Poona, had the same experience. The eager mob almost broke the doors of the cinema in Poona. In Madras, *Lanka Dahan* collections had to be carried in a bullock cart with the help of police.'[14]

Phalke received several offers at this point from financiers interested in collaborating with him.[15] One of the industrialists who offered to invest money in a film was Walchand Hirachand Sethji (1882–1953, founder of the Walchand Group). Phalke's blunt manner, however, put Walchand off. The industrialist wanted Phalke to make a film within three or four months, but Phalke refused to accept this restriction, saying he was a creative artist and could not guarantee when the film would be completed. Gangadhar Pathak, the owner of Aryan Cinema, arranged the meeting, and he recounted Phalke's words: 'This Mr Walchand is a capitalist. They know all about investments. All they know is how to put forward terms and conditions.' Walchand could not take what he called Phalke's 'whimsical' behaviour, and the talks ended acrimoniously.[16]

At this time, Phalke was also in talks with Fatima Begum, an actress (whose daughter Zubeida went on to star in *Alam Ara*, India's first talkie film, in 1931). Fatima Begum wanted to offer Phalke one lakh rupees. Before the matter could be settled Phalke withdrew from Fatima Begum's offer[17] because he had managed to secure finance from a group of five industrialists in Bombay—V.S. Apte and his business associates. However, Tatya's son, Bhausaheb, clarified in later years that the offer from Tatya and his associates was less a business proposition, and more a response to a request made by freedom fighter Lokmanya Tilak.

While Tatya refused to discuss his experiences of the Hindustan Film Company in the *Kirloskar* magazine interview around 1947, Bhausaheb was not so reluctant to talk about it. In an article written in the late 1970s, titled 'Dadasaheb Phalke and his financier Tatyasaheb Apte' and based on interviewing Bhausaheb, the journalist C. Antony Louis recounts: 'When DG Phalke was looking for some financiers to expand his Phalke Films ... he was introduced to Vaman Shridhar Apte, alias Tatyasaheb, by a note given to him by Dr Bhadkamkar [an eminent scholar of Sanskrit] which the latter had got from Lokmanya Tilak. Phalke first met Tilak on board the ship which Tilak was taking on his way to England as leader of an Indian delegation and this is how they came to know each other briefly.' This note was delivered to Tatya when he was in a business meeting with his associates, Mayashankar Bhatt, Gokuldas Damodar, Madhavji Jesing and Laxman Balwant Phatak. Tatya introduced Phalke to these men and passed around the letter of recommendation from Lokmanya Tilak. Now Tilak had only four years previously returned from prison in Mandalay, Burma, after a six-year imprisonment for sedition against the British and was a great national hero. This group of businessmen had such a high regard for Lokmanya Tilak that they all agreed to finance Phalke despite not knowing anything about film production.

Phalke needed 60,000 rupees to make a film called *Kaliya Mardan*. Having agreed to supply him with this amount of money, it was then decided that Phalke should immediately set off for Nasik, where he had set up a studio in a bungalow called 'Haudacha Bangla', and begin work on the film.[18] Phalke chose Nasik because, he said, 'the climate there is most suited to photography' and because there were useful places nearby where he could shoot his films, such as 'oriental jungles, historical places and rivers'. Phalke was familiar with the region, and it was cheaper to run a studio in Nasik as compared to Bombay.[19] Phalke Films was incorporated into a new company called the Hindustan Film Company. This meant that Phalke's previous films—four features and sixteen short films—became the property of the Hindustan

Film Company.[20] Due to this financial assistance, Phalke was able to build a pucca studio at Nasik. According to Bapu Watwe, Phalke's biographer, the Hindustan Film Company was formed on 1 January 1918.[21] The business address of the Hindustan Film Company was 125 Narayan Mansion, Girgaum Back Road, Bombay,[22] not far from Tatya's residence and his MJ Market pedhi where he traded textiles.

However, after Phalke began shooting *Kaliya Mardan* at Nasik, he appears to have suddenly changed his mind. He put the project on hold and embarked instead on making a film called *Shri Krishna Janma*. The making of *Shri Krishna Janma* was not without a few comic asides: for the scene of baby Krishna's naming ceremony, the five male actors who normally played female roles dressed up for the shot. But Phalke needed to show a crowd of women for the scene, and hence every staff member who was willing to don a sari was required to do so; even Phalke's cook was not spared. It was a terrible sight—none of these impromptu extras looked even remotely feminine. Eventually Phalke shot the scene by mainly showing the backs of their heads. In a triumph of trick photography, Phalke showed several avatars of Krishna in one shot—each one wielding a different weapon against his uncle Kansa, who had imprisoned him—by using the same film ten times over to shoot Krishna in different corners of the frame.[23] In another scene, he managed to show Kansa hallucinating that his head was cut off and was floating away in a spurt of blood. Film historian Chabria notes unconfirmed reports that the blood in this scene was hand-tinted in red, creating a 'coloured' scene.[24]

Till the film was completed, all five of Phalke's financiers were blissfully unaware that Phalke was shooting a film called *Shri Krishna Janma*, instead of the agreed-upon *Kaliya Mardan* project. Thus, the very first silent film produced by the Hindustan Film Company was *Shri Krishna Janma* in 1918, and only later did Phalke complete *Kaliya Mardan*, which was released in 1919. Both films were extremely successful. *Shri Krishna Janma* was released on 24 August 1918 in Bombay's Majestic Theatre, which had opened in Girgaon earlier that year. It had a length of 5,500 feet, its six reels running for about 90 minutes.* It made a profit of 3 lakh rupees, an enormous sum at the time.[25] At the Majestic Theatre itself it ran for eight consecutive weeks, an unheard-of record.[26] The title card of the film read: 'The Hindustan Film Co. Presents their First Grand Production SHREE KRISHNA JANMA (Birth of Shree Krishna) Produced by Mr DG Phalke The Pioneer Cine Artist of the East'.

Despite the fact that the Hindustan Film Company had proved, in its very first film, to be an incredibly shrewd business investment, Tatya and his four partners were not pleased with Phalke's way of doing things, and summoned him to Bombay. They argued that Phalke should have stuck to the original agreement to make *Kaliya Mardan* first, and did not wish him to use their money to finance films of his own choice, that too without informing them. Louis' article states, 'During this meeting, tempers rose high, heated exchanges took place and Phalke asserted he was a top class artiste and that he will not be dictated to by his financiers.'[27]

It appears to have been a classic clash of art and business. While Phalke no doubt surged forward on his creative impulses, and in fact came up with two winners in both the films he made, his financiers would have none of it—the world they came from was based on financial contracts and solid business commitments. They could hardly be expected to waft along on creative fancies and were not about to invest money in a venture that did not produce what was agreed upon in the first place. (One can imagine the annoyed discussion among the five financiers, none of whom had so far had the slightest exposure to the world of films: '*Tell me*

---

* Silent films ran at 60 feet a minute. Phalke mentions in an interview that *Raja Harishchandra*, at 3700 feet, took about an hour to show (Anon. 1913b).

Vaman Seth, what if I agreed to sell you silk and showed up with a bale of cotton instead? Even if it was the finest bale of cotton, would that be any way to run a business?')

Kaliya Mardan, a six-reel film of 6,000 feet that ran for 100 minutes, was released on 3 May 1919, also in Bombay's Majestic Theatre. Phalke's five-year-old daughter, Mandakini, played the lead role of Krishna, and audiences loved her. She would dress up as Krishna at the Majestic Theatre for the eager crowds, and some touched her feet in reverence even if she happened to be walking on the road.[28] According to film historian B.V. Dharap, during a triumphant aarti scene, which is shown after Krishna subdues Kaliya the snake, audiences would start singing devotional songs and shouting nationalist slogans, equating the defeated snake with colonial rule.[29]

Kaliya Mardan did such excellent business that there were not enough prints of the film to keep up with the demand. It ran at the Majestic Theatre for ten months; and for the next ten years, it could be found playing somewhere or the other in India.[30] However, despite this second success on the heels of the first, Phalke quit the Hindustan Film Company the same year due to differences with his financiers.

Phalke did not help his own cause, for his nature was temperamental and inflexible, which often alienated his business partners and contributed to the Hindustan Film Company's on-again-off-again relationship with its most well-known film-maker—a situation which lasted for years. Phalke's biographer Bapu Watwe writes, 'Phalke would not hesitate to speak bluntly to his partners. His nature was obstinate, whimsical, stubborn and hot-headed. He was never able to balance the requirements of business and art, which was an important factor in the immense success of [for example,] Prabhat Films.' For instance, during the filming of *Kaliya Mardan*, one of the five business partners, L.B. Phatak, was present at the shooting. There were several re-takes of a shot. Seeing this, Phatak spoke up. 'How will the Hindustan Film Company be able to afford it,' he asked Phalke, 'if you waste so much film on a single shot.' Phalke was not the sort of person to tolerate being questioned. His reply was scathing. 'Phatak,' he said, 'you are a contractor by profession. What do you know of the art of film-making? This job needs brains which the Almighty has given me, and not you, so kindly sit still and do not poke your nose into my shot.' It is not clear from Watwe's biography, in which this incident is recounted, as to how Watwe came to know the words that were exchanged. However, the caustic tone of the exchange is clear, and must have caused immense harm to Phalke's relations with Phatak, a man whose support he so obviously needed.

There were other disagreements with his financiers: there was an incident where one of the partners, Mayashankar Bhatt, sent the negatives of *Lanka Dahan*, *Shri Krishna Janma* and *Kaliya Mardan* to America to get prints made, with his nephew who was going there to learn film-making; Phalke was of the opinion that there was no need to put the company to this expense when the prints could have been made in India. In another incident, an American, Captain Rowan, was appointed as the manager of the Hindustan Film Company on a salary of 1700 rupees per month; again, Phalke objected to the unnecessary expense, pointing out the vast disparity between the American manager's salary and the normal salary scale of the company, which ranged from 15 rupees to 100 rupees per month. In both these cases, it is clear that Phalke may have indeed had a valid point. But it appears that most of the time he was not able to disagree in a tactful manner. He could not bear anyone to interfere in his creative vision, and the main bone of contention with his financiers was that he did not care about the money or time taken to achieve his creative vision.

After just two films, *Shri Krishna Janma* and *Kaliya Mardan*, it was clear to Phalke that he could not work with the five financiers, and he decided to resign from the Hindustan Film Company. His lawyer, though, had some bad news for him—it was not going to be so easy to resign. The reason for this was that Phalke had signed a fifteen-year agreement with the Hindustan Film Company, in which one of the conditions was that if he were to leave the company earlier, not only would he not get his share of the profits (which, so far, amounted to about 1 lakh rupees), but he would also have to pay the company 50,000 rupees.

While Phalke found himself in this unfortunate position, Tatya and his four business partners were worried about the future of the film company. It was clear that Phalke wanted to leave. But if he left, who would run the company? With this worry in mind, the partners summoned Phalke's staff, especially old and trusted staff members like Mama Shinde, Krishna (Anna) Salunke, Gajananrao Sane, Trimbakrao Telang, Dutta Telang and Nath Telang, who had been with Phalke through thick and thin since the days of *Raja Harishchandra*. These staff members were told that the partners did not want Phalke to leave the company, but also did not wish to force him to stay. After he left, the only alternative to shutting down the company was for the old, experienced staff members to take over the film-making. The partners said that winding up the company would be of no consequence to them, since none of them was financially dependent on it, but that it would have a devastating impact on the employees who would suddenly find themselves without jobs. Taking stock of this situation, the staff agreed to stay on in the Hindustan Film Company despite Phalke's departure. After many years of irregular and uncertain salaries, the staff were now enjoying the stability of salaries being paid regularly and on time, and no doubt this played a part in the collective decision. So it was that the Hindustan Film Company continued on the basis of the old and experienced hands, so well trained by Phalke over the years.[31]

In 1970, Phalke's son, Bhalchandra, wrote about his father's disillusionment with the Hindustan Film Company: 'One of the unaccomplished and highly cherished goals of my father's life was to bring colour photography on the Indian screen. That was one of the reasons why he joined hands with financial interests in a partnership firm like the Hindustan Film Company. But he soon realised that finance was of no use unless supported by firm determination and ambitious spirit. He saw that though there was no dearth of money, there was no intention to spend it for a solid, purposeful scheme. He also wished his old equipment to be replaced by the latest one but that too did not happen.'[32]

It is not clear to what extent the partners eventually enforced the financial penalties of Phalke's contract, but nevertheless a disillusioned Phalke moved to Benares with his family in 1919.

Film Production With and Without Phalke

Phalke's departure created upheaval in the Hindustan Film Company. Four of the five original financiers, Bhatt, Phatak, Jesing and Damodar, were not interested in looking into the running of the company. And so, with Phalke gone, most of the responsibility of film production fell onto Tatya, for he was the managing partner. With the help of Phalke's well-trained studio assistants, Tatya took on a far more active role in the production of films. He could no longer be just a financier of the Hindustan Film Company, for the situation had evolved. He now had to run the company and take the lead in producing films. The film historian B.V. Dharap writes, 'This was a real testing period for the Managing Partner [Apte]. But he rose to the occasion with a will and determination to continue producing films. With the aid of Phalke's assistants, he kept the production going … With the sudden exit of Phalke …, Apte seems to have learnt another important lesson in film production, i.e. not to depend only on one man if the production is to carry on uninterrupted.'[33]

So it was that the Hindustan Film Company not only got different people to direct its films, but in 1921, Tatya also set up a second film company, the Bharat Film Company, in Pune: 'Apte, therefore, extended an invitation to two other technicians, Karandikar and Divekar, from Patankar Friends and Co., another early production company. Apte provided them with finance and asked them to set up a studio in Pune. Thus Apte's other film unit started in Pune, the new studio named Bharat Film Company. Within two years—1921 and 1922—Bharat Film Company produced ten pictures, all mythologicals.'[34] The filmography of the Bharat Film Company (Appendix 3) shows that Vishnupant Divekar and A.P. Karandikar worked as a team on all ten feature films, the former as director and the latter as cameraman.

From 1921 onwards, coinciding with the establishment of the Bharat Film Company, the Hindustan Film Company found itself on a firm footing and produced films at a steady clip for the next decade. In 1918, it made one film, in 1919, two and in 1920 it made three films. But in 1921, production jumped to eight films and remained steady at eight to ten films a year. The year 1925 was a peak year, with thirteen films being made. It was only in 1930 that there was a visible slowing down, with only five films in 1930, four in 1931 and then one final film in 1932. (See the filmography of the Hindustan Film Company in Appendix 2).

The first film to be produced by the Hindustan Film Company after Phalke's exit was *Ahilya Uddhar*, followed by a film called *Ushaswapna*.* Meanwhile, seeing that *Shri Krishna Janma* and *Kaliya Mardan* had brought in excellent financial returns, and realising that Phalke was living without much money in Benares,

* The film *Ushaswapna* does not appear in the filmography of the Hindustan Film Company, but was mentioned by Bhausaheb, based on his personal recollections, in his interview with C. Antony Louis.

Tatya decided to send him 500 rupees by money order every month. But Phalke was too proud to accept it, and the very first money order was returned to Tatya.[35]

Despite their differences and diverse styles of working, Tatya and Phalke collaborated on another project at this point even though Phalke had left the Hindustan Film Company in a huff. It was a stage show called *Rangbhoomi*, staged in Bombay's Baliwala Theatre in 1922, and then in Pune and Nasik. Phalke wrote and conceived of this play during his stint in Benares, after leaving the Hindustan Film Company. It involved a revolving theatre and was to be viewed over two consecutive nights. It had seven acts, four acts to be viewed on the first night and three on the next.[36] Tatya listened to the play read out to him by Phalke, and realised that in his disillusionment Phalke had included several direct and indirect barbed references to Tatya and the other financiers of the Hindustan Film Company. But he decided to overlook this aspect of the play and agreed to provide finance since the idea of a revolving theatre appealed to him as something novel and original. Phalke even prepared a papier-mâché model of the revolving theatre to demonstrate how it would work. Tatya invested about 90,000 rupees in the venture.[37] (Bapu Watwe's biography of Phalke gives an alternate figure of 70,000 rupees as the production cost of the play[38]).

Narayan Hari Apte, who was a well-known novelist, short-story writer and scriptwriter (and no relation of Tatya), was roped in by Phalke to write the play, but there were too many disagreements between them. Narayan Hari Apte later recounted that Phalke was too extreme in his criticism: 'Phalke wrote the play because he felt that his partners [in the Hindustan Film Company] behaved badly. But in truth, I never felt that they had behaved badly.'[39] Phalke felt that his film fans would want to see his play as well, but unfortunately audiences didn't like the production. Apart from the problem of its length, the play's subject, and even its humour, was based on the problems of the theatre world, which most people couldn't relate to. The play flopped and most of the money was lost. Phalke's son later recounted that his father had lost 40,000 rupees in the venture.[40] While Phalke was busy with the play, he had declared to the newspaper *Sandesh* that as far as films were concerned, he was dead. *Sandesh* then published an article titled 'The Death of Phalke'. The article created a flurry of readers' letters expressing dismay at Phalke's self-imposed exile and pushed Phalke to return to Nasik,[41] where the Hindustan Film Company was still in full swing.

So it was that three years after leaving the Hindustan Film Company in 1919, Phalke and his family returned from Benares to Nasik in 1922 for a brief period—perhaps a trial of sorts. During this stay, before he left for Benares again, Phalke guided and advised the technicians of the Hindustan Film Company on various production matters, particularly trick photography, in which he was an expert. Journalist Louis writes, 'Perhaps here lies a true measure of the greatness of the man and the artiste. For whatever were his differences of opinion with Tatyasaheb and others, when it came to giving himself to the art to which he was devoted, he gave all of himself.'[42] (Of course, the fact that Tatya had just financed his *Rangbhoomi* may also explain this to some extent.)

During his stay in Nasik, Tatya invited Phalke back to work as an advisor, to which Phalke agreed. By 1922, the Bharat Film Company, which Tatya had started the previous year in Pune, was not doing well, and Tatya perhaps felt that Phalke's inputs would be helpful not just to the Hindustan Film Company, but to the Bharat Film Company as well. Though Phalke was no longer a partner, and was a paid employee on a salary of 1,000 rupees a month, Tatya and the other partners continued to treat him as an equal. He didn't need to sign an attendance roster, nor were there any restrictions on him as for the other employees, and a horse carriage was provided for his use. If he left the sets in one of his famous hot tempers nobody stopped him, and whenever he chose to return nobody questioned him. But once again, there was a clash of art and business; the old disagreements with the partners arose again, and Phalke was never comfortable with the requirements of the business side of film-making. He spent a great deal of money, for example, on re-shooting portions of his films if he happened to find a location better than the one in which the shooting had already been completed. On the other hand, it must be noted that though Phalke gave little thought to expense, this also meant that he created stunning visuals on screen that others would have thought impossible.[43]

A strong point of the Hindustan Film Company was that Tatya managed to ensure that its success was not reliant on Phalke's presence. While Phalke had been away in Benares, the Hindustan Film Company had become an extremely profitable venture. Film historians Bapu Watwe and B.V. Dharap have both noted that this was due to Tatya's management and business sense. He had managed to get Phalke's old assistants to make profitable films, and while the cost of making one film was 10,000 rupees, the monthly earnings of the film company were 40,000 rupees. Tatya had also apparently found a way to manage his relations with Phalke in a way that would be agreeable to all.[44] Many of my interviewees referred to Tatya's skills in dealing with people in an amicable and fair manner, and his flair for maintaining good relations with his associates; his relations with Phalke, which were regularly renewed and soothed, would appear to support these statements.

Film historian Dharap writes:

> Even after the return of Phalke to the Hindustan fold in 1922, Apte took care of production work and saw to it that at least six or more pictures were produced every year—with or without Phalke. As a seasoned businessman, Apte had already set up

> a distribution office of Hindustan Film Company in Bombay early in 1919 and with the combined products of Hindustan and Bharat Film Company he opened another distribution office of Hindustan Film Company in Madras in 1922. It was because of these marketing arrangements that Apte could keep the production rolling year after year. When he saw that he could not divide his attention between Nasik and Pune, he decided to close down the studios of Bharat Film Company in Pune towards the end of 1922 and concentrated mainly on Nasik. Apte's distribution offices were managed initially by his Hindustan partner Mayashankar Bhatt along with his relative Dabke [Tatya's son-in-law, who had married his daughter Durga in 1913] ... it was Apte who continued to produce pictures until the advent of talkies in 1931. In all, Apte produced 96 feature films for Hindustan between 1920 and 1931 in addition to 10 features produced by Bharat Film Company in 1921-22.[45]

The Hindustan Film Company was known primarily for making mythological films. Indeed, Phalke was the pioneer of this genre. His trump card—special effects—was perfectly suited to the requirements of mythological stories and legends. He was a film-maker and inventor of real genius. Only a few fragments of the Hindustan Film Company's films remain today, housed in the National Film Archive of India, but they give a wonderful insight into what a Hindustan Film Company hit looked like. There are scenes in those fragments where the special effects are brilliant by any standards, despite the unsophisticated technology at his disposal. In *Kaliya Mardan* (1919), the scene of baby Krishna wrestling with a monstrous snake in the river creates the illusion that the fight is really taking place underwater, thanks to bubbles rising around the action. The snake, with its tail lashing out in the water and its coils slithering around Krishna, is visibly fake but appears fearsome nonetheless. Likewise, *Shri Krishna Janma* (1918) included the wonderfully eerie scene where the head of the evil Kansa floats away from his body.

Phalke also made imaginative use of outdoor locations, such as the panoramic opening shot of *Kaliya Mardan*, with a small Krishna looking at the river and wandering about in the foreground, the wind rustling through the trees and through his hair, and with the silhouettes of three figures by the riverbank in the background. Phalke's indoor scenes sparkled as well: there is a lovely play of light and shadow in the same film, when a female character looks out of a window grill and is covered in dappled sunlight. *Bhakta Prahlad* (1926) had a marvellous set full of opulent pillars, carpets and lamps in the court of Hiranyakishapu. Historian Chabria writes of this film: 'With a rocking camera and superimposed streaks of lightening shooting out as the pillar bursts open to reveal the wrathful [half-man, half-lion] Narasimha, this is perhaps Phalke's most brilliantly executed and elaborate special effects sequence.'[46]

The company did, however, sometimes make social-themed films as well. One of its very successful socially oriented films was titled *Municipal Elections*, made by Phalke and released on 24 May 1924. A reviewer in *Navakaal* newspaper wrote: 'Who will you give your vote to? To Mr Daatkore *["Mr Toothpicker"]* or Mr Bheekmage *[Mr Begging-for-donations]*? … The Hindustan Film Company has prepared this film to publicise the rights of the people, as well as to warn people to stay away from candidates who make false promises, and is a comic film well worth seeing!' Another review appeared the following day: 'The film … shows the monkey-antics of crazy candidates in a wonderful manner. The municipal elections have been justly made fun of.'[47]

Despite successes like these, Tatya had to continually deal with the unpredictability of Phalke leaving and rejoining the film company—he did so no less than three times, starting in 1919, when he went to Benares, before finally leaving for good in 1929. During one of these departures, Gangadhar Pathak, the owner of the Aryan Cinema in Pune, which had profited greatly from Phalke's hit *Lanka Dahan*, took it upon himself to bring Phalke back to the Hindustan Film Company. He later recounted: 'I went to meet Vamanrao Apte. He told me, "Phalke is an intelligent man. But I will not go to invite him back." So I went to Dadasaheb [Phalke] and said, "Look, I am acting as the mediator. You had better go back to the Hindustan Film Company." To my surprise, Dadasaheb said, "When did I ever have an objection to that?" It was on the terrace of my house that the understanding was reached. I felt very satisfied with this turn of events.'[48]

The Hindustan Film Company and the Business of Silent Films

The wider film industry context in which the Hindustan Film Company operated, and in which various film companies jostled for space and exhibitors, centred to a large extent on Bombay. Film historian Suresh Chabria writes: 'In the silent era, as it would also be in later decades, the Bombay film industry was the leader and the ultimate badge of success was to have made it there. In the 1920s … "masala" cinema was already being created. It was, of course, partly the product of Bombay's cosmopolitan character and partly an offshoot of its commercial dynamo which made capital more accessible.'[49]

The most important and prolific film production company in Bombay was Dwarkadas Sampat's Kohinoor Film Company launched in 1918, which made the highest number of silent films and had famous stars like Zubeida, Gohar and Sulochana (Ruby Myers). Its main rival was Ardeshir Irani's Imperial Film Company established in 1926, which had a string of successful silent films. Other major studios were Sharda Film Company started in 1925 by Bhogilal Dave and Nanubhai Desai, specialising in exotic adventure and stunt films starring Master Vithal, who was advertised as India's Douglas Fairbanks;* Chandulal Shah's Ranjit Film Company set up in 1929; and Surya Film Company set up by Haribhai Desai in Bangalore in 1929, which went on to become the largest film producer in South India in the final years of silent films.

By the mid-1920s, writes Chabria, 'India had a large and flourishing studio system ... Films were made in nine broad genres—the mythological, the devotional, the social, the historical, the costume movie, the stunt movie, the comedy, the literary adaptation and the crime movie.'[50] Most film companies specialised in a particular genre of film. For example, Prabhat Films did mainly mythologicals and some social-themed films, Wadia did films with action and an 'Arabian Nights' flavour, Minerva did film adaptations of plays from the Parsi theatre, and Bombay Talkies did socials. Among its contemporaries, the Hindustan Film Company was known for almost exclusively making mythologicals.[51] One of the reasons was that Phalke felt that only mythological films would have an all-India market. In his oral evidence to the Indian Cinematograph Committee† in 1928 he said, 'If I produce Shivaji's life, it will never be appreciated in Bengal or Madras [since Shivaji is a folk hero revered only among Marathi people] ... Only for mythological films we can have an all-India market; for other films, we will have only a provincial market.'[52]

---

* Master Vithal's Douglas Fairbanks was just one example of the popular custom of promoting Indian actors by comparing them to American stars: Ermeline was publicised as the 'Indian Mary Pickford' and Nandram was promoted as the 'Indian Eddie Polo' (Chabria 2013a, p. 20).

† The Indian Cinematograph Committee was set up by the Government of India primarily to examine the system of film censorship in India, as well as to examine the desirability of encouraging the production and exhibition of films made in India. The committee was made up of British and Indian members, and headed by high court lawyer Diwan Rangachariar. The committee travelled around India, recording oral evidence and written statements from over 400 people (Indian Cinematograph Committee 1928a, pp. xi–xii).

To put the entire Indian film industry into context, it is also worth noting that at the height of the silent film era, in 1926–27, only 15 per cent of the feature films released in India were Indian films. Of the films released at this time, 85 per cent were foreign, and mainly American.[53]

What was the Hindustan Film Company like in its day-to-day operations? One can put together a mosaic of its functioning from information about how Phalke went about making his films and from more general information about the business and technical aspects of making silent films in that era.

Phalke's discipline on the sets was extremely strict. His daughter, Mandakini, was not allowed onto the sets at all, unless she was there specifically to act. She recounts that once when he caught her looking into the mirror to practice the facial expressions he had taught her, he lost his temper and threatened to beat her if he caught her doing it again—the only time she was allowed to look in the mirror was when applying make-up. His staff were, according to his biographer Watwe, terrified of him—none of them would have dared to be seen by him while smoking a beedi or chewing on a paan.[54] Given that most of the key staff had been trained by him, it is safe to assume that even during the periods of Phalke's absence, the work ethos at the Hindustan Film Company would have run along similar lines.

The food served at the Hindustan Film Company for the staff was strictly vegetarian, and milk was supplied to add to the healthy diet. Every morning a doctor was on hand to check on the staff. It was compulsory to exercise every day, for which equipment, like horizontal and double bars, was purchased from a circus. Coaches were employed to teach exercises, fighting and fencing. The studio also maintained a farm and garden which were used for outdoor shooting and also to supply vegetables to the studio kitchen. This self-contained world of the studio even had a library, reading room and miniature zoo.[55]

It is likely that the studio space used for filming was akin to a warehouse, with minimal indoor facilities, and was most likely open-topped because most silent films were shot in natural light.[56] Open-topped studios sometimes had a white cloth stretched overhead to get soft, diffused sunlight to shine through.[57] What is accepted as standard equipment today was seen as incredible innovation at the time: 'VB Joshi created a sensation when he introduced the reflector (a wooden plank covered with aluminium foil) to control the direction of the sunlight while shooting a film. Soon there were "light boys" perched on studio roofs, breaking through the white canopy manipulating beams of sunlight with mirrors, silver paper and aluminium sheets.'[58] Due to this reliance on sunlight, silent film production usually ceased during the rainy season.[59]

Most of the shooting of the Hindustan Film Company took place outdoors, taking advantage of the natural settings around Nasik of jungles and wilderness. On outdoor shootings, all the actors would get dressed for their roles before dawn and walk two or three miles to the location. Phalke, the cameraman and the camera would follow in a car.[60] There was also a lorry available for outdoor shootings with 'Hindustan Film Company' written in large letters on the side.

There was no hierarchical division of labour in the Hindustan Film Company and everyone, even an actor, was expected to do everything. Everyone was a permanent employee of the film company, receiving a monthly salary. There was no 'star system' in silent cinema at this time—film historian P.K. Nair notes that the bulk of Hindustan Film Company films were made prior to the emergence of a star system in the late 1920s. For instance, the actor Vasant Shinde recounts how actors in the Hindustan Film Company doubled up as housekeepers: 'The shooting for the film *Shathmukhi Ravan* was on a mountain in Trimbakeshwar. At the foot of the mountain a large house was rented for everyone to stay in. I, along with Gangaram Nhavi, who later played the role of Prahlad in *Bhakt Prahlad*, had no part to play in the film. So our job was to sweep and clean the house. When the meal was ready we had to arrange for it to be sent up the mountain. And in the evening, we had to lay out everyone's bedding.' Narayan Tambat, a storekeeper employed by the Hindustan Film Company, recounts that he often had to dress up as a woman to play a minor or background character.[61] The filmography of the Hindustan Film Company (Appendix 2) also illustrates the fact that while some employees played fairly set roles in the company (Gajanan Sane was the director of a large number of films, while Bhaurao Datar was a lead actor in most of the films) others played more fluid roles: Anna Salunke was the chief cameraman, but also appeared as an actor in some films, while Ganpat Shinde was director, cameraman and actor at various points of time.

In keeping with this mode of working, it was routine that well into the 1920s, films did not name any individuals in the credits other than the producer and perhaps the 'scenarist', which has often caused filmographers to speculate on the people behind the making of a film. It has also led to generalisations like attributing all Hindustan Film Company films to Phalke. Similar generalisations can be found pertaining to other film companies as well.[62]

It was still very difficult during most of this era to get women to play female characters due to the stigma of women being associated with films. The first women to act in silent cinema tended to be prostitutes and dancing girls. Many were Anglo-Indians, Jews or foreigners, such as Ermeline or Renee Smith.[63] Still, Kamlabai Gokhale, who was the first Indian film actress, and who had acted in Phalke's *Mohini Bhasmasur* in 1914 with her mother, Durgabai, also came to Nasik to work in some of the films of the Hindustan Film Company. She reminisced in later years about the atmosphere at Phalke Films, no doubt recreated by Phalke at the Hindustan Film Company, surely contributing to her decision to once again work in the family-friendly atmosphere: 'It was usual to treat women with dignity. One observed norms of propriety … Phalke's wife Saraswatibai was very considerate and [my mother and I] used to help her washing the film at night … in a fountain in the backyard … used as a developing tank.'[64] Nevertheless, the stigma of women working in films could not always be contained, and Nalli Paranjape, granddaughter of Tatya, remembered how the women in Nasik would talk amongst themselves, criticising Kamlabai, saying things like 'look at this woman, why is she working in films'. In only one instance, Nalli's sister, Kamla, a baby at the time, was hurriedly placed in front of the camera during a shoot because a baby Krishna was needed for the shot. This was never repeated.

In fact, in the early days, Phalke had a great deal of difficulty in getting any actors at all, male or female, whom he found acceptable. Silent film star Jairaj reminisced in an interview, 'Can you believe it, even prostitutes wouldn't act on screen … Actors were considered immoral. My own brother didn't talk to me for years. He told everyone I had joined the bioscope.'[65] Apart from the stigma of acting in films, it was also believed by some that exposure to the camera lens was harmful to one's health. (It was also believed in the 1920s that recording for the gramophone would harm the quality of one's voice.)[66] In 1918, Phalke wrote in *Navyug*: 'In this tropical country of India, I get only dark, ugly and emaciated persons for actors … I always require handsome, finely built actors … The stage for a screen actor is not limited to twenty square feet. It extends over acres and miles on the world's stage. He must know climbing a tree, riding a horse and swimming. He has to run … and move about in the sun. Hence he is required to be healthy and he must have boldness as well.' He further described, in rather scathing words, his travails in getting actors for his first four films, prior to the formation of the Hindustan Film Company:

> I advertised, 'Wanted fair, good-looking actors'. To my surprise, I found that most of the applicants flocking at my door were ignorant even of the meaning of the word 'good-looking'. Hence, in subsequent advertisements I began to specify that 'ugly, lack-lustre or deformed actors need not take the trouble of visiting me…' [But] they were an ugly lot with lean faces, buck-teeth, malformed eyes and noses, with hollow cheeks scarred with pock marks—in short, the type of faces which were created by the God Brahma at the end of his working day when he had run out of material.[67]

Apart from the problem of getting suitable actors, Phalke's evidence given before the Indian Cinematograph Committee of 1927–28 gives some interesting insights into the workings and problems of the Hindustan Film Company. For a start, he verifies before the committee that the company was now 'a paying concern', and that the company produced twelve to fourteen films a year. He stated that it cost about 10,000 rupees to make a film, and a good return on this amount was obtained—it took about six months to recover the cost of the film, and after that period all the earnings were profits. However, costs sometimes went up because projectionists spoiled the films, necessitating more prints to be made: 'Generally a film should last at least for four months but sometimes they are spoiled owing to bad operation and bad machines within three or four weeks … the usual projection speed should be about three to four thousand feet per hour but sometimes the projectionists even show about eight to ten thousand feet per hour, with the result that the film is easily spoiled.'[68]

It appears from the findings of the Indian Cinematograph Committee that by 1928 the business of producing good quality Indian films was a highly profitable one and that, for Indian film producers, it was a seller's market. Kohinoor's studios often churned out three films a month, while the Ranjit Film Company, like the

Hindustan Film Company, produced about twelve films a year. Some companies wrapped up films in ten days, with only three or four prints released for the whole market.[69] The Hindustan Film Company was clearly, therefore, a lucrative business for Tatya and the other partners. Indeed, it was more expensive for an exhibitor to buy Indian films as compared to Western films. The Indian Cinematograph Committee report noted:

> Although the exhibitor pays more for the Indian film, his gross receipts are greater owing to a much larger audience. The crowds which flock to witness a popular Indian film (and many of them are popular) are really remarkable ... Exhibitors cannot always obtain Indian films, as the demand is greater than the supply; in particular there is some difficulty in obtaining the better productions, which command relatively high prices as compared with the ordinary Western films ... A good Indian film is extremely profitable to the producer; even an indifferent film generally yields a fair margin of profit.[70]

Other interesting facts about the operations set up by Tatya emerge from Phalke's evidence to the Indian Cinematograph Committee: in 1928, the capital of the company was 3 lakh rupees; while the chief office was in Bombay, there were branches in Calcutta and Madras; in some other parts of India, the company employed agents; the company also sent films for exhibition to Singapore, Rangoon, Zanzibar and other foreign locations, and made profits on the export; in Nasik there were ninety-five permanent employees of the company, including fourteen women, and so there was no need to make use of any outside amateur actors; the employees included three photographers and three or four directors who had all been trained by Phalke; the Hindustan Film Company kept up with film industry developments in the West through subscriptions to movie magazines like *The Bioscope* and *Moving Pictures*; and the company made its own electricity for using arc lights using two engines and two dynamos, though

Phalke said the electricity produced was not enough for the company's needs.

Unfortunately, Phalke was the sole representative to be interviewed from the Hindustan Film Company by the Indian Cinematograph Committee, and so we do not have an insight into the viewpoints of Tatya or the other business partners with regard to the business operations. (Though at the precise point of giving this interview on 13 February 1928, Phalke was not officially with the Hindustan Film Company—he was on one of his self-imposed absences, telling the committee, 'I have retired, being disgusted with it ... I do not care so much for money. I care more for technicality and first-class production. I could not succeed and so I left off.')[71]

All the equipment used by the Hindustan Film Company—and by all other film companies in India—was imported. The film stock, cameras, lights, laboratory equipment for film processing, printing machines, editing machines, negative cutting tools and film projectors would have all been imported from France, Germany, England and the United States of America. Some of the manufacturers whose equipment was used included Houghton-Butcher, Zeiss Tessar and Pathe. Film stock was generally imported from DuPont or from Kodak in America.

The technical challenges presented by early film stock, and the solutions found, help to create a vivid picture of what the Hindustan Film Company's sets must have looked like, as well as the appearance of its actors in full costume and make-up. Early film was not sensitive to a wide spectrum of colour. For example, it was not sensitive to red. Therefore, film-makers avoided using red, as well as colours that contained red, in sets and costumes. Green colours worked very successfully, and sets were often painted in different shades of green to achieve gradations in tone.[72] Costumes that needed to be shown as white were made of light yellow or blue cloth. Make-up took a long time to apply. It often came from a German firm called Leichner. The colours were mixed by the actors themselves and applied on the face, neck, hands and arms. While a pink powder was used as a foundation, the eyebrows and lips were dabbed with black and dark red, creating a mask-like effect which was necessary for filming on stock that was not sensitive to all colours.[73]

In 1927, Kodak came out with a 'panchromatic' film negative which was sensitive to all colours of the spectrum. Cameras and lenses also improved by this time, and lighting equipment became more versatile, allowing film-makers to create films with better contrast and more variation and subtlety in their tones of black and white and grey.[74]

The operations of the Hindustan Film Company appear to have been fairly typical of the time—most other studios also kept a permanent staff of actors and technicians, and often took four to six weeks to complete a film. However, one particular problem faced by many studios appears to have not touched the Hindustan Film Company: film historian Chabria notes that barring a few of the larger studios, 'many of the production companies were short-lived with brittle partnerships and the shifting financial backing constantly leading to realignments and the setting up of new concerns'. In many cases, shortage of capital was a recurring problem and even major studios often had to take loans at high interest rates from moneylenders.[75] Film-maker Ardeshir Irani, for example, talked at length in his oral evidence to the Indian Cinematograph Committee about how it was difficult to get investors to put money into the business despite the promise of good returns, due to the stigma associated with the film business.[76] In contrast, given the backing of five financiers, none of whom were dependent on the film business for their wealth, the Hindustan Film Company was a stable concern and never faced the problem of shortage of capital.

Tatya and his wife Yamuna (who came to be known as Kaku) used to visit the film studio in Nasik now and then, usually staying only for a couple of days before returning to Bombay. On rare occasions, say during the summer holidays, they would take Kamla and Indu, their eldest grandchildren, with them and sometimes brought back some films to Bombay to show them to the family at home in Peerbhoy Mansion, where they had moved into apartments.

In Nasik, the family would visit the nearby sights, such as the caves of Pandavleni or the temple at Saptashrungi, which could only be accessed by climbing. Tatya's mother-in-law, Rahtyachi Aai, had also visited Nasik. She was a great one for climbing, banging her walking stick on the ground, leading the women and children from the front while a doli made for Tatya's daughter Durga followed, as she was not able to undertake the climb. On holidays, when no one was around, Kaku would take Kamla and Indu for outings in the film company's lorry. Two drivers, Vishwanath and Keshav, taught Kamla to swim in the pond next to the bungalow when she was seven years old, though five-year-old Indu was too scared to learn. There was a man called Shinde mama who used to show the children the developed films at night. Old film was given to the children to play with. The girls also knew a man called Karmarkar, a tailor who used to stitch the actors' costumes on a sewing machine, and a man called Jairam Mistry, who worked as a carpenter. The girls addressed Phalke's wife as 'Kaki', and she used to invite them for tea in the evenings.

Back in Bombay, films were advertised in publications like *Bombay Samachar*, *Bombay Chronicle*, the *Times of India*, *Moving Picture Monthly* and *Mouj Majah*. Once the films were certified by the censor board (which was set up in 1920) and released, the women and children would sometimes get passes to go see them in the cinema—Kamla and Indu would be accompanied by Kaku, their aunt Manorama, their mother Durga and sometimes

Saraswati, wife of Tatya's nephew, Balasaheb. They were never accompanied by the men. Just occasionally, in the Peerbhoy Mansion apartment, Shinde mama would arrive from Nasik with a film and put up a white screen so that the film could be viewed by Tatya to check if it had been developed properly and if the acting was alright.

The Silent Film Experience

What was it like watching a silent film? Once the films had left the studios of the Hindustan Film Company and been distributed for exhibition, what were the conditions under which those films were viewed? Since Tatya produced over a hundred silent films, understanding the experience of watching a silent film seems essential to an understanding of the texture and lived experience in this phase of Tatya's life.

In the earliest days, particularly outside the urban centres, the setting would more often than not have been a tent in which the unevenly lit image would flicker onto the screen, the projector would growl and whir, and the band would begin playing amid beedi smoke, the calls of snack vendors and the sounds of the audience shifting on their wooden benches.

Often the tents were temporary ones put up by travelling showmen who toured the country on bullock carts with two or three film shows. Sometimes the exhibitors had to accept entrance fees in commodities like rice, which they later sold at a village market.[77] The larger cities later had permanent cinema theatres, such as the Electric Theatre in Madras built in 1913, Calcutta's Elphinstone Picture Palace built in 1907, and various cinema halls in Bombay set up in the 1910s by Abdulally Esoofally, who had started his career by touring the country with his cinema tent.[78]

While early films were about half an hour long, by the 1920s they were about two hours long. A harmonium, a tabla and sometimes a sarangi would play during the screenings. The musicians were permanent employees of the cinema theatre. They were usually stage performers, so they knew what kind of music to play to suit the film, since many of the films were based on plays or well-known mythological stories. They would often improvise along with the film, sometimes taking song requests from the audience.[79] Apart from the entertainment value of the music, it also provided the service of drowning out the whirring of the projector since there was not much sound-proofing between the audience and the projection equipment.[80] During this period, novel methods of producing a life-like cinematic experience were developed. In addition to the live music, there were innovative sound effects—the sound of galloping horses, for example, was produced by banging coconut shells together, while the musicians shouted or stamped their feet depending on the requirements of the scene.[81] 'Thus songs and musical sequences,' notes film historian Chabria, 'which are the most common features of our sound films, were, in a sense, already a part of silent film viewing.'[82] While pictures from the West were mainly accompanied by a piano and a violin (and sometimes a small orchestra), film historian Chandavarkar also writes of 'blazing rolls on the tabla' to accompany the swordfights of Douglas Fairbanks, while the harmonium players 'supplied rapid *taans* in *ragas* to suit the climactic end of these blood-curdling fights'.[83]

In the early days, among the most popular films were documentaries like Queen Victoria's funeral or news from the Boer War. Foreign feature films, like Melies' *A Trip to the Moon* and *Gulliver*, or Porter's *The Great Train Robbery* and *Uncle Tom's Cabin*, played all over India for several years. Feature films were often screened along with shorter documentary or comic films, particularly in the later silent era.[84]

It was common for the best theatres in the big cities to be reserved for American films, which was the preferred kind of film among the Indian and European elite. However, the majority of people preferred Indian films, despite the relatively poor conditions of the theatres showing them.[85] Theatre owners adopted various means to lure people to their shows; Phalke, as we have seen, hired dancing girls to attract people to his very first screening. In Pune's Aryan Cinema, the owner, Gangadhar Pathak, offered to grind one measure of grain into flour for each ticket bought.[86] In the better theatres that showed Western films, Europeans and the Indian elite would sit in the best seats, priced at around two rupees, often wearing full evening dress for night shows.[87] Some of the theatres even had bars to serve alcohol.[88] Silent film-maker J.B.H. Wadia wrote about the VIP treatment offered to the moneyed patrons at the best cinema theatres:

> The door-keeper would enter pompously … holding a silver *pigani* of rose water in his hand. He would then walk from one end to the other, sprinkling it liberally on and over the occupants who would go into a flitting reverie as if they had been supplied with Hashish. Those enterprising Parsee exhibitors, the Wellington Brothers (Seth Rustomji and Seth Ruttonsha Dorabji) would even present rosebuds to each of their regular patrons; and in the splendid Indian way of life not only enquire of their health but also of their entire families.[89]

In Bombay, the elite theatres showing only Western films tended to be centred around Fort, while theatres showing primarily Indian films were located around Girgaon.[90]

Actors often mouthed their dialogues, which were then written or explained on 'title cards' that appeared in between the action. Sometimes the musicians provided live dialogue for the most important scenes. Many producers, particularly for films releasing in cosmopolitan Bombay, liked to use title cards in four languages simultaneously: English, Hindi, Gujarati and Urdu. Cinemas often had a commentator who would read out the title cards for the benefit of illiterate people in the audience, and sometimes mouth the dialogues in a kind of on-the-spot dubbing.[91] The Indian Cinematograph Committee of 1928 took note of the need for such commentators since audiences were mostly illiterate: 'The confused murmur which greets the appearance of the caption on the screen ... must be familiar to those who frequent Indian cinemas.'[92]

J.B.H. Wadia gives a striking account of watching films as a boy during the silent film era:

> We would rush to Lohar Chawl where stood the old Alexandria Cinema in all its tin-roofed splendour ... [where] enthusiastic crowds of cine-goers ... enjoyed unrestricted liberty of movement, jostling, pushing, dragging and bedraggling one another so as to reach the front line of the box-office ... Then there would be a veritable stampede of cinegoers in the auditorium ... I would try to secure the best seats possible on the wooden benches by laying myself prostrate on one of them. This was the accepted technique for reservation of seats ... [and] one witnessed the strange spectacle of the first batch of cinegoers all lying supine and glued to their respective areas, motionless like so many corpses ... But as soon as their friends turned up they would jump up and accommodate them ... In those days Pista-Badamwalas had free access in the auditorium. Even in the midst of ... the film they would shout out their consumer goods ... A slapstick comedy preceded the main film ... Film fans would roar with laughter... obliviously slapping the thigh of their neighbours in unbounded appreciation.

Wadia then goes on to describe how emotions ran high when the villain of the story tried to man-handle the heroine: 'Sitting in the auditorium we would also become furious ... We would threaten the lecherous assaulter with dire consequences ... We would hurl a verbal hailstorm of forceful obscenities ... When the hero popped up in the nick of time ... and gave the villain the thrashing of his life, we would jump in our seats and welcome the saviour with massive ejaculations of "*Dey, dey—Maar saaely ko*".'[93]

The Beginning of the End

As we have seen, the Hindustan Film Company was a profitable business and a significant player in a vibrant film industry. Tatya was instrumental in keeping film production rolling with the support of the other four partners, despite Phalke's disagreements with them and his frequent absences. There came a time, however, when the business ceased to be sustainable.

The first time Phalke left, in 1919, and then returned to the Hindustan Film Company, Tatya had offered him a salary of 1,000 rupees per month, with perks like a horse carriage. The second time he left and returned, the partners decided to decrease it to 500 rupees per month, probably to express their displeasure and perhaps to cover any expenses that might have been incurred due to his exit. And the third time he left and returned, Tatya was surely a party to his salary decreasing to 250 rupees per month—by this time it is highly likely that Phalke had squandered away any goodwill left towards him among the partners. As to why Phalke precipitated and accepted this downward slide, his biographer, Bapu Watwe, expresses his complete bafflement, given that he was a proud man and an accomplished artiste. His son, Prabhakar Phalke, later recounted, 'Though my father's partners and associates were good, he was never able to get along with anybody.'[94]

The immediate reason for Phalke's final departure in 1929 was a showdown with Tatya. Phalke had long chafed at what he saw as the restrictions of making films under the discipline of a company run by someone else. When he had owned and managed Phalke Films, he was free to operate as he pleased, but the result had been a terrible financial instability despite the success of his early films. When Phalke Films became the Hindustan Film Company, it immediately became a stable, profit-making venture that paid salaries on time and dispelled any anxiety about getting the capital needed to make the next film. Whereas for his early films Phalke himself had to go collect his money from theatres and bring back coins in gunny bags in a bullock cart, later it was the Hindustan Film Company that took care of distribution and networks while Phalke could concentrate on the technical and creative aspects of his work. Tatya had even managed to create an amicable working relationship with Phalke. But Phalke was unable to work with his business partners and there were constant differences of opinion. He had started feeling the need to be his own boss again, and began trying to generate capital from people in places as diverse as Bombay, Indore and Ujjain, to start his own film company. When Tatya heard about this he was not pleased, and it may have been the straw that broke the camel's back. He spoke bluntly to Phalke, pointing out to him that he was an employee of the Hindustan Film Company, and under these circumstances, it was not appropriate for him to try and generate capital from elsewhere. He gave him an ultimatum—if Phalke wanted to continue working in the company, he would have to stop this outside activity or otherwise leave the company.

What was the rationale behind the ultimatum? Phalke's attempts at generating capital to branch out on his own do not appear to have negatively affected the work he did for the Hindustan Film Company. It is most likely that Tatya felt that Phalke trying to generate outside capital, while still working for the Hindustan Film Company, would create a bad reputation for the company, giving the impression that it was not doing well and was in need of resources. It would have hurt the wider business standing of the partners. After this exchange of words, it was inevitable that Phalke would choose to leave, given his proud streak of independence. He was hurt and angered by Tatya's words and vowed never to come back. His biographer Bapu Watwe notes that for Phalke this was the beginning of the end of his career as a film-maker.[95]

But Tatya may have been blissfully unaware at this point that, for entirely different reasons, it was soon to be the beginning of the end for the Hindustan Film Company too—because the year was 1929, the same year that India's first Hollywood talkie, *Melody of Love*, was screened in Calcutta's Elphinstone Picture Palace, the first theatre in India to be equipped for sound.[96]

The era of Indian talkie movies was only a couple of years away.*

One Last Encore

Incredibly, there is a postscript to Tatya and Phalke's parting of ways. This final break turned out to be not so final after all. After everything that had occurred between them, ending with Phalke's bitter departure, Tatya ended up financing yet another film made by Phalke. What happened to precipitate this complete turnaround in their relations?

Having left the Hindustan Film Company, Phalke had gone about setting up a new film company called Phalke Diamond Company. He had approached Mayashankar Bhatt, one of the original five financiers of the Hindustan Film Company. It appears that Bhatt had withdrawn from partnership in the Hindustan Film Company at some point before this period. In addition to

* Hollywood had experimented with sound in short films since 1926, but the first feature-length sound film was *The Jazz Singer* (1928); though even this film included sound in only about a quarter of the film, for the musical numbers and a few dialogues. The first feature film with all of the dialogues recorded was *Lights of New York* (1928). *Melody of Love*, advertised as a '100 per cent talking picture' appeared shortly afterwards in 1928, and released in India in early 1929. By the end of 1930, more than thirty of India's 370 cinema theatres had installed sound equipment (Pfeiffer 1925, Hall 1928, Chatterjee 1999).

his textile and other business interests, he was responsible for introducing Agfa and Gevaert film in India in 1920–24 as a selling agent, and later made an outright purchase of the Sharda Film Company in 1930.[97] Of course, Bhatt was well aware of Phalke's extravagant spending. But he also knew that every paisa of this extravagance went towards the making of the film, because Phalke was a perfectionist. Keeping this in mind, he agreed to give Phalke 50,000 rupees on the condition that the entire film must be completed within this amount, and that he was not prepared to invest any more than this. The project that Phalke had in mind was a mythological film based on the Ramayana, called *Setu Bandhan*. It was about the building of the bridge across the sea by Ram and his army, to reach Lanka. Work was on in full swing—body builders from Bombay were chosen to play the roles of Ravan's monsters, an actress to play Sita was, with great difficulty, found in Madras, and the sets were constructed in Nasik. But Phalke's habit of excessive spending could be seen here too. Gangadhar Pathak, owner of Pune's Aryan Cinema, recounts an incident during the making of this film, where 5,000 rupees were spent on looking for a particular kind of tree which was to appear for only a moment in the film. A large staff would accompany Phalke in hunting for the ideal tree, with all the attendant expenses of vehicles, board and lodging.

By the time the film was only half complete, Bhatt's 50,000 rupees had all been spent. Bhatt was adamant that he would not part with any more money. Phalke was once again on familiar territory—he could not pay the staff's salaries and, in the absence of any other solution, he wearily told his staff to sell off the company's equipment and take their salaries from that money.

At this point, Tatya heard of Phalke's troubles and went to have a look at his sets. He liked what he saw, and felt that he would like to let bygones be bygones and help Phalke. This was a generous offer, as there was no need for Tatya to invest in a film outside his own company. Phalke was in no position to refuse this offer of help. So it was that Tatya shifted all the *Setu Bandhan* sets and equipment to the Hindustan Film Company's premises, and paid all pending salaries to Phalke's staff. The film would now be produced under the banner of the Hindustan Film Company. It was then decided that the film would be completed in Bombay at the Imperial Film Studio, and the whole assemblage of people and sets was shifted there. The filming in Bombay was not without its troubles and unexpected costs—most importantly, a key actress called Iqbal said she would go to Calcutta to finish two or three days of shooting for another film, and immediately return. But there was no sign of her for two months. Replacing her was not an option because that would mean re-shooting the portions in which she had already appeared, including re-erecting those sets. The expense would have been great. As it was, the expense of waiting for her was also not inconsiderable. During those two months, the board, lodging and salaries of all the staff, including forty young men who had been hired as actors, had to be paid. Eventually Iqbal returned and the filming resumed. Filming also took place along the coastline of Ratnagiri and in Rameshwaram.[98]

It took two years to complete *Setu Bandhan* and cost almost 2 lakh rupees.[99] Unfortunately, in the interim, Imperial Studios had released a film called *Alam Ara* on 14 March 1931. This was India's first talkie film, and it was in Hindi. Two more Hindi talkies were released soon after, and following on their heels was *Ayodhyecha Raja*, the first Marathi talkie, made by Prabhat Film Company.* All these films were extremely successful. *Setu Bandhan* was, of course, a silent film. But the era of silent films was now over.

---

* The Hindi version was released on 6 February 1932 as *Ayodhya Ka Raja*, while the Marathi version was released four weeks later (Jasraj 2015b, pp. 97–98; Gvalani 1938, p. 122).

The Talkie Era

In 1932, seeing that the talkie era had truly arrived, and that the process of film-making was henceforth going to be much more complicated, Tatya decided to close down the Hindustan Film Company. It was proving impossible to even get a theatre for the release of *Setu Bandhan*. Tatya decided to permanently withdraw from the film line. But before doing so, he paid the staff of the Hindustan Film Company a bonus salary of one year. Underlining how unusual this gesture was, Phalke's biographer Watwe writes: 'There will perhaps never be a film producer more generous than Vamanrao Apte.'[100]

By the end of the silent era, between 1,313 and 1,700 silent feature films had been made in India.* Of these, over 55 per cent were produced by fourteen film companies, most of which operated from what was then called the Bombay Province. Topping the list was the Kohinoor Film Company, which produced ninety-eight films, and the second place was taken by the Hindustan Film Company, which produced ninety-seven films (as well as twenty-six short films like documentaries).[101]

What became of *Setu Bandhan*? It remained unreleased in most of India when the Hindustan Film Company shut down. It had only a limited release in south India in 1932, where it managed to recoup some of its costs. Phalke could not accept that all the effort had gone to waste. Like the other employees of the Hindustan Film Company, he too had received a one-year bonus. On the suggestion of Imperial Studio's Ardeshir Irani, he decided to dub *Setu Bandhan* in Hindi, using 40,000 rupees of his own money. It took another year to dub the film, and by the time it was finally

* The 1,313 figure is quoted by Dharamsey in his filmography (Dharamsey 1994, p. 69), while P.K. Nair estimated, in his interview, that about 1,700 silent films were produced in India.

released in 1934, as India's first dubbed film, it was too late. The film was dated, and it flopped.

With hindsight, the decline of silent films and the advent of talkies may appear to be a foregone conclusion. But at the time, there was no consensus as to which way the wind would blow either in terms of what audiences would want to see or whether the available technology would support the widespread introduction of sound in films. Three full-page advertisements in the August 1931 edition of the magazine *Cinema*, published in Lahore, are illustrative of the conflicting views—and something close to panic—at the time with regard to the coming of 'talkies'. An advertisement from Universal Sound Systems (India) Ltd in Bombay confidently states that talkies are the future of cinema: 'CINEMA OWNERS! "TALKIES" INCREASE YOUR PROFITS! Install "Universal Sound System Equipment". It will pay for itself in a few months ... Now every cinema, however small or large, can possess the tremendous attraction of Talkies ...'

In contrast, an advertisement from film distributors Famous Pictures of Lamington Road, Bombay, urges cinema exhibitors to stick with silent films: 'YOUR POLICY OF SOUND PICTURES IS UNSOUND,' begins the advertisement, going on to question why exhibitors would want to spend their 'hard earned money for the so-called Talkie'.

And apparently trying to have it both ways is the Prabhat Film Company of Kolhapur, putting out an advertisement that states that while talkies are merely a passing fad, Prabhat is ready to fulfil the demand for it: 'A lot of tomfoolery is going on at present in Sound pictures which they call the "Talkies" of India. As time passes this fad will hardly have the public support. And the "Talkie" policy ... will be looked down upon as another disaster to the Motion Picture Industry of India. ... But ... "Prabhat Talkies" will be as good as their silent pictures. Prabhat Talkies will be made on the same machinery as biggest pictures are made in

Hollywood ... PRABHAT'S PERFECT TALKING, DANCING, SINGING PICTURES ARE COMING.'

It is not surprising then that Tatya might have thought the uncertainty and the complications of changing to a new technology were not worth the risk of continuing film production—but nor is it surprising that Phalke soldiered on with *Setu Bandhan* and then tried to make the leap from silent to talkie films by dubbing it. Indeed, film historian Feroze Rangoonwalla notes[102] that silent films continued to be made till 1934 by some die-hard producers, and finally faded out as an increasing number of cinema theatres were re-equipped for sound.*

Apart from the arrival of talkies, Tatya had another reason for withdrawing from cinema production. Like an old-fashioned gentleman, he feared the influence of the film world on his children, nephews, nieces and grandchildren. (Perhaps he was justified—after more than a decade of making mainly religious and mythological films with names like *Hanuman Janma* and *Pandawa Vanvas*, the last year of production produced a distinct change of tone with the release of two movies titled *Mohabbat Ki Putli* and *Shaitan Ka Shikar*.) He rarely spoke about the Hindustan Film Company to other family members, and was even reluctant to talk about it years later during the *Kirloskar* magazine interview when journalist Parvate asked him why he left the film business. Tatya said in the interview:

> I can understand that you want to ask me this question. But I find it difficult to speak on this subject ... I did make money in that business too; but the kinds of people one has to associate with, and the kinds of things that go on in that business—an old-fashioned

---

* In America, Charlie Chaplin too soldiered on with silent films, making his *City Lights* in 1931, three years after Hollywood started releasing talkie feature films. Chaplin writes in his autobiography, 'I was determined to continue making silent films, for I believed there was room for all types of entertainment' (Chaplin 2003, p. 322).

> Brahmin like me could not accept; that is why I withdrew from it. I did not wish my children, my nephews and my grandchildren to get involved in that business. Please do not ask me anything further on this subject, I will not say anything further. It is true that there is no harm in doing any kind of business if one does it with honesty and goodness. But often there is a great difference between theory and reality. I am absolutely clear that women of good background should on no account step into this business. Of course I am not talking about all cinema companies. I also know of good examples. But otherwise it is already clear to you what my opinion is.[103]

The stigma of women working in films and the general lack of respectability of this line of work had continued well into the 1930s, reflected in a talk given by Phalke around this period, where he lamented the fact that film studios were compared to brothels since women of 'good families' did not want to work in films. His talk provides an insight into what appears to have been a dire situation regarding the personal safety of actresses:

> By God's grace if these vamps are replaced by a few ladies from good families, the whole atmosphere in the film studio will entirely change, and the black spot of its being compared to brothels will be completely wiped off ... The moment these virtuous ladies enter this profession the chaotic atmosphere in the studios must change. If unfortunately this does not happen, and these wolves continue molesting them, I would request my professional sisters, that their own look should scare these scoundrels like an electric shock ... If even this does not suffice, keep a small sharp instrument always with you, and be bold to use it in an emergency.[104]

Despite the reasons stated by Tatya for leaving the film line, a few questions remain unanswered. From a business point of view, it is clear that he was not risk-averse—indeed, the range of his business interests indicate that he seemed to thrive on an element of risk in his openness to new ventures (his other businesses are described in subsequent chapters). So why did he not see the arrival of the talkies as an interesting new business opportunity, rather than shying away from it altogether? And why did he dismantle the Hindustan Film Company instead of simply selling it to another investor or film producer? Second, from the very beginning, women of 'good background', in Tatya's words, had never been a part of the film industry. Why, then, did Tatya suddenly develop a desire to protect his family from the film line after sixteen years in the business? No clear answer emerges to these questions; it seems most likely that the reasons for Tatya's withdrawal from the film business were, eventually, a combination of factors. Perhaps he genuinely did not believe in the potential of the talkies; perhaps he was fed up with the way in which *Setu Bandhan* was made, with all its delays and costs; perhaps there were some incidents towards the end which appalled him enough to want to dissociate himself with the film line once and for all.

Whatever the reasons, so firmly did Tatya hold on to his view that the film line would be highly undesirable for the next generation, that he appears to have never spoken about it subsequently to anyone in the family. It is truly remarkable that though my extensive interviews with family members revealed a great deal of information about Tatya's other business interests, nobody knew much about his extremely successful career as a silent film producer. Various family members could only give me scraps of information, sometimes inaccurate, which had to be pieced together to try and create a whole. Most of my information eventually came from researching books and archives. Poignantly, only a few things that belonged to the Hindustan Film Company—some furniture, a few carpets, a foot-operated harmonium—remained with Tatya, and these were to be seen in subsequent years in Tatya's new bungalow, Woodlands, on Pedder Road. And there was an old film camera which, at some point, was simply gotten rid of.

Tatya had no further business dealings with Phalke* after the closure of the Hindustan Film Company. However, a family connection remained, for one of Phalke's sons, Neelkanth Phalke, later worked as a German language tutor for Tatya's youngest grandson, Arvind.

It is worth pointing out that information about the Hindustan Film Company obtained from books and articles exists mainly because the renowned Phalke was associated with it; the extensive documentation of Phalke's life and times (including through his own writings) has meant that, luckily, some of the history of the Hindustan Film Company has also been preserved. The Indian Cinematograph Yearbook of 1938 declared, 'No tribute is too great for this Grand Old Man of the Indian Cinema World.'[105] Since 1969, the Government of India has presented an annual Dadasaheb Phalke Award for an outstanding contribution to Indian cinema. These are but two examples illustrating the reverence in which he is held in India. No doubt this factor—along with sheer serendipity—also provides some explanation for the fact that fragments of the Hindustan Film Company's films are still to be found in the National Film Archive of India in Pune, when the vast majority of silent films, made by so many other studios, have been lost forever.† Major reasons for the

* Phalke continued making films after the Hindustan Film Company had closed down. His last film was *Gangavataran* made in Hindi and Marathi in 1937.

† The National Film Archive of India (NFAI) acquired the surviving films of the Hindustan Film Company as late as 1969, thanks to the persistent efforts of P.K. Nair, assistant curator of the NFAI at the time. Just a few years earlier he had tracked down the first reel of *Raja Harishchandra* (1917) which was with Phalke's daughter, Mandakini. In 1969, he realised that Phalke's son, Neelkanth, who lived in Dombivili, Bombay, had two rusted cans of film, which turned out to be the last reel of *Raja Harishchandra*, and the negatives of *Sinhastha Mela*, a short documentary from the early 1920s. The indefatigable Nair then travelled to

loss of silent films are that old nitrate film is highly flammable and it decomposes easily in hot weather. In addition, films were often destroyed through wear and tear, particularly when used by touring exhibitors, while old film was often sold as junk to dealers who bought it to extract silver from the nitrate content of the film.[106]

Despite the repeated help offered by Tatya to Phalke, and the way Phalke often ended up alienating his partners through his undiplomatic style of working, a notion remained that Phalke was unfairly treated and was simply a victim of misfortune. This view appears in Phalke's son's account given earlier in this narrative, and can also be seen in the Indian Cinematograph Yearbook 1938, where an extensive profile of Phalke ends by saying, 'The life of Mr DG Phalke has been one of romance and tragedy, in that throughout his career, fortune has not played fair with him and his destiny has repeatedly dragged him to the very pit.'[107] In the late 1970s, when journalist C. Antony Louis interviewed Tatya's son, Bhausaheb, it was with a similar view in mind. Louis writes:

> At the institute in Pune, while lecturing on Indian film history, the curator of the National Film Archive of India had referred to certain unsavoury facts concerning how the financiers of his [Phalke's] films, including in particular Vaman Shridhar Apte, had unscrupulously exploited Dadasaheb Phalke. So … I casually asked Bhausaheb if he knew or was in any way connected with the Apte who was the financier of some of Phalke's films ….

Nasik, where Phalke's youngest son, Prabhakar, lived. He found that Prabhakar had almost all of *Kaliya Mardan* (1919), the second film made by the Hindustan Film Company. Working on the limited budget of the newly set up NFAI, Nair transported the film in a taxi used to ferry newspapers between Nasik and Pune, a rather risky journey due to the inflammable old film: 'The journey was long and tedious. I was … always conscious of the archival reels kept behind us, and every time the car bumped, my heart took a jump. The transport of inflammable nitrate film was indeed risky, but we had to go through with it to save the film. We reached Pune by evening, deposited the tins at the Archive's temporary shed, and heaved a sigh of relief' (Nair 2017, pp. 42–44).

> Bhausaheb gazed at me with an immensely amused look, and said, 'Well, I must say "yes" to both your queries, considering that he was my father.' Then he guffawed heartily.

During this interview, and taking the *Rangbhoomi* theatre experience into account, Bhausaheb summarised his thoughts regarding his father's association with Phalke in these words: 'It hurts me deeply to be told that in certain circles the rumour prevails that Tatyasaheb, my father, exploited Phalke's lack of business sense and made money for himself. The truth is that my father suffered financial loss, in the final reckoning, out of his association with Phalke.'[108] This of course contradicts Tatya's own evidence that he did make money in the film business; but the notion that Tatya took advantage of Phalke appears highly improbable given the events narrated above, and given Tatya's wider reputation as a person who was fair and upright in his business dealings.

There is a small postscript to Tatya's career in films: as late as 1943, more than ten years after his last film production, Tatya was still receiving requests from people interested in hiring films that had been made by the Hindustan Film Company. There is a letter that survives dated 9 July 1943 from the Private Secretary to the Maharajah Raj Saheb Bahadur of Dhrangadhra asking for the rates to hire 16 mm films 'on different subjects', no doubt alluding to the many short documentary films made by the Hindustan Film Company alongside its feature films. By this time of course the Hindustan Film Company no longer existed; the letter is addressed to the apartment at Peerbhoy Mansion and must have been redirected to Woodlands where Tatya had moved in 1938. There is another letter from a company called Saalfeld and Fink in Tehran, Iran, dated 3 April 1943, marked 'Original by Air Mail, Copy by Sea Mail'. It asks for a list of feature films, preferably with English, Persian or French titles, with a view to purchasing them for Iranian audiences. It is not known whether Tatya continued hiring out old films of the Hindustan Film Company in response to such requests.

As an aside, it is also interesting to note that Tatya's involvement with films indirectly extended to Burma—the New Cinema de Paris theatre in Rangoon, with seating for 825 people, was held by him as collateral for a 15,000-rupee loan extended to its owners on 16 November 1928. The loan must have been repaid, as the theatre never came into Tatya's possession. I went looking for the cinema in Rangoon at 55 Phayre Street (now Pansodan Street) but it no longer exists.

Chapter 5

The Phaltan Sugar Years 1932–52

Moving into Sugar

TATYA CLOSED DOWN THE HINDUSTAN FILM COMPANY IN 1932. He was now fifty-seven years old and, given the conventions of the era, he might reasonably have been expected to hang up his boots at this point and let the younger generation get on with things. However, the old man had another iron in the fire.

All through his career as a film producer, he had never moved away from his core business of textiles. Now, while keeping the core textile business running, he decided to move—apparently seamlessly—from film production into sugar production. Just as he had entered the film industry at exactly the moment it was taking off, he also managed to get into the sugar business as it was about to take off. He had been among the pioneers of film production. Now, at the ripe old age of fifty-seven, he was willing to make yet another pioneering move, because sugar production in India, and particularly in the Bombay Deccan, was very much a fledgling industry. He decided to create a sugar factory in the arid, barren landscape of the small princely state of Phaltan, several hours drive from Poona. His wife, Kaku, initially objected to this scheme. You are almost sixty years old, she said, why are you doing all this at your age? Never mind, was his answer, it will be a bit of extra pocket money for Madhav and Arvind.

It defies the imagination as to how Tatya thought that creating an enormous sugar factory out of nothing was simply a way of generating some 'extra pocket money' for his grandsons. It shows an enviable, easy-going confidence in himself—but it also speaks volumes about the level of wealth he had already generated from his textile and film businesses.

The Setting

The state of Phaltan was ruled by Malojirao Naik Nimbalkar, the Raja of Phaltan, also known as Maloji Raje. He and his wife, the Ranisaheb, held progressive views and were both closely involved with educational and social activity in the state. Maloji Raje had abolished the veil system early on in his rule, though it was a tradition in his family for women to be veiled. The couple had great respect for the social reformer Maharshi Karve, who had been a central catalyst in promoting women's education, and in 1939, they celebrated Karve's eighty-second birthday on a grand scale in Phaltan. Maloji Raje also took an active part in politics.[1]

The scholar Donald Attwood, writing in 1992, paints an evocative picture of the landscape in which Phaltan was situated:

> For those who have travelled the backroads of Maharashtra, it is not difficult to imagine what the region may have looked like in the middle of the 19th century. The land would have looked much the same: wide river valleys and rolling plateaux, separated in places by mountain ridges and steep scarps. Except for a few

> trees and fields of grain growing in the folds of hills, at the foot of scarps, and along the rivers, the land was dry and rocky … sun-bleached and dusty … Villages and hamlets were clustered near streams and rivers, which were dry for much of the year. Houses were built of mud, brick and stone, and temples of carved stone were found in every large village, as were mansions belonging to notable families. Within a day's walk of most villages, there was a market town, which also served as the administrative centre for a group of perhaps 50 or 100 villages. The climate and economy of this region were shaped by the coastal mountains which guarded its western marches. Clouds sweeping inland from the Arabian sea collided with the mountains and released their rain, which drenched the steep and humid coast. Further east, the Deccan plateau lay in the rain shadow of the mountains. A wide belt, running parallel to the coastline just west of Pune city, was known as the famine zone.[2]

The average rainfall in this 'famine zone' was so uncertain that farming was a gamble, even though the staple crops, sorghum and millet, were sturdy and drought-resistant. If at all it rained, it was almost exclusively from June to November. This meant that the farmers had to sow millet (bajri) in June, while sorghum (jowar) was sown around October so that it would ripen in the winter. The farmers protected themselves to some extent against the uncertain weather by building small-scale irrigation works, such as small weirs and diversion channels in nearby streams. Deep wells were dug, and if a farmer was lucky, a well could irrigate two or three acres. Teams of bullocks were used to draw water out of these wells, with the water coming up in large leather buckets. Sometimes the wells provided water to vegetable gardens, fruit trees and even small plots of sugarcane. But most fields had no access to irrigation, and they produced no more than one crop a year and sometimes less.

The British ruled the inland plateau region of what is now western Maharashtra, including the 'famine zone'. They called this territory the Bombay Deccan, which was a part of the Bombay Presidency. The British directly administered the districts of the Bombay Deccan with orders coming from Bombay via Poona, the capital city of the Deccan. Scattered among these districts were various princely states, such as the princely state of Phaltan, which were subject to indirect British rule and were nominally independent.

The princely state of Phaltan was situated in the midst of unfriendly, semi-arid land, though the Nira river flowed nearby. To provide the land with protection against drought, the British government had built the Nira Left Bank canal in 1885, diverting some of the river water into the canal that flowed past Malegaon and Baramati, on the left bank of the river. However, the British government found that the canal water was not much in demand in years when there was no drought—even though it flowed through arid land, and even though the charges for irrigation were kept very low for subsistence crops. They found that there were three main reasons for this: first, farmers did not want the additional cost of preparing their fields for irrigation, which would require levelling, as well as preparing ditches and dykes; second, there was a shortage of plough cattle, which were essential for ploughing the heavy black soil when irrigated; and third, adding irrigation during a year of normal rainfall did not increase the crop production in proportion to the increase in costs. Since most of the subsistence crops of millet and sorghum were intended by farmers for home consumption, they could not justify spending money on irrigation. In addition, since the subsistence crops were adapted to the semi-arid conditions, the farmers usually managed to get some kind of crop except in the most severe drought conditions. Unfortunately, since farmers did not use the canal water in normal years, this meant that when there was indeed a drought, their lands were not well-prepared to make full use of the canal water that was made available to them.

Due to the lack of perennial rivers in the Deccan area, the British had built large storage dams to provide canal water, making the Deccan canal water the most expensive water in the country. Given this expense, and given that the Deccan canals were not being used sufficiently by subsistence farmers, there was a need to find another use for the water. Among the viable crops in the region, sugarcane was found to grow well under canal irrigation. Sugarcane needed water year-round, and the British could charge a substantially higher rate for canal water used for sugarcane than for subsistence crops. Apart from needing to generate some kind of revenue for the canals, there was no particular reason for the British to push for sugarcane farming—neither was sugar an export crop, nor were there any British financial interests tied up in it (only one British-owned sugar factory was ever established in the Deccan area, the Belapur Sugar factory). From 1901 onwards, a successful system of sugarcane irrigation, known as the 'Sugarcane Block System',* was initiated, which also included canal irrigation for other crops. Farmers on the Nira canal took to this system with enthusiasm, and the land under sugarcane cultivation increased dramatically. This encouraged the government to build more canals in the Deccan region.

---

* Under the 'Sugarcane Block System' a farmer agreed to pay for canal water for six years for a certain area of land (i.e. a 'block' of land), where the water supply was guaranteed by the government. Farmers were more willing to invest in preparing their land and planting sugarcane knowing that irrigation was guaranteed for a period of several years. Second, rates were fixed per acre, regardless of the crops grown. This eliminated any potential confusion of different rates being charged for different crops. Third, year-round irrigation was provided for one-third of the block of land, making it suitable for sugarcane cultivation. The rest of the block would get seasonal irrigation, and could be used for growing seasonal crops. While sugarcane was a cash crop, the seasonal cultivation of, for example, food grains, functioned as a subsistence crop for the farmers (Attwood 1992, pp. 61–62).

The Beginnings of a Sugar Industry

Though India was an important world supplier of sugar in the eighteenth century, the development of sugar beet in Europe as a source of sugar, under the patronage of Napoleon, had almost wiped out the Indian sugar industry. The first modern sugar mill was established in India only in 1902.[3]

Up to the early 1930s, India used to import vast amounts of sugar from Java, and to a lesser extent from Mauritius. There were only twenty-nine sugar factories in India, mostly in Uttar Pradesh and Bihar, which had sprung up during the 1920s and produced about one lakh tons of sugar annually. Given the competition from imported sugar, it was not feasible for an indigenous sugar industry to find a foothold. This situation changed when the government decided to give protection to the Indian sugar industry by passing the Sugar Industry Protection Act in 1932. This act imposed a tariff on imported sugar for a period of fourteen years, with the proviso that the tariff could be increased if it was found that sugar imports were adversely affecting the Indian sugar industry.[4]

The sugar tariff had an astounding effect on the Indian sugar industry. From twenty-nine factories in 1930–31, the number rose to 140 sugar factories by 1936–37, a period of just six years. The annual production of white, industrial sugar rose from 1,20,000 tons to 11,29,000 tons in the same period. The result was that imports fell from 8,09,000 tons to 22,000 tons per year. Of the 140 factories, most were in the north—Uttar Pradesh and Bihar accounted for 109 factories, producing 83 per cent of Indian white sugar by 1936–37.[5]

Following the passing of the Sugar Industry Protection Act in 1932, several industrialists in Bombay, among them Tatya, suddenly became interested in the potential of this new industry. By 1932, there were several new canal systems along the Nira river (including on the right bank of the river, near Phaltan), where the land and irrigation potential were under-utilised and therefore available at affordable rates. This situation allowed industrialists from Bombay to set up a system of factory-run plantations—a system that had never been tried before in India because it had been impossible to get a large amount of good land in a compact area. But now, with canal irrigation available, large tracts of land with good potential were suddenly available cheaply. Due to the Great Depression which began in the United States in 1929, and which had hit the countryside in India, many farmers agreed to sell or lease out their lands at relatively cheap rates to the industrialists.

The only factory that had attempted a plantation-type system so far was the Belapur Sugar factory, which was started in 1918 by a British company. It could do so only with special assistance from the Bombay government, which acquired 7,300 acres along the new Pravara Canal by compelling the owners to sell their land. This land the government leased out to the factory for ninety-nine years, and guaranteed perennial irrigation on a third of the cultivable area. In 1921, the Indian Sugar Committee noted that Bombay was the only province in the country where land had been compulsorily acquired for this purpose, and recommended against it in the future. Nevertheless, the Belapur Sugar factory provided a blueprint of sorts for the running of plantation-type factories. The Bombay government once again considered helping the new factories through compulsory land acquisition along the new canals in 1932, but nothing came of this idea. On the contrary, in 1938 the Irrigation Inquiry Committee emphasised that this should never be done: 'If any pressure is put by Government on local occupants to part with their lands either by acquisition or by compulsory leasing, there will be a storm of opposition and the situation may develop into one of Capital versus Labour.'[6] However, the government did help the new sugar factories—not by compulsory land acquisition, but by providing irrigation on special terms. The government guaranteed perennial canal irrigation for a certain area per factory, and gave the factories the first claim on canal water in these areas. Still, factories often found it difficult to gain compact blocks of good lands, since farmers did not want to part with their best lands. Often factories ended up with poor quality fields in scattered locations, and spent much time and money to clear the rocky and scrub land and enrich it with manure.[7]

The 1932 tariff, along with the availability of irrigation, created a situation whereby the new sugar factories of the Bombay Deccan could become successful and thrive. Though the government intervened once again in 1934, this time to impose an excise duty on factory-produced sugar (and also to introduce a minimum cane price to be paid to farmers),[8] most of the new factories became profitable within a few years and performed better than the average for the rest of India; sometimes their cane yields and the amount of sugar they extracted from cane could be compared with the best in the world. The efficiency of these new factories was due to the temporary availability of cheap land and a guaranteed supply of water, both of which made a plantation system possible. The arrival of the new sugar factories in the 1930s meant that there were now two systems of sugar production in the Bombay Deccan: on the one hand, there were the local villagers who grew cane and processed it into *gul*, or jaggery, along the older parts (and some of the newer parts) of the canal. On the other hand, were the new entrants who set up factories to produce white sugar from cane that was mostly grown on their own plantations. By the late 1930s, these two systems had taken over nearly all the available canal water.[9]

The Phaltan Sugar Works

In the early 1930s, Tatya became aware of the potential of the sugar business because he had very recently bought shares worth

20,000 rupees in a sugar factory in North India, belonging to a Marwari friend; and in the very first year, had made a profit of 35 per cent.

Soon after the sugar tariff was imposed in 1932, Tatya sent an exploratory team to Phaltan state, comprising of his son Bhausaheb, son-in-law Baburao Dabke and nephew Balasaheb. They were to meet the Rajesaheb of Phaltan to get preliminary information and discuss the possibility of setting up a sugar factory there. Tatya's wife, Kaku, also decided to accompany the young men. On arriving in Phaltan, they first met Dr Bhadkamkar, a close friend of the Rajesaheb of Phaltan and Tatya. Along with Dr Bhadkamkar was Rao Bahadur Godbole, the diwan (prime minister) of Phaltan who was known for his disciplined and honest administration of the state. The two briefed the Apte delegation about what kinds of concessions they could expect from Maloji Raje, the Rajesaheb of Phaltan, for setting up a sugar factory there. The following day was the meeting with the Rajesaheb himself, who urged them to come to a decision soon because he was also negotiating with another industrialist who wanted to set up a sugar factory in Phaltan. A point in favour of the Apte delegation, as Balasaheb recounted later in his memoir, was that 'the Rajesaheb had a soft corner for the Apte family because Tatya had built up a good rapport with him in Bombay'. After meeting the Rajesaheb, they visited Hol village to see a plot of land and met a farmer called Chitale, who explained to them various ways of achieving the desired tonnage of cane for different varieties of cane. He also explained to them how crops differed depending on the type of plot and land. Basic groundwork done, the group returned to Bombay.

Tatya then began correspondence and negotiations with the Phaltan Durbar. Along with his old textile associates, Seth Mafatlal Gagalbhai and Seth Nahalchand Laloochand, he decided to raise capital of 10 lakh rupees to set up a sugar factory in Phaltan. Accordingly, they set up a private limited company called The Phaltan Sugar Works Ltd, with its head office in Phaltan. The three founders appointed themselves as permanent directors and decided that 12.5 per cent of the net profit of the company would be distributed amongst themselves.

Tatya was appointed as the managing director of the company. Therefore, of this 12.5 per cent, he was to get one-eighth, while the balance seven-eighth would be shared among the three founders, Mafatlal, Nahalchand and Tatya, in the ratio of 4:3:3. The share holding of the company was distributed amongst them at the same ratio. It was agreed that Mafatlal Gagalbhai would have a higher share in the investment because he had three sons, while Tatya and Nahalchand Laloochand had only one son each.

Why did these three gentlemen choose Phaltan as the location of their new venture? First, Tatya was well connected in Phaltan due to his acquaintance with the ruler Maloji Raje, who was very keen that a sugar factory should be set up in his state. Second, Tatya was a close friend of Dr Bhadkamkar, a well-respected personality residing in Phaltan. Dr Bhadkamkar proved to be a valuable go-between in negotiations between the sugar factory founders and the ruler of Phaltan. He also had his own farm and was knowledgeable about local agriculture.[10] And third, there was the prospect of getting income tax concessions from the Rajesaheb's durbar, as the new sugar factory would contribute to development in the state.

In fact, Tatya had initially approached his old Marwari friends, the Khaitans, to set up the sugar factory jointly. At this point, the land around Phaltan was still undeveloped and barren, with no irrigation facilities or other infrastructure. In the summer months the River Nira was dry and had to be crossed by bullock cart. There was no railway connection and no bridge. The Khaitans were aghast at what they perceived to be a wilderness—Vaman Seth, where have you brought us, they asked, taken aback—and immediately opted out of the venture. But Tatya, convinced of the potential of the venture, had persisted with the idea and approached Mafatlal Gagalbhai and Nahalchand Laloochand. How did Tatya manage to rope in Mafatlal and Nahalchand, given that they had no background in sugar? The answer is that they had faith in Vaman Seth. Of course they saw the potential to make large profits in the sugar business, but one of their conditions of investment was that it would be Vaman Seth who would manage the running of the factory, while the two of them would only be on the board of the company.

In 1933, barely a year after the Hindustan Film Company was shut down, an agreement was signed between the Phaltan Durbar and The Phaltan Sugar Works Ltd. Under this agreement, Phaltan Sugar Works got permission to set up the factory near a place called Pimpalwadi. In addition, the durbar gave an assurance that it would either acquire, or provide under lease, land up to a total of 3,000 acres for the use of the company. The durbar also agreed to provide land for experimental purposes and for building a trolley line. It agreed to waive income tax for a period of ten years, starting from the year that sugar production began. After ten years, the company would have to pay a tax of only one anna in a rupee (i.e., 6.25 per cent, as there were 16 annas in a rupee). For fifteen years, the company would be exempt from paying any tax on the import of raw materials or finished products, and after fifteen years the tax would be 5 per cent, but only if an import tax was not already paid in British India. And finally, the durbar agreed to construct a three-and-a-half-mile road, of a width of 24 feet, up to the factory. For its part, the Phaltan Sugar Works agreed to set up a factory as soon as possible with the capacity to crush 450–500 tons of sugarcane per day. The Phaltan Sugar Works also got permission from the irrigation department to cultivate sugarcane on an area of 1,500 acres, along with an assurance for the supply of water.

With all agreements and assurances in place, the sugar company proceeded with alacrity. Of course Tatya himself had no experience in the sugar industry, but he knew someone who did. Just as Killick Nixon & Co. were the managing agents of Kohinoor Mills, there was a British company called Brady & Co. who were managing agents for textile mills and also for the Belapur Sugar factory which they had founded in 1918. Tatya approached Sir Joseph Kay, who was the chairman of Brady & Co., for guidance. Sir Joseph recommended that Tatya order machinery from Duncan Stewart, a Scottish firm that also supplied sugar equipment to the Belapur Sugar factory. Tatya then sent his son-in-law, Baburao Dabke, to Mauritius to have a look at the functioning of the sugar industry there. Finally, with all the groundwork done, the Phaltan Sugar Works placed an order with Messrs. Duncan Stewart in Glasgow, for a sugar plant with a 450-ton crushing capacity. The cost was 6.5 lakh rupees, and it would be delivered to India within six months. The company then bought 1,000 acres of land at a cost of 5,000 rupees for the purpose of building the factory and a residential colony for the staff. The contract for constructing the factory was given to Messrs L.B. Phatak & Co., a well-known firm in Poona. They were also charged with constructing a workshop, a laboratory, stores, a go-down and the offices of the manager, chemist, engineer and the proprietors.

The closest railway station was almost 20 km away from the factory site, at a place called Lonand. This made transporting heavy machinery very difficult. Nevertheless, the machinery started arriving at the site of the factory in mid-1933, and the construction of the factory and workshop were completed in early 1934—all within a year of placing the order for the machinery. Messrs Duncan Stewart sent a Scotsman, one McAskill, to erect the machinery. While he was in Phaltan, a chief engineer, Uplekar, as well as several local staff like engineers and fitters, were appointed under him and received valuable training.

Thus began the trial season of the sugar factory in February 1934 under McAskill's supervision. Over 5,000 tons of cane were purchased from farmers, and 3,500 bags of sugar were produced. This performance was deemed satisfactory, and so Messrs Duncan Stewart were paid in full and McAskill was free to return to Scotland. In the same year, Tatya appointed his nephew Balasaheb as the general manager of the sugar factory. Balasaheb was the only son of Tatya's older brother Dada, and had previously worked for Tatya in the textile business. Tatya had sent him to Calcutta three years earlier to look after textile trading there. Now Tatya needed a trusted manager at the Phaltan Sugar Works, and asked him to take on the job. Accordingly, Balasaheb started work as the General Manager on 1 September 1934, just a few months after the sugar factory had produced its first batch of sugar. This post was to remain Balasaheb's for decades. He retired only in 1970 after thirty-six successful years at the factory.[11] The factory had some of its most prosperous years under his direction, and his detailed chronicling of the Phaltan Sugar Works since the days of its inception has been essential to this narrative. Tatya also appointed Annasaheb Divekar as the deputy general manager of the factory—Annasaheb was the grandson of Tatya's beloved elder brother Baba, who had passed away in 1903.

Meanwhile, Tatya personally looked after the sale of sugar. Sugar merchants would come to meet Tatya and make deals for a few hundred or a few thousand sacks of sugar. Demand was high, so there was no need for Tatya to go looking for business, and nor was there any particular need to develop a brand for the sugar. Nevertheless, the sugar produced at Phaltan Sugar Works did have a brand—it was called 'Rising Sun'. (Perhaps it was a reference to the Kohinoor Mills icon—a crowing rooster standing on the globe—which had proved to be so lucky for Tatya; a rising sun may have been an apt pairing in Tatya's mind. This is purely speculation, of course.)

As noted earlier, the government helped the new factories of the Bombay Deccan by providing irrigation on special terms and guaranteeing perennial canal irrigation for a certain area per factory, thus giving the factories the first claim on canal water in these areas. The Phaltan Sugar Works was among the factories that benefitted from this help—the irrigation department issued a gazette whereby first, Gates 7–17 and Gates 22–27 of the canal were designated as part of the Phaltan Sugar factory's area, and second, a supply of water was guaranteed for 2,500 acres of cane cultivation.

The leasing of more land from farmers was continuing rapidly to ensure a good supply of sugarcane to the factory. The leasing was done as per guidelines from the Phaltan Durbar. However, some of the additional land was almost 18 miles away from the factory. The cost of transporting sugarcane to the factory would therefore have been very high. So a decision was taken to build a small railway line exclusively for the use of the sugar factory, for the purpose of transporting raw materials as well as finished goods. A few miles of railway line and two steam engines were bought from C. Comens, a firm in Calcutta. A few more miles of line were purchased from a company in Chinchwad, near Poona. The railway line was completed by the end of 1937, and was 33 miles long. The cost ran into lakhs of rupees due to the topography of the land, with its steep ups and downs, as well as the need to build bridges over several nallahs and streamlets. A railway maintenance workshop was set up near the factory. The narrow-gauge train line, which operated on diesel, ran from the factory to a place called Nira where there was a go-down. From Nira, the train would transport sugarcane to the factory, while the finished sugar would be transported to Nira for distribution to wholesalers. On both sides of the factory's railway track were the sugar plantations.

In his memoirs Balasaheb describes the early years at the factory:

> When I joined the Phaltan Sugar Works [as General Manager in September 1934] there were four to five bungalows, a factory building in cement concrete, one go-down, and a workshop, part of which was for storage. For middle income staff there were four to five quarters built in stone and for workers bamboo huts were provided .... Annasaheb Divekar and my family used to live in the same house. That house was originally a sulphur go-down. With a few alterations and additions of bathrooms it became habitable. The house had no plinth. There was a nice courtyard. No drinking water facility was available. People drank water from the canal's phata [gate] #13. But immediately on my arrival I started work on digging a well in an outlet of a canal between the factory and Pimpalwadi. Fortunately the water was of a good quality and in plenty. An electric pump and an overhead tank of a capacity of 48,000 gallons was erected and before January 1935 the bungalow was supplied with tap water. In the colony, workers were given common taps. In addition the factory was also supplied water from this source because the canal water had a lot of rubbish.

Lessons were drawn from nearby settlements too: the year after Balasaheb joined the sugar factory, he visited the nearby Kirloskar Wadi to learn from their colony development. He writes, 'They [Kirloskar Wadi] had an acute problem with water supply. Because of the canal being close to us, we used to get water quite easily. Another well was dug up in the colony near a canal phata [gate]. There we struck water in plenty. Since the workers used to do all their washing etc. there, we made enough space available for them and provided two or three water wheels to draw water from the well.' Balasaheb notes that caste discrimination was not tolerated with regard to drawing water, or in other areas of colony life: 'We issued an order to prevent caste discrimination and to make the wells free for all. However, initially a Brahmin person objected to a Mahar using the well. But he was summoned and told off. In our colony no caste considerations were ever observed.'[12]

Farming the Land

As per canal regulations, the Kharif season was from 15 June to 15 October. The Rabi season ran from 16 October to 15 February. And finally, the summer crop was from 16 February to 14 June.*

The sugarcane that was planted during the Kharif season was called *adsaali*, and the cane planted during the Rabi season was called *suru*. Once the cane had been harvested, it was allowed to grow again for the following year, and this was called *jodva*. If the *jodva* cane was allowed to grow once again after harvesting, it was called *nidva*. *Nidva* was not used by sugar factories.

The *adsali* crop gave the highest output, since it was allowed to grow over two monsoon seasons, and was of 16–18 months' duration. Eventually the Phaltan Sugar Factory was allowed to increase its *adsali* crop to 60 per cent of its farming. The general pattern of cane production was that the *adsali* crop would give 60 tons of sugarcane per acre, the *suru* crop would give 35 tons per acre, and the *jodva* crop would give 30 tons per acre.[13]

A Disappointing Start

Despite the trial crushing of February 1934 being encouraging enough for the directors to relieve McAskill of his duties, the ensuing performance was disappointing. The first crushing season of the Phaltan Sugar Works was in 1934–35, but the factory faced two problems: neither was there an adequate supply of sugarcane nor was the machinery running efficiently. The crushing lasted only for eighty-three days with 21,000 tons of cane crushed. The factory had the capacity to crush 450–500 tons a day, but the first crushing season had only managed to crush about 253 tons per day. The company made a loss of about 1.5 lakh rupees over the

* Kharif and Rabi are terms for farming seasons, derived from the Arabic words for autumn and spring.

trial season of 1933–34 and the first crushing season of 1934–35. The next season, beginning in August 1935, was not much better. Only 325 tons of sugarcane were crushed per day, while fuel worth 60,000 rupees was used.

Tatya, Mafatlal Gagalbhai and Nahalchand Laloochand put their heads together and began rethinking the viability of this new venture they had got themselves into. As a first step, they decided to once again approach the manufacturers of their cane crushing plant, Messrs Duncan Stewart, for advice. The manufacturers responded by sending out an expert engineer from Glasgow to India, called Houghden. Houghden made a detailed study for a period of eight days, and then declared that Uplekar, the chief engineer at the sugar works, did not have the required knowledge to run the machinery and was completely unable to control the steam requirement. If an expert engineer could be hired, he said, not only could the machinery crush up to 500 tons a day, but even the fuel consumption could be reduced.

So it was that Uplekar was asked to leave, and on the recommendation of Messrs Duncan Stewart, a Scotsman called William Buchanan arrived to take up permanent residence in Sakharwadi. Sakharwadi, meaning 'sugar hamlet', was the rather lovely and evocative name given to the staff colony.

A Magic Wand from Scotland

William Buchanan had worked in Africa for over a decade, and since then had erected sugar producing machinery for three factories in India. Balasaheb, in his memoirs, likens Buchanan's presence in Sakharwadi to a 'magic wand'. In the very first season after his arrival, the 1936–37 season, the fuel bill came crashing down from 60,000 to 20,000 rupees, while the rate of crushing went up to 480 tons of sugarcane per day. For the first time, the company made a profit: a total of 1,12,000 rupees. After that, there was no looking back.

William Buchanan, sometimes referred to simply as 'W', set up his residence in Sakharwadi. Initially he came on his own, but three years after his arrival in Sakharwadi he married his second wife, Aileen, in Bombay in 1940. He had met her in the United Kingdom where she worked at Messrs Duncan Stewart. (His first wife, whom he had married in Africa when working there, had died in childbirth some years previously, on a voyage from Africa back to the United Kingdom.)

Buchanan made forays into Poona to shop at Dorabjee's to buy tinned food and other essentials necessary for a Scottish family.* He had a refrigerator that ran on gas cylinders, which was probably an addition made to his house after he got married, along with other Western-style additions like a bathtub. He listened to the BBC on the radio and smoked a pipe which he tucked into his long socks. When at work, he wore khaki shorts and shirt, a felt cap and long socks. He was an engineer with a hands-on approach, and he had no qualms about getting his hands dirty. A son and daughter were born in Poona. Though he and his wife did not mix too much with the local folk at Sakharwadi and tended to be a bit aloof, they were sure to be present at any public function. Balasaheb's daughter, Usha Karandikar, remembered the Buchanans attending the Ganpati celebrations in Sakharwadi, mainly when there was a programme of instrumental music. During the Second World War, when sugar was being rationed in the United Kingdom, he and his wife gave up eating sugar even though they were living and working in a sugar factory. After the war ended, Buchanan informed Tatya and the other partners that he would like to leave by April 1947 since it would be difficult to

* Established in 1911, Dorabjee's sold household provisions and imported goods in Pune's cantonment area, and was frequented by British officers and civilians. It is now a supermarket chain.

provide his children with a good education in Sakharwadi. It is possible that India's forthcoming independence and the political turmoil in the country may also have been factors in wanting to return to Scotland. Buchanan's presence being very valuable to the sugar factory, the partners suggested that he and his wife stay on for another three years and offered to pay for his children's education in Scotland. But Buchanan and his wife did not want to live apart from their children—their daughter was four years old and their son only three. Eventually it was agreed that instead of paying for the children's education, Buchanan's wife and children would return home and the Phaltan Sugar Works would pay 3,000 rupees for Buchanan's airfare to go to Scotland for one month every year.

Buchanan's family returned to Scotland in 1947. Meanwhile, Buchanan stayed on in Sakharwadi, going home to see his family on his annual holidays at Christmas. In 1950, Buchanan retired to Scotland with a gift of 1,500 rupees from the Phaltan Sugar Works—but he was still retained as a consultant, so till around 1958 he would come to Sakharwadi for three months every year during the cane crushing season. The person appointed as chief engineer in his place had been trained by Buchanan himself over the four years prior to his retirement.[14]

Balasaheb's daughter, Usha Karandikar, reminisced: 'Buchanan did not mix with the local people, but he had good relations with the officers. He was good at his work. But otherwise, he would be alone in his bungalow, reading and so on. He did not go to the [staff] club to mix. If there was a function he would attend it. Sometimes we would go there to play [with his children]. But it was comparatively little. There was no regular coming and going.' Tatya's grandson, Madhav Apte, described Buchanan's style of working: 'He was very upright, very hardworking and totally trustworthy, dedicated to the job. Very meticulous. He was conservative in terms of the use of machines. He would not flog the machines. The other theory was to flog the machine, extract as much as you can out of it and then throw it out, which meant that you would make more profits while the machine was there. But Buchanan was more concerned about the working efficiencies, the extractions, whether sugar losses could be reduced to the minimum, etc. And he himself would be on the job—although he was chief engineer, he was not shy of soiling his hands. His successor, G.K. Joshi, who was trained under Buchanan, also adopted similar practices.'

In 2009, I made contact with William Buchanan's son, Ian Buchanan, and met him in London. He gave me a lucid description of his father's life in Sakharwadi, though he had no memory of his own childhood in India:

'My father was born in 1900, and went into the navy for one year during the First World War, till 1918. In the 1920s after an apprenticeship with Duncan Stewart, he went to Africa and moved through a number of jobs, ending up at a sugar factory there … He had trained as a plant engineer and his forte was working with machinery. … In Africa he was robbed twice and was left with nothing other than the clothes he was wearing; that would freak us in modern terms, but that generation seemed to get on with it.

'My father was in three different sugar factories in India before coming to Phaltan Sugar Works. I think his most enjoyable time was in Phaltan. He had a slightly hard time in Africa. In some of his other projects he started off living in a tent, and started building the factories. So he obviously had a tough approach to life.

'His daily routine in Phaltan was that he was up early and out to the factory. When sugar was in production, the factory was running 24 hours a day. Otherwise, he would be servicing and maintaining and upgrading the machinery. He was very interested in sugar technology—he had many old text books on sugar refining.

'Regarding his interaction with the three partners of the Phaltan Sugar Works—I know he spoke very highly of them. There was obviously a mutual respect …

'He was very comfortable to be isolated in India—though there were lots of British people happy to be in Poona and Bombay which had a social infrastructure. My folks didn't take part in the expat British life of India—to some extent they couldn't afford it, as they weren't wealthy.

'At that time, the roads from Poona to Sakharwadi—they were dirt roads—took maybe about three hours. My parents rarely went to Poona and Bombay. But every year they did go to Mahabaleshwar—because there were certain phases to prepare and plant the crops. While the crop was growing you did the factory maintenance, and when the crop was ready the factory started. So there were quiet periods when they could go to Mahabaleshwar. I think there was an expat club in Mahabaleshwar in the 1930s and 1940s, when there were strong ethnic divisions between whites and native people.'

Running the Sugar Factory

The total land in the possession of the factory soon grew to 9,000 acres. The factory directly owned only 600 acres of farmland, of which 200 acres had been bought from the Rajesaheb of Phaltan. The rest was leased from farmers. Of the 9,000 acres, about 7,000 acres was fit for cane cultivation.

How was this enormous amount of land farmed, administered and managed? All the land in the factory's possession was divided into seven or eight divisions or 'circles'. Each circle had several hundred acres of land under cane cultivation. Each circle was independently supervised by two managers with a BSc in agriculture, who were given motorcycles to move around. In addition, every circle had three foremen, a clerk and some other staff. The administrative staff were given stone houses, while the workers lived in huts. One of the circles, named Phaltan Circle, comprised only 150 acres of cane, and so had only one manager. Thirty or forty bulls were maintained since every circle had bullock carts.

This system of farm management continued till 1936, when it was decided that it was not working satisfactorily in terms of maximising cane production—what was needed was a single expert agriculturalist to take charge of the entire operation, rather than running each circle independently. So an estate manager, Deshpande, was appointed—he was given charge of the entire agricultural operations, and agricultural equipment was purchased according to his advice.

By 1938, it was becoming more and more likely that war would break out in Europe. At the same time, since the sugar works had attained a degree of stability, it was decided to begin an expansion programme and increase production even further. It was imperative that the machinery needed to expand production should arrive from Europe before war broke out and impeded its delivery; and so an order for the machinery was placed urgently. Before the Second World War was declared in 1939, the machinery had been delivered to the factory, erected and put to work. The full benefit of this decision came in the first subsequent season itself—in the 1939-40 season, the factory worked for 236 days, and crushed 1,24,000 tons of cane, i.e., 525 tons per day. The crushing capacity and sugar yield had risen so dramatically during this season that the company made a profit of 8 lakh rupees. In the next season in 1940-41, it made a profit of 12.5 lakh rupees, and the following year a profit of 12.75 lakh rupees.

With these profits, Tatya and the other company directors could make further improvements to the worker's colony that had already been set up five years earlier.

It is worth noting that Tatya was among the pioneers of the modern Indian sugar industry, having entered the business at just the right moment, on the back of the government's 1932 protection to the indigenous sugar industry. The result of that government protection was immediate and immense—the output of Indian sugar increased six-fold in the brief period from 1931–32 to 1935–36. By 1938, total Indian production had increased by a further 33 per cent to 12.8 lakh tonnes annually.[15] The Phaltan Sugar Works rode on this wave of growth and success for the Indian sugar industry as a whole—it was a result of Tatya being in the right place at the right time, and being savvy enough to be aware of the opportunities arising from the new legislation of 1932.

It was during this phase of success that Tatya moved his family from the apartments in Peerbhoy Mansion in Girgaon to the decidedly upmarket location of Pedder Road. From the mid-nineteenth century onwards, wealthy Indian businessmen had started moving from their traditional wadis and neighbourhoods to areas like Malabar Hill, Cumballa Hill, Breach Candy and Mahalaxmi, which were residential areas mainly occupied by European businessmen and officials.[16] Tatya followed this trajectory himself, and in 1938, just two decades after moving out of his two-room chawl dwelling, he bought Woodlands, a sea-facing mansion with sprawling grounds on Pedder Road, for the sum of 3,30,000 rupees.

A Workers' Colony: Sakharwadi

The Phaltan Sugar Works had started a small one-room school in 1933, with the school's sole teacher running three classes in what was, essentially, an outhouse. In the same year, a small clinic was constructed with a doctor and an assistant where workers could get treated for minor ailments at no cost.

In 1934, the company began construction of a housing colony for the staff, where initially there had been only makeshift accommodation. Three or four wells were dug, and diesel pumps were used to deliver tap water for drinking to the colony. Nevertheless, despite the construction of four or five large capacity steel tanks for storing water for the factory and the colony, as well as a filtration plant, water shortage continued to trouble the colony for years.

Around 1934, a decision was taken to turn the workers' colony into a self-contained village unit called Sakharwadi, with facilities like a post office and a school. In 1934, a post office was begun on an experimental basis, with most of the expenses borne by the company. In later years, as the activities of the colony grew, the company built a permanent post office and rented it out to the postal department at 40 rupees per month. In 1936, given the lack of any facilities for entertainment around Sakharwadi, two recreation clubs were started—the men had the Sakharwadi Recreation Club while the women had the Vanita Samaj. The company constructed a building for the men's club, while the women's club was given a room within that building.* However, women could become members of the men's club by paying an extra fee. The facilities of the two clubs developed over time, with members playing cards, carrom, chess and volleyball. In 1952 a large hall was built for playing badminton, which doubled as a library and reading room for all workers free of cost. The Recreation Club celebrated an annual day, when an eminent person, say an economist, would be invited to give a lecture. The Vanita Samaj and the library celebrated their own annual days.

The Vanita Samaj made foods that would be useful to members and other local residents—it ran a shop called the Vanita Vastu Bhandar where people could buy cloth, stainless steel utensils,

* Much later, in 1956, the company constructed a small, independent building for the Vanita Samaj.

pickles, papads and so on, at reasonable prices. It also provided a small income to poor women in the locality who helped to produce some of the eatables. The Vanita Samaj soon turned into a hub of activity. It regularly invited scholars for religious discourses or lectures on various subjects. Balasaheb, in his memoirs, recounts an amusing episode where the members of the Vanita Samaj felt that they were unfairly compared to the workers who toiled in the sugarcane fields all day and were thought of as not being able to do any manual work. There was, of course, some truth to this view of the Vanita Samaj members as most of them were women from a middle-class background, the wives of engineers and supervisors who worked in the sugar factory. However, to prove whether they could undertake manual labour, the company gave 1.5 acres of land to the Vanita Samaj, along with an assured water supply, and asked them to grow seasonal crops. The members of the Vanita Samaj took on the challenge, manually watered the fields and tended the plants, and successfully managed to produce four or five crops which were distributed equally among the participants.

Around 1936, a dairy was established for the benefit of the workers, with 150 cows and buffaloes. The company's policy was to keep the price of milk at a steady, reasonable rate through the year so that workers would not be adversely affected by seasonal price fluctuations of milk available in the bazaar. For a while, two veterinary doctors who had retired from the Bombay government were appointed to the dairy operations. The dairy ran at a loss of about 20,000 rupees per year, but continued providing subsidised milk.[17]

In 1939, well before the Provident Fund Act was passed by the government in 1952, a provident fund scheme was started whereby each worker had to mandatorily contribute a month's wages to the scheme, which would be added to his savings.

Balasaheb's daughter, Usha Karandikar, described the sense of community that had developed at Sakharwadi, when she and her siblings lived and attended school there: 'We really enjoyed ourselves. Everyone was known to us, and even when school finished we used to see the same people every day. A different kind of attachment was built up among all the staff. My father kept the atmosphere very lively. When he was in the office, he was the boss. But when he went to the recreation club, he used to play with everyone. That was his nature. So we were also brought up in that way, [learning] that you should mix with everyone from top to bottom. We were all like relatives, all the children in the colony were our friends. And the atmosphere was really very good, it is very difficult to express it.' Balasaheb apparently had the ability to compartmentalise his work and recreation—a keen bridge player, he would regularly use the recreation club to play bridge with his driver, who was excellent at the game. While playing they were friendly opponents, but there was no question of the driver saying a contrary word to Balasaheb during working hours.

Tatya had a similarly down-to-earth reputation—the workers in the factory would tell of how, when he came to the factory and saw a stalk of sugarcane lying around on the road, he would pick it up himself and take it to the factory for processing. Such was the trust placed in Tatya's and Balasaheb's running of Sakharwadi, that when the farmers went away on pilgrimages or long journeys, they would bring their valuables in a box to put it in the factory's treasury room, which had a big safe and a guard stationed there. There were no signatures taken, no questions asked. There was simply the faith that their possessions would be well looked after.

By 1943, following the enormous profits of the company between 1939 and 1942, the staff colony had grown much larger, and there was a major expansion of facilities for both the school and the clinic. In the 1940s, the Sakharwadi community numbered between 2,000 and 3,000 people, including the workers' families. Since the nearest maternity homes of good quality were several hours away in Satara and Poona, the company built a small hospital and maternity home at a cost of 75,000 rupees and appointed an additional doctor and two nurses. It was inaugurated in 1943 by the Ranisaheb of Phaltan. Meanwhile, the school was also expanded in the same year. The company constructed a school building of five rooms, inaugurated on the auspicious day of Dassera, and took over the running of the school. Education was provided free of cost. In 1947, a secondary school was started with the further construction of three rooms. Over the years, additions were made as necessary, till, in the mid-1950s, the primary school building had eleven classrooms, an office and a library; a playing field with a small pavilion; and the facility for students in the secondary school to study up to the SSC examinations at a nominal cost. The company spent 50,000 rupees per year on both the schools, along with a grant of 18,000 rupees from the government. In addition, the older boys were given agricultural lessons while the girls had sewing lessons. Balasaheb writes in his history of the Phaltan Sugar Works that Tatya 'was very affectionate towards the school and he was very keen that education pertaining to agriculture and commerce be taught in the school'.[18]

In 1935, the workers and staff began a tradition of collecting contributions for the ten-day-long Ganpati festival—each worker pitched in with a day's wages. The money was then used to celebrate the festival with great gusto. A committee was formed for organising the festival, headed by Balasaheb. In addition, there were twelve committee members, including one female member from the Vanita Samaj. Over ten days, there would be an event organised every day, such as drama, music, dance or sports. Traders associated with the factory sent in monetary contributions as well, while the company organised a decorative Ganpati shamiana, lighting, stage, transport and accommodation for guests. The company also sponsored a wrestling competition by contributing a prize of 100 rupees. Balasaheb writes, 'It would not be an exaggeration to mention that apart from the city of Poona, festivities on this scale are not celebrated in this entire region.'[19]

The festivities included a drama competition, field sports and, every alternate year, an art exhibition. So great was the enthusiasm and participation of the factory workers, that eventually in 1948 a large hall was constructed for celebrating the Ganpati festival, including a stage. It was also rented out to workers for marriages and other functions for a nominal fee. Tatya was a great supporter of the Ganpati celebrations and particularly liked to make sure that he was there for the drama competitions.

All these schemes and facilities were put into action by Balasaheb with the full permission of Tatya, without whose support, of course, none of these developments would have been possible. The development of facilities and infrastructure continued even after Tatya's death in 1952, under Balasaheb's guidance.

Tatya used to visit Sakharwadi very often. Perhaps he enjoyed the rural peace and quiet as much as he enjoyed seeing the progress of the factory. There was a particular tree he enjoyed sitting under, to eat his packed lunch. If Tatya's family happened to be in Sakharwadi in the winter, the adults and children would sometimes enjoy hoorda parties in the late afternoons at one of the sugarcane farms—they would either hitch a ride to one of the farms on the narrow gauge train or drive there by car. With everyone settled down for an outdoor picnic, the local farmers would bring them the hoorda, cobs of young, green bajri or jowar. The whole cob was roasted and threshed, and the grains mixed with lemon, salt and chilli powder. There would also be some roasted brinjals to eat, and lots of sugarcane juice. Invariably, nobody ate much dinner that night! At this time of the year the sugar factory would have been working at full speed—after the harvest, the factory started working around October and continued running till about February or March, depending on the availability of cane.

Every year the factory started work on a Friday, because it was Tatya's lucky day. Even if there was any other 'inauspiciousness' attached to that day—such as amavasya, a moonless night—the factory would be sure to begin crushing sugarcane on a Friday, with a family member doing a puja on the occasion.

Success and Tragedy

Though the years 1938–40 were bumper years in terms of profits for the Phaltan Sugar Works, the same three years brought three tragedies one after another. A large ditch had been dug behind the workshop in which the contractor Phatak had stored some dynamite in wooden crates. He was the contractor who had built the factory and was still developing the facilities. In the sweltering heat of May 1938, the storekeeper took out those wooden crates to hand them over to Phatak for some work related to the wells. At 11.30 a.m. that morning, the crates caught fire and began smoking. The fire engineer Khambete and some other workers rushed to the spot and tried to douse the fire by spraying it with water. It was too late, however—the dynamite exploded, killing the fire engineer and eighteen other men. Tatya and his family were in Mahabaleshwar for a family holiday when they heard the news. His granddaughter, Kuma Rajwade, recounted that the news gave him such a terrible shock that it contributed to his developing diabetes shortly afterwards. The Phaltan Durbar appointed a justice to conduct an inquiry into the incident. The company was ordered to pay out a compensation of 47,000 rupees, and was also accused of not storing dynamite as per the rules of the Explosives Act.

The second tragedy unfolded in the same year, affecting two of the three founders. Seth Mafatlal's eldest son, Pransukhlal, who was a director of the Phaltan Sugar Works, passed away. It was a double tragedy, for not only was he Seth Mafatlal's son, he was also the son-in-law of Seth Nahalchand.

And then just two years later, in 1940, Seth Nahalchand himself passed away. He was the eldest of the three founders of the Phaltan Sugar Works, and his great store of experience was sorely missed.

Meanwhile, there had been some severe disagreements between the Phaltan Sugar Works and the Phaltan Durbar, with regard to the tax exemptions that the durbar had granted to the company. The company had been promised tax exemption from all profits for a period of ten years. However, the durbar spotted a loophole: the agreement made no mention of any tax exemption for dividends received by Tatya, Seth Mafatlal and Seth Nahalchand. Taking advantage of this loophole, the durbar began charging tax on the dividends. To counter this, and to strengthen the company's finances, the three founders made plans to keep the entire profits in a reserve fund instead of declaring dividends. Unfortunately, this did not help them. There was a provision in the law whereby if 60 per cent of the profits were not distributed as dividend, then the income tax officer could treat 100 per cent of the profits as taxable. So it was that till 1942 Tatya and his two partners in the sugar works did not receive the tax breaks they had anticipated, and jointly paid around 25 lakh rupees in tax to the Phaltan Durbar.

The War Years: 1939–45

In 1939, the Second World War broke out in Europe. The price of commodities went up and private sugar factories had a boom in profits.[20] Though these were profitable years, the profits were limited by the rising costs during the war.

As costs went up substantially, some items, such as sugar and grain, became harder to procure in the shops and prices began to rise steeply. In 1942, sugar was among the items that the government decided to ration and control. Prices were fixed according to the quality of the sugar. The price for the quality of sugar produced by the Phaltan Sugar Works was fixed at 12 rupees per maund (i.e., per 37 kilos). Initially the company was entitled to keep 100 bags of sugar to be used for the benefit of the workers. Later this was reduced to 50 bags.

This sugar was distributed among the workers by the company according to the rules of rationing—since these rules were issued by the Phaltan Durbar and were more generous than those being imposed in British India, the workers were happy with it. During this period, sugar from the Phaltan Sugar Works was distributed mainly to princely states like Kurundwad, Jamkhindi and Sawantwadi, in what is now southern Maharashtra.

From around the mid-1940s, the Phaltan Sugar Works provided the workers with rations at lower rates. At times the amount of grain produced on the factory's land was insufficient for the workers' needs, so the factory imported grain from Uttar Pradesh and Saurashtra and supplied it to the workers at a concessional rate. The Phaltan Sugar Works incurred a cost of 3–3.5 lakh rupees over five or six years for doing so.

The war years also brought wage increases due to general price rises. In 1941, the company gave a 20 per cent dearness allowance for workers because prices had gone up due to the war. In 1943, the dearness allowance was increased to 40 per cent. The same year, during the 1943-44 season, the factory workers went on strike one day at 4 a.m. in protest at rising costs. The strike lasted only four hours because Balasaheb met the workers and assured them of wage increases. As a result of the strike, the workers' wages went from 6 annas per day to 7 annas per day.

The following year, during the 1944-45 season, there was a more serious strike. This time the strike lasted for about a week, with the workers demanding higher wages. They were asked to resume work till the issue was put to Tatya and the other owners of the factory. After seven days, the workers voluntarily resumed work, but the strike meant that the daily workers lost their daily wages. The cane in the factory yard dried up, and the factory had to run an extra week in the summer, causing a loss due to reduced sugar production. In the end the wages went up from 7 annas per day to 8 annas per day. There was also an increase in the basic wage and scale of the skilled and unskilled workers. Despite all this, relations between workers and the management remained cordial. Costs remained high even after the war ended in 1945, so in 1946 the dearness allowance of the workers was increased from 60 per cent to 90 per cent. In 1948 the company gave a special dearness allowance of 3 annas per day to daily workers and 5.25 rupees to monthly workers.[21]

As far as profits were concerned, the boom that had begun in the war years peaked in 1947–48 with the factory's largest profit ever of 31,57,000 rupees. Feeling that the workers should also get a share in the profits, Tatya and his partners had started giving a bonus to employees in 1941; and in 1947-48, the management declared a bonus of six months' pay and distributed almost 4 lakh rupees among the employees. One of the reasons for the unexpectedly good profit that year was that the government had removed sugar rationing on 1 December 1947.

Going Public

It was during the war, in 1942, that Tatya, Mafatlal and Kantilal (the late Nahalchand Laloochand's son) decided to take the Phaltan Sugar Works public. They converted the company's reserve fund of 30 lakh rupees, comprising profits, into share capital, bringing the total share capital to 40 lakh rupees (including the original share capital of 10 lakhs). Out of 80,000 shares, with each share valued at 50 rupees, they offered 24,000 shares for sale. One enterprising individual bought the entire 24,000 shares for 125 rupees each, bringing in 30 lakh rupees to the three partners. In addition, of course, the value of the remaining 56,000 shares, i.e., 70 per cent of the shares, which were still held by them, increased dramatically. (The person who had bought the 24,000 shares also made a tidy profit by selling them on to the public at rates ranging up to 175 rupees per share.)[22]

After the Phaltan Sugar Works became a public limited company in 1942, instead of having permanent directors, a new private limited company was formed to act as managing agents of the sugar works. The new company was called MAK, which was short for 'Messrs Mafatlal, Apte and Kantilal'. The Phaltan Sugar Works would pay MAK a managing agent's commission (in addition to the dividends the owners received as shareholders). An agreement to this effect was drawn up between MAK and the Phaltan Sugar Works for a period of twenty years. The shares of MAK were divided between the three partners in the same proportion as the original division of the share holding of the Phaltan Sugar Works—4:3:3, with Seth Mafatlal allotted the largest share. Before the war ended came a difficult time for the Phaltan Sugar Works when, in 1944, Seth Mafatlal died of a heart attack. He was one of the three original partners, and director and chairman of the Phaltan Sugar Works. He had been a close associate of Tatya since their early textile days and, like Tatya, was a self-made man. Starting from humble beginnings, he had become one of the most prominent and wealthy business leaders of the time. After him, his second son, Navinchandra Mafatlal, and grandson Arvind Mafatlal, took on his duties.

Only Tatya was left of the original three founders, and he was now sixty-nine years old. Shortly afterwards, in 1945-46, Tatya more or less retired from his textile business, leaving his son Bhausaheb in charge. He did, however, retain an active involvement in the Phaltan Sugar Works.

In 1948-49, sugar production in the country went down and prices went up. The government brought in total control over sugar and sugar prices, and began a scheme whereby those factories who produced more sugar than a set target, could sell 50 per cent of the excess production on the free market. Though many companies benefitted from this, the Phaltan Sugar Works did not benefit due to a shortage of cane.[23]

We get a fascinating insight into Tatya's thinking with regard to the Phaltan Sugar Works in the *Kirloskar* magazine interview around 1947. It is worth noting here, that it appears to be a peculiarity of Tatya's to say he didn't really want to do something, but then went ahead and did it anyway. Just as, in the case of the Hindustan Film Company, he declared that he had been unwillingly dragged into film production, so he speaks of his great reluctance at starting a sugar factory in Phaltan. In both cases, nothing at all about his management of the film and sugar businesses suggests any hesitancy whatsoever. On the contrary, he clearly put every effort into making a success of film production and sugar production and made enormous profits from both. Was it a sense of modesty that prevented him from taking full credit for his ideas? Was he trying to downplay the fact that he had shown brilliant business sense in investing in the film and sugar industries? Whatever the reason, though he speaks to the *Kirloskar* journalist about his hesitation at starting the sugar factory, it is also obvious that he takes pride in what had been achieved in Phaltan.

In the interview, Tatya says,

> You know, I was completely against going into those jungles of Phaltan to plant sugarcane there and start a sugar factory. But I went on the encouragement of the Rajesaheb of Phaltan, Dr Bhadkamkar and Mafatlalbhai. Today 3,000 acres of land are irrigated by the Nira river. Eight to ten thousand people have found employment in the sugarcane fields and in the factory. We

> have laid down a 33-mile-long railway to transport sugarcane and sacks of sugar to and fro! Every day we produce 700 sacks of sugar. We have 40 lakh rupees invested in the factory. We pay 10–11 lakhs in excise duty and income tax to Phaltan state every year.

But in the same interview Tatya adds a sobering note to the story of success, recounting the challenges encountered along the way. When the journalist asked him why he did not start another sugar factory in Phaltan, Tatya said, 'In reality business does not proceed as easily as you make it out to be. Now you only see the profits we are making; but what about the losses we had in the beginning? To get water from the irrigation department to Phaltan state, we had to put in an iron plough worth 1 lakh rupees into the ground, to break the rock there—only we know the struggle and efforts that went into that. But this is how it is for each new venture.'

More Sugar: The Princely State of Sangli

Looking at the success of the Phaltan Sugar Works, Chintamanrao Patwardhan, the ruler of the princely state of Sangli felt that his state too could benefit from the development of a similar industry. At this time, Sangli state had a major investment in a sugar factory called Ugar Sugar. Ugar, now in Karnataka, was an area of Sangli state. The sugar factory in Ugar had been started by the Shirgaonkar family from Kolhapur. They had previously held the managing agency for Kolhapur Sugar Mills, in which the Rajesaheb of Kolhapur had a stake. After losing the managing agency of Kolhapur Sugar Mills, the Shirgaonkars had started the Ugar Sugar factory, with the Sangli Durbar holding a large stake in it. However, by around 1944–45, Ugar Sugar was not doing very well. Given the achievements of the Phaltan Sugar Works, Chintamanrao Patwardhan felt that Tatya should take over the running of the Ugar Sugar factory as well. He came one day to Woodlands, Tatya's residence in Bombay, for afternoon tea, to suggest this; it was a rather grand occasion, with sandwiches and cakes ordered from the Taj Mahal Hotel for the Rajesaheb's visit. The Rajesaheb also sent shares of the Ugar Sugar factory to Balasaheb, who was managing the Phaltan Sugar Works, saying that the Aptes should keep the shares and take over the management of the factory. In response, Tatya sent Balasaheb and William Buchanan to Ugar to have a look at the factory—but they came back saying that the factory and machinery were far too old and they didn't think much could be done to revive the factory. It would be far better, they said, to set up a new sugar factory. Tatya, however, decided to take a more ambitious approach. He returned the Ugar shares to Chintamanrao Patwardhan and said that if the Sangli state could provide the land, he would set up not only a sugar factory but an entire industrial complex, including a tobacco curing plant, an oil mill, a vegetable ghee plant and a textile mill.

To explore the possibility further, and to discuss things in person, Tatya made a trip to Sangli, taking along with him his son Bhausaheb, his grandsons Arvind and Madhav and some of his friends and potential investors, including an Egyptian Jewish friend called Framji. The party travelled to Sangli via Poona, stopping at Lucky Restaurant at one end of Fergusson College Road. In Sangli they stayed in one of the guest houses belonging to the Rajesaheb. For the meeting with the Rajesaheb, seating was arranged under a tree in a large garden, probably at the mansion known as the Maal Bangla, and lassi was served. Dinner was a royal affair with fine silverware, and Tatya's two young grandsons were seated at a nearby table while the elders sat together. Coincidentally, the eleven-year-old Arvind's future wife, Suneeti, who was the Rajesaheb's granddaughter and princess of Sangli, was very likely somewhere in the Maal Bangla as a one year-old while this meeting was taking place.

An agreement was reached with Chintamanrao Patwardhan whereby the Sangli state provided 3,000 acres of land for sugarcane cultivation in Sangalwadi, which included land leased from farmers. Like the Rajesaheb of Phaltan, he also agreed to provide tax concessions. Sangalwadi was a few kilometres outside Sangli town, on the banks of the Krishna river; unlike in Phaltan, there was no canal system in Sangli, and water would have to come directly from the river. The sugar machinery would have to once again be imported from Scotland and, though the war was coming to an end, it would still be a while till it arrived in India. However, the equipment for the oil factory—'expellers', which were machines that crushed oil seed to extract oil—was available in India. So the industrial complex began by starting the oil mill as well as a vegetable ghee (dalda) plant. The tobacco curing plant could be started also, since Sangli and nearby Nipani were tobacco-growing areas. Meanwhile, the sugar factory was on the drawing boards and would be started a bit later. Eventually there was to be a textile mill as well. To manage this large industrial complex, Tatya formed a syndicate in which he was a major shareholder. Two companies were formed—Sangli Planters for the cane growing and sugar factory, and Sangli Industries for the other mills and plants. An office was opened in Sangli town, near the well-known Ganpati Mandir. The other partners in this venture were Natu and Divekar, two former school teachers who had gone into the power loom and textile business—they had a spinning mill in Madhavnagar, near Miraj, and had also put up Swastik Textile Mills for weaving. During the Second World War they had started weaving nine-yard saris, as well as printed saris, which were a novelty at the time, and had become extremely successful. Coming from a textile background, they no doubt had much in common with Tatya. Other partners in the syndicate were Purshottam Badyani from East Africa, who had gone into textiles and put up Sadhana Mills, and a group of several other

Tatya's eldest brother, Govind, known as Baba

The second brother, Balkrishna, known as Anna

Anna's wife, Radha

The third brother, Ganesh, known as Dada

Dada's wife, Anandi

Tatya's wife, Yamuna, known as Kaku
(1883–1946)

Vaman Shridhar Apte,
known as Tatyasaheb
(1875–1952)

Khatryachi Chawl in Girgaon, where Tatya lived from around 1894 to 1912

The first floor balcony of Khatryachi Chawl

Peerbhoy Mansion on Sandhurst Road, where Tatya rented apartments from 1912 to 1938

The title card of *Shree Krishna Janma*, the first film produced by the Hindustan Film Company in 1918. Tatya was living in Peerbhoy Mansion at the time.

Tatya's son, Bhausaheb, with Gotu Mule, who was their right-hand man at the MJ Market pedhi

Kohinoor Mills advertisement, with VS Apte & Son mentioned as the cloth selling agents. Tatya's good friend, Nahalchand Laloochand, is mentioned as the yarn selling agent.

The main gate of Kohinoor Mill No. 1 in later years, when the mill had ceased to function

In Kohinoor Mill No.1, the office building where Tatya used to sit.

The Viceroy and Governor-General of India, the Marquess of Linlithgow, visited the Morarjee Gokuldas Spinning and Weaving Mills in 1941. Tatya was the chairman of the mills at the time. Above, he is seen to the left of the Viceroy. Below, he stands towards the front of the stage, on the left, wearing his distinctive pagdi. The commemorative photo album also included an evocative picture of the workers at the mill on the day of the Viceroy's visit.

The Phaltan Sugar Works

Tatya in a sugarcane field. Standing next to him in a sweater is his nephew, Balasaheb, who was the general manager of the Phaltan Sugar Works.

Conveyor belt carrying sugarcane at the factory

From left to right, Annasaheb Divekar, William Buchanan and a smiling Balasaheb.

The sugar factory at Sakharwadi

Four Cousins

Tatya's son, Bhausaheb (Laxman)

Anna's elder son, Baburao (Mahadev)

On the left is Dada's son Balasaheb (Keshav) and on the right is Anna's younger son, Raghunathrao.

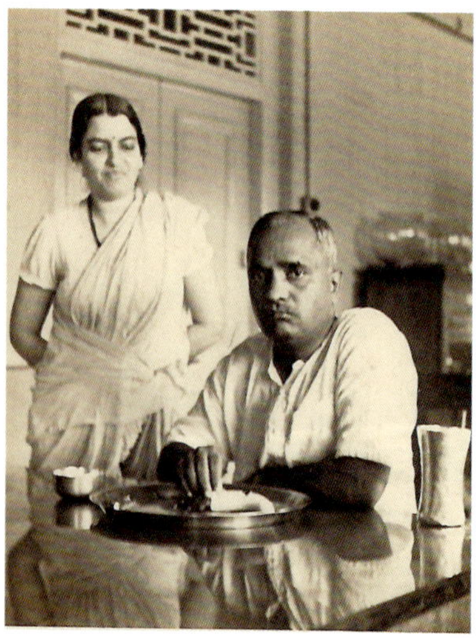

Bhausaheb and his wife Manorama, at Woodlands

The family in 1944, on the occasion of Tatya and Kaku's fiftieth wedding anniversary, at Woodlands.
Tatya is sitting in the centre, holding a walking stick, next to Kaku.

Manorama with her children. L to R: Madhav, Kuma, Arvind, Manju

Kuma and Arvind, around 1950

Kaku at her daily puja in Woodlands

Tatya and Kaku

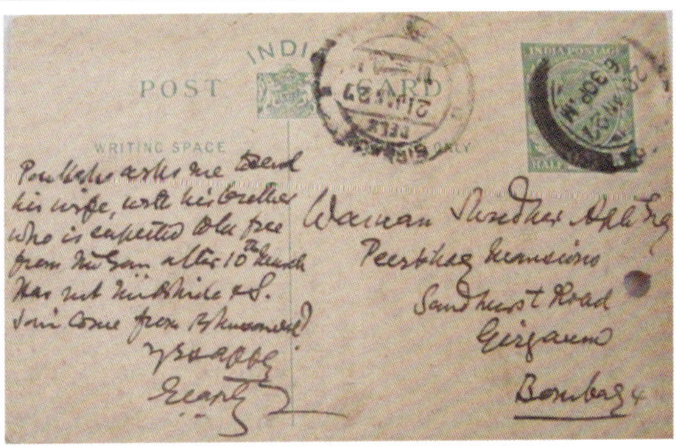

One of a series of postcards from Dada to Tatya, between August 1926 and November 1927

Tatya having his meal in Woodlands with his granddaughter, Manju, in attendance

Manju married Kamlakar Modak in 1946. The wedding was held at Woodlands with almost 2,000 people attending the wedding dinner.

In 1951, this portrait of Tatya was put up at the Brahman Sabha in Mumbai where he was a trustee and advisor for several years as well as a regular donor. The portrait was taken down sixty-seven years later, in 2018.

Tatya's grandchildren. L to R: Nalli, Khandu (Durga's children), Manju, Arvind, Kuma, Madhav (Bhausaheb's children). Durga had three older daughters too.

Tatya's son-in-law, Baburao Dabke. He married Durga in 1913.

Manorama and her son Arvind in Woodlands.

The Woodlands bungalow on Peddar Road, which Tatya bought in 1938

Tennis court at Woodlands

Kaku and Tatya

Kaku's mother, known as Rahtyachi Aai

Tatya with his youngest grandchild, Arvind

small shareholders, including the Near East Trading Company, which was run by Bhausaheb's close friend Nana Apte. Balasaheb and one Sathe also invested some money in the Sangli venture. A managing agency was set up to oversee the functioning of the industrial complex. Just as Tatya had appointed his nephew Balasaheb to manage the running of the Phaltan Sugar Works, he now dispatched his daughter-in-law Manorama's brother, Anant Ganu, to be the man on the spot in Sangli.

By early 1948, lakhs of rupees had been invested in the Sangli venture, and work was proceeding without any hitches. The oil mill was up and running. The machinery for the refinery and dalda plant had arrived and was lying in Sangli and Bombay, awaiting transportation to the site. Parts of the sugar factory, such as the pumping station, had been built. Sugarcane plantation on 30 acres had begun, and the same building contractors who had built the Phaltan Sugar Works staff colony started work on building a housing colony.

Problems with Land

Back in Phaltan, however, the company was facing problems with farmland. Almost from the beginning, despite the overall profitability of the Phaltan Sugar Works, the company had faced problems with regard to the land used for cane cultivation. Balasaheb's memoir extensively deals with the technicalities of the matter and goes into the details of various arbitrations and court cases. Suffice to say here, though, that despite the rosy picture of the Sakharwadi workers' colony with all its facilities and club houses, as far as many of the farmers were concerned, things were not satisfactory. The land lease issue was a bone of contention between the company and many (not all) of the farmers for several years. As early as 1941, the Phaltan Sugar Works had sought to mitigate the problem by, for example, buying additional cane from farmers to help them tide over the drop in jaggery prices, though it was not under any obligation to buy the extra cane planted by the farmers, thus incurring losses. But it did this in the hope that it would make the farmers cooperate on the land lease issue. This strategy, though, was not successful.

The problem was that much of the land that supplied sugarcane to the factory had been leased from farmers for a period of twelve years. Not all of this had been done voluntarily by the farmers—some of the leases had been obtained as a result of pressure from the Phaltan Durbar. The twelve-year leases that were made during the period 1933–35 were due to expire in 1946–47. The company, however, wanted to continue leasing the land. The company therefore offered to increase the rental to be paid to the farmers who owned the land (and who were cultivating the sugarcane on it). Some farmers agreed to this arrangement. Many farmers, however, insisted on getting the lands back as the rightful owners. They did not wish to lease the land to the company anymore. The Phaltan Durbar tried to help with negotiations and, when this did not work, eventually decreed that the farmers would once again have to lease out their lands to the company. But this time around, unlike a decade earlier, the intervention of the durbar did not work. Times had changed.

The company's position was that to ensure its stability, it would need the land for at least another thirty years. Despite the opposition of farmers, and despite the fact that the land leases had expired, the company refused to let go of the land. It suggested other remedies, like paying the farmers a higher rental, paying rents in proportion to profits earned or paying rent in proportion to the price of sugar. The farmers were having none of it. In the face of the company's opposition, some farmers forcibly took control of their land and started ploughing it. The company filed court cases against such farmers. The farmers were represented by communist workers and former freedom fighters. Angry speeches were made in the local bazaar in support of the farmers. The atmosphere was bitter and inflammatory, and nobody took any heed of the Phaltan Durbar's interventions.

At the beginning of 1947, the farmers also demanded that they should be paid higher rates for cane retrospectively for three years, despite having accepted the rates without objection for the past three years. The company offered to fix a higher rate for the future, but not retrospectively. The farmers, however, were adamant. On the Phaltan Durbar's suggestion, the company agreed to this demand since the atmosphere was already unsettled due to the unresolved land lease issue.

In order to try and settle the matter of the land leases, an arbitration committee was set up in consultation with the company, the farmers and the durbar. It was decided that in time, this committee would become an advisory body that would forward suggestions to the durbar. The durbar, in its turn, would give a legal status to those suggestions and make them binding on all parties. Accordingly, a committee of five members who were acceptable to all parties was set up, including a retired high court judge from Bombay. However, before the arbitration committee could do anything meaningful, the whole situation was overtaken by a historic and unprecedented series of events that swept through all the princely states.

The Merger of the Princely States with India

On 22 March 1947, Lord Mountbatten arrived in India as the new viceroy. From that very day, religious violence broke out in Delhi, Punjab, Calcutta, Patna and various other places, continuing into April. On 30 March, on the festival of Ram Navami, three separate riots broke out in Bombay between Hindus and Muslims. In June, the partition of India was announced by Jawaharlal Nehru and Mohammed Ali Jinnah.[24]

On 15 August 1947, India's independence was celebrated with great pomp at Sakharwadi, though celebrations were marred by the knowledge of the horrifying violence that had accompanied independence and the partition of India.

So far, the princely states were differentiated from British India in that for most internal matters, they were under the control of their hereditary rulers. But in the run up to independence, the Indian National Congress had started talks with them for a full merger with India. Their rulers had widely differing views on merging with India. Many resisted the idea of having to give up their privileges and rights as rulers. In 1946, the rulers of some of the Deccan princely states, including the Rajesaheb of Phaltan, had proposed the idea of a federation of Deccan princely states as a way of presenting a united front in the face of negotiations with the Indian National Congress. The Rajesaheb of Phaltan communicated the proposal to Nehru, who was not averse to the idea. Accordingly, K.M. Munshi, a leading Congressman, drafted a covenant for the formation of a United Deccan State, including the creation of a Council of Rulers made up of the Rajesahebs of all the participating states, as well as a constituent assembly, High Court, Judicial Commission and an interim government for the United Deccan State.

By the time India became independent on 15 August 1947, all the participating princes (and, in fact, the vast majority of princes in India) had been persuaded to sign an Instrument of Accession with the Indian government, whereby they legally gave up control over three areas of government—defence, external affairs and communications—but retained all other privileges and powers within their states as before. Since previously the British had, in any case, held powers over these three areas of government, most princes did not mind signing up to this.

Shortly after Independence, in October 1947, the covenant to form the United Deccan State was formally ratified by eight princely states: Phaltan, Aundh, Bhor, Kurundwad Junior, Miraj Senior, Miraj Junior, Ramdurg and Sangli. The inauguration of the new United Deccan State was fixed for December 1947 in Miraj.

By this time, however, Nehru and Sardar Vallabhbhai Patel, who was the minister of states, had changed tack. With the assistance of V.P. Menon, who was secretary to Sardar Patel, they had begun pressuring the princely states to go one step beyond 'accession' to India: they now wanted the princely states to undertake a full merger with India. This would mean dissolving each princely state as an independent entity and fully integrating it with India. In return, the rulers would be permitted to retain their titles, palaces and other personal properties, and would be paid an annual privy purse, i.e., an annual allowance. The idea of a full merger did not go down well with many princes across the country, who had hoped that 'accession' to India would be all they would need to commit to.

In Miraj, the day before the inauguration of the United Deccan State, the Rajesaheb of Jamkhindi dropped what Balasaheb called 'a bombshell', on the rest of the hopeful princes: he would not consider joining the federation of Deccan states after all, and had decided to merge with Bombay Province (and thereby with the rest of India). Other princes too began to realise the futility of resisting a merger with India. As an alternative, they suggested that the United Deccan State could merge with India as a single entity and that the provisions in their covenant, with regard to their personal wealth, should be retained. This idea was struck down by Sardar Patel, who said that since the United Deccan State had not yet been formally recognised by the Government of India, its covenant had no validity. Therefore, he said, the princely states would have to merge individually. Meanwhile, Nehru and Sardar Patel were pushing recalcitrant princes across the country for a full merger with India, alternately threatening them with military force and negotiating deals to sweeten the blow.[25]

As far as the Phaltan Sugar Works was concerned, Tatya and the other partners in the company were keeping a close eye on these developments, because all the agreements regarding land and tax had been signed with the state of Phaltan. The question loomed as to what would happen if the state of Phaltan became part of a new federation of princely states. To what extent would the existing arrangements continue to be honoured? What would be the fate of the arbitration committee that was to deal with the thorny issue of land leases? As the proposal for the new United Deccan State gathered pace, the company approached the Phaltan Durbar and requested that whatever the Phaltan Durbar had agreed regarding arbitration with the farmers should also be binding on the new federation of states. The Phaltan Durbar consented to this request.

But as the idea of a United Deccan State began to disintegrate by January 1948, the Phaltan Sugar Works was once again in a quandary. If the Rajesaheb of Phaltan agreed to a full merger with India, the Phaltan Durbar's assurances on arbitration regarding the land leases would become meaningless. The company's policies would have to stand up in a court of law in independent India, and it was by no means clear what the outcome would be. As Tatya and the other partners were deliberating on what was to be done next, and as negotiations between the Deccan princes and the Indian government continued, historic events overtook the situation once again.

On 30 January 1948, Mahatma Gandhi was assassinated. Tatya's grandson, Arvind, and his mother's brother, Anant Ganu, were playing tennis at Woodlands when the news came in. Gandhi's murderer, Nathuram Godse, was a Maharashtrian Chitpavan Brahmin. His act unleashed fury against all Brahmins, and particularly Chitpavan Brahmins. Godse's partner's surname was Apte, though not related to Tatya's family. Brahmin homes, businesses and individuals all over Maharashtra were attacked by angry mobs. The Phaltan Sugar Works was no exception. In fact, apart from the factory workers, the entire management was Brahmin. Over a period of about ten days, 75 acres of sugarcane were burnt down. Rioters attempted to throw the company's train over a bridge. They managed to destroy about fifteen transport bogies by doing so, but the engine proved to be too heavy to topple over, so they used hammers to damage it. To quell anxiety, Balasaheb, who was the general manager, and the civil overseer, Sadubhau Deshpande, visited the farms every day to urge people to remain calm. The Rajesaheb of Phaltan also intervened to keep the peace and sent police to assist at various locations. Despite that, the violence was brutal. Sadubhau Deshpande, who had made regular forays to the farmlands to maintain calm, was himself hacked to death with an axe in Sakharwadi. He was a Rashtriya Swayamsevak Sangh (RSS) man, and used to run an evening RSS shakha at the sugar factory. On that day, a truckload of people came from Phaltan town to the sugar factory, dragged Deshpande out of his house and beheaded him in front of his wife and son. Luckily, another son of his had gone out and was not present. Balasaheb only had one watchman with a rifle, but he managed to bring the wife and son to his own home.

News of terrible violence in Sangli and Miraj kept coming in too. Dr Bhadkamkar's house in Miraj was burnt down by local rioters—a great shock for the doctor who was well known for treating poor local patients, and who had continued providing treatment to his patients even after being afflicted by paralysis in 1946. (He never recovered from the shock of losing his house, and passed away in 1949.)[26] In Sangalwadi, the oil mill that had been set up so recently was burnt down by mobs from Sangli town. The oil seeds easily went up in flames. The machinery was set on fire and also hammered to pieces. The machinery for the vegetable ghee plant was in the process of being erected at the time—it would not burn, so the mob hammered it apart. With most of the machinery and buildings damaged, the loss to Tatya and his partners in Sangli was almost 20 lakh rupees: the mill had been insured for fire, but not for arson. A phone call to Bombay at 4 a.m. informed Tatya about what was happening. His first instructions were to get all the people associated with the Sangli factory out of the area. Fortunately, there were no casualties at the factory.

In the midst of the violence, unable to control the situation, the Rajesaheb of Sangli, Chintamanrao Patwardhan, and the Rajesaheb of Miraj, Narayanrao Patwardhan, finally agreed to merge with India. Following suit, the Rajesaheb of Phaltan, Malojirao Nimbalkar, realising that he too was unable to control the situation, also agreed to merge with India and requested the Indian government's help. The same evening, the inspector general of police of Bombay arrived with a police force at the Phaltan Sugar Works, which had been closed for thirteen days, and brought the rioting under control.

Immediately, the Indian government started putting in place new administrative arrangements. The Phaltan Sugar Works put forward a strong representation to make Phaltan a part of Poona district, since the go-down as well as the irrigation department's offices were in Poona. However, Phaltan was made a part of Satara district, which meant that the company would henceforth have to deal with two sets of officials in the two separate districts of Poona and Satara.

Second, the Phaltan Sugar Works requested the new government administration to begin work on the arbitration of the farmland dispute. However, there were sugar factories in other princely states, such as Kolhapur Sugar Mills in Kolhapur and the Ugar Sugar factory in Sangli, which were also facing problems of land disputes. The government decided, therefore, that since several sugar factories were facing land problems, it would not be appropriate to appoint an arbitration committee simply for the sake of one factory. So it was that the arbitration committee that had been set up by the Phaltan Durbar was wound up once and for all.

From the point of view of the Phaltan Sugar Works, there seemed to be no end in sight to the land dispute. The company was still in possession of farmlands where the tenure had expired two or three years previously. Rather than dragging things on any further, these lands were simply returned to their owners along with a payment for the additional use of the land. From the point of view of the farmers, of course, things had gone well and the rightful owners finally had their lands back.

Having returned this land to the farmers, the company lost access to around 1,250 acres of land. This was a great loss because these lands were close to the factory, were very well cultivated and gave a good yield. Meanwhile, the land still held by the company, which was not as well suited for cultivation, was deteriorating. The costs of labour and administration were going up, and the total area of land under sugarcane cultivation—which had been 7,000 acres in the factory's early days—kept reducing. By 1949, the land with standing cane had been reduced to 1,665 acres.

While Phaltan had been an independent princely state, the durbar had set the tax rates and concessions for the Phaltan Sugar Works. For its part, the Phaltan Sugar Works had tried to minimise its contact with British India, even closing down a small office in Bombay and moving its staff to Phaltan, to ensure that it would not attract tax in British India. But now that Phaltan was a part of India, there was no particular reason not to have an office in Bombay again. A small office was reopened in Bombay in 1948–49, and then a much larger office was opened in February 1952 in the Sangli Bank Building, near the Reserve Bank of India in Fort.

Around 1953, shortly after Tatya had passed away, the company's shares began to be traded on the Bombay Stock Exchange.

When Tatya died in 1952, the Phaltan Sugar Works was still a profitable concern. However, it did not survive the changing political and economic climate of subsequent years. State-supported cooperative sugar factories sprang up from the mid-1950s onwards, and private sugar factories found it difficult to compete with them. In 1961, agricultural land ceiling laws restricted land ownership. This meant that the Phaltan Sugar Works lost almost all of its land to the Maharashtra State Farming Corporation (MSFC), retaining only 18 acres of farmland, while the compensation received for the lost land was negligible. This also meant that the sugar factory had to now buy cane without being assured of the supply or the price. A combination of high cane prices set by the state, unreliable cane supply and rising expenses made the Phaltan Sugar Works increasingly unviable. In an effort to find a middle ground between being a private company and a cooperative, a new unlisted public limited company was launched in 1985 called the New Phaltan Sugar Works. This was a joint stock limited company in form, but was run like a cooperative by including farmers as shareholders. The day-to-day management of the factory was done by the farmer directors. This too proved financially unviable. The sugar factory was eventually taken over by new owners.

Chapter 6

Oil, Paper, Cans, Land:
Other Business Ventures

WHILE TATYA'S CORE BUSINESSES REMAINED TEXTILES AND sugar (with the long interlude of film production), over the years he also diversified into various other businesses. In this sense he was a trader as well as an institution builder. He had a long-term vision for his family, whereby the wealth he was generating would outlast him and be safeguarded through a three-tiered combination of, first, stability through the core businesses; second, risk and growth through diversification; and third, a long-term safety net built into his real-estate purchases. Of course, it was the stability of his textile and sugar businesses that allowed him to take risks and attempt growth through diversification. Unlike textiles, films and sugar, however, he embarked on his later ventures when he was much older—he was seventy years old when he began paper manufacturing, and seventy-five when his oil and can ventures were launched as a way of partially salvaging the disaster of the Sangli industrial complex. Perhaps his advancing years played some part in blunting his business instincts, or perhaps it was simply bad luck, for these businesses did not do well. This made little dent in his fortunes as a whole, since his textile and sugar businesses continued to thrive. In these later years, apart from his core businesses, his acumen proved to be sharper for real-estate deals as compared to his other ventures.

Andhra Paper Mills

Around 1944, about ten years after Tatya had started the Phaltan Sugar Works, a proposal came to him to buy a paper mill in the Madras Presidency, in an area that later became the state of Andhra Pradesh. The paper mill was in the town of Rajahmundry on the banks of the Godavari. It was a small mill, with the paper made from bamboo. Tatya travelled to Rajahmundry to see the mill, along with an entourage which included his son Bhausaheb and his grandsons Arvind and Madhav, all travelling by train in terrible heat. At train stops along the way, merchants associated with Kohinoor Mills came to the train station to receive Tatya and send him on his way with flowers and sweets. Tatya felt that buying the paper mill would be a good diversification of his investments. A managing agency called Khaitan, Apte & Co. was set up—Tatya's partners in the Andhra Paper Mills were the same Khaitans who, a decade previously, had declined investing as partners in the Phaltan Sugar Works. A general manager called Chaudhury was appointed to run the mill and report to Tatya.

It turned out to be a bad investment. From the beginning, affected by war-time shortages of coal, caustic soda, chemicals and other supplies, the mill did not do well. Without the necessary supplies, it was not possible to make white bleached paper, which would have given better returns, so mainly brown paper was produced. It was also too far from Tatya's home base in Bombay for him to be closely involved in the running of the mill. In addition, the political climate was not conducive to it: a movement to create a separate Andhra state for Telugu speakers had been simmering for years, and there was hostility towards outsiders coming in and buying a factory.

Given all these problems, within two or three years Tatya took the company into voluntary liquidation. The venture incurred heavy losses, by one estimate around 20–25 lakh rupees, which would be like losing crores of rupees today. It adversely affected Tatya's health. He was already more than seventy years old by this time, and was simultaneously overseeing the new Sangli venture—and though his spirit of entrepreneurship remained as strong as ever, it would perhaps not be an exaggeration to say that Vaman Seth had finally overstretched himself.

An Oil Mill at Sakharwadi

After the devastation caused by the 1948 rioting in Sangli, Tatya had decided there was no point in trying to resume work on the sugar, oil and ghee complex at Sangli. He had taken a philosophical approach to the disaster, saying, 'I am the one who made the money in the first place, and I am the one who has lost it.' However, he lost interest in doing anything further in Sangli. Meanwhile, the Phaltan Sugar Works had built up a substantial reserve fund from its run of good profits. Development of its infrastructure had continued with, for example, the construction of a 20,000-gallon steel tank built in 1948, supplied by well-water. The time seemed to be right for the Phaltan Sugar Works to use the money in its reserve fund to invest in some other industry. So in 1949, the Phaltan Sugar Works bought all the undamaged machinery from the Sangli venture at a cost of about 6 lakh rupees and started an oil mill, refinery and vegetable ghee plant at Sakharwadi instead. Several lakhs of rupees were spent in constructing a power house, buildings to store groundnuts, and oil tanks on trolleys to transport the groundnut oil.

The oil mill began operating on the auspicious day of Gudi Padwa, on 30 March 1949. But it ran only for three years. It was discovered to be unsustainable as there was no steady supply of groundnuts within 75 miles around the mill, while the most suitable market for the oil was as far away as Bombay. It also turned out that the raw materials needed to run the oil mill were more expensive than they would have been in Sangli. In its second year of running, the oil mill broke even; but in 1952, in the third year of its operations, it made a loss of 3 lakh rupees, and Tatya decided it was time to close it down and sell off the machinery.

The incomplete ghee plant was sold to a businessman from Africa. The buildings which had been constructed were eventually used as sugar go-downs for the Phaltan Sugar Works, while the oil tanks were used as storage for diesel. The power house was used to convert small engines and pumps to run on electricity, and many of the factory workers' chawls were given electric lights. The oil mill was sold much later, in 1956, about four years after Tatya died, and even then some refinery machinery was still unsold.[1]

The Oriental Can Manufacturing Company: 1949

As part of the preparations of setting up a vegetable ghee plant in Sangli, Tatya had purchased can-making machinery from the Burma Shell oil company which had been using the machinery to make cans for packaging their oil. Tatya's plan was to use the machinery to make four-gallon rectangular tin cans to package the vegetable ghee and seed oil in Sangli. This machinery was lying in Bombay, waiting to be transported to Sangli, when the 1948 riots broke out and the Sangli factory was destroyed.

In 1949–50 Tatya decided to use the machinery to start a can-making company in Bombay, called the Oriental Can

Manufacturing Company. He already owned a large property of 30,000 square feet of built-up area at Haines Road in Worli, Bombay, which he had bought around 1946 from Tansukhrai Karundia for about 6 lakh rupees. This was chosen as the location for the factory. Natu and Divekar, as well as Nana Apte, who had been partners in the Sangli venture, became partners in this company as well. Since Tatya's son, Bhausaheb, was mainly interested in looking after the textile business, the can business was left to Natu and Divekar to look after, which they did as per the singular arrangement they had developed when running their textile business—each partner managed the business for six months at a time, handing over charge to the other one at the end of that period.

The Oriental Can Manufacturing Company was sold a few years after Tatya passed away.

Real Estate: Bombay, Panvel and Poona

Tatya started buying real estate in Bombay, Panvel and Poona beginning in 1938 when he bought the Woodlands bungalow on Pedder Road as his residence. He was very keen to also buy the property adjoining Woodlands, called the Hermitage & Green Gables, about a third of the size of Woodlands. It belonged to his neighbour, Sir Narayan Mandlik, a Chitpavan Brahmin like Tatya. Sir Mandlik was single and had no child to leave the property to. At one time the Hermitage and Woodlands had been connected, and there was still a path from the Hermitage leading directly to Woodlands. In fact, Woodlands itself had been bought by Tatya from Sir Mandlik. But he wasn't very keen on selling the Hermitage. To try and sweeten the deal, Tatya bought another property in 1945 for 70,000 rupees from Sir Mandlik: 800 acres of land in Kundevahal, Panvel, just outside Bombay. Of 800 acres, about 80 acres were cultivated with rice, while the rest was jungle.

From the property, rice, vegetables and mangoes would sometimes arrive at Woodlands, with the sacks of rice stored on the terrace in Woodlands where the women of the family would sit to clean the grains.

Tatya then proposed that he would pay the full market value of the Hermitage to Sir Mandlik right away, but that Sir Mandlik could continue living there rent-free for the rest of his life. Sir Mandlik thought this over for a day or two, and then came back to Tatya with the memorable reply, 'Vamanrao, I would not want to do that. It will shorten my life. Because every morning you will be praying that since you have already paid for my property, that this old man goes. So the deal cannot be done.' Sir Mandlik died around 1948, and after his death the family of the Maharajah of Baria lived there for a year or two. Around 1951, the Hermitage was auctioned off, and Tatya once again tried his luck. He sent his elder grandson, Madhav, who was in college at the time, along with his manager Gotu Mule, to bid for the property. His instructions were to bid up to 3.5 lakh rupees. But the property was sold for more than 4 lakhs, and Tatya lost his chance even as he watched the auction from the balcony of the Woodlands bungalow.

Chawls in Phanaswadi and Chowpatty

In the mid-1940s Tatya bought a group of buildings known as Jagannathachi Chawl in Phanaswadi, in the heart of Girgaon. The chawl was made up of five or six buildings, occupied by lower middle-class Brahmin families living in dwellings of one or two rooms. In other words, exactly the sort of chawl where Tatya had himself once lived. The rent was collected by Tatya's trusted right-hand man, Gotu Mule. After just a few years, though, Tatya found that it was too much of a bother to deal with so many tenants as well as the maintenance and repairs. He found a buyer willing to pay a good price, and sold the chawl at a profit.

After selling off Jagannathachi Chawl, Tatya bought Latif Mansions at Chowpatty around 1946—this was a group of buildings and chawls with about fifty tenants. It was an old property and was well known for its Wilson Restaurant, right behind Wilson College. Tatya's grandsons, Arvind and Madhav, sometimes used to go there from school to eat traditional Bohra food, which they enjoyed.

Tatya planned to demolish Latif Mansions. One of the options he had in mind was to build a cinema theatre at the site. He had even asked a builder to prepare plans for a cinema, but this did not materialise, and Latif Mansions was sold after Tatya passed away.

Raja Dhanraj Girji property, Pune

Around 1945 Tatya bought 7 acres of land in Poona from the Raja Dhanraj Girji family for a sum of 80,000 rupees. It was a beautiful sprawling property with a large house with marble fittings, gardens and horse stables. Today it is the Residency Club. Tatya bought this property as an investment, but also intended to use it as a residence for his family, since they all visited Poona frequently. Poona was an essential stop-over for Tatya's visits to the sugar factory in Sakharwadi. Tatya enjoyed staying in Poona, often going on a Friday evening to spend the weekend there, and the family and children also often vacationed in Poona during school holidays.

To date, Tatya had always stayed in the old, traditional part of the city in the Deccan Gymkhana area of Poona where his nephew, Balasaheb, had built a house. Balasaheb had bought the plot on Prabhat Road (called Vallabh Mandir Road at the time) in 1938, an area of around 11,000 sq ft at a cost of 5,500 rupees.

Since Balasaheb himself lived in Sakharwadi with his family, Tatya decided to rent the house from Balasaheb for an annual sum of 2,100 rupees. A housekeeper from Sakharwadi was employed to look after the place, and Tatya would visit Poona and stay in this bungalow at least twice a month, along with Kaku and other family members. There was a private balcony attached to Tatya's bedroom, where he enjoyed sitting and looking out over the quiet tree-lined road.

In contrast, the Dhanraj Girji property was in the cantonment area, very cosmopolitan and completely at odds with the cultural environment that the family was used to. In particular, Kaku and their daughter-in-law Manorama did not take to the idea of staying outside the traditional heart of Poona. Tatya also found that since the property was in the cantonment area, the rules for developing it were rather cumbersome, and subject to special army regulations. In the event, Tatya continued staying at Balasaheb's bungalow whenever he visited Poona.[2]

The question now arose as to what to do with the sprawling new property. Friends of his son Bhausaheb, including Nana Apte, Kesi Ibrahim, Madanraiji and Keshavlal, proposed to Tatya that they would run it as a hotel. Tatya agreed to rent out the property to them. The Kohinoor Hotel opened around 1948–49, but did not do well. In those days Poona was a sleepy university town. It did not have a culture of people going to hotels and restaurants. Even though the Kohinoor Hotel was located in the cosmopolitan cantonment area, its main customers were people who came to Poona during the racing season between July and October. Room rates were very low, and they did not manage to get a liquor license for the hotel. Around 1950–51 when Tatya's daughter-in-law, Manorama, was recuperating from an illness, she stayed at the hotel for several days along with other family members. The stay was only one indicator of how times were changing: in this orthodox Chitpavan family, Tatya's grandson Arvind's first ever taste of mutton was when staying here with his sisters Manju and Kuma, and Manju's husband Kamlakar. He remembered it later as a fun stay on a fabulous property. However, the hotel closed within three years. Soon after Tatya's death in 1952, Bhausaheb sold it to seed merchants Cooper & Co. for about 2 lakh rupees and bought a property on Prabhat Road opposite Balasaheb's bungalow. Bhausaheb built a new bungalow on the property and gave it his wife's name, Manorama—the very same elegant art deco structure full of polished dark wood, and the oil portraits of Tatya and Kaku, with which we began our narrative.*

* Manorama is now a nineteen-storey apartment building, constructed in 2024.

Chapter 7

The Family

TATYA HEADED A LARGE BUT CLOSE-KNIT FAMILY, AND HIS WIFE, Kaku, was a steadfast presence in his life. Over time, they found themselves negotiating changing milieus as Tatya's wealth grew, and as they moved to an upmarket part of the city and social norms changed. Just as Tatya's story of entrepreneurship is understood more fully by examining the historical and business contexts of the industries in which he operated, so it is relevant to consider his personal relationships and the social context in which he lived, to understand Tatya's personality, his outlook on life and the paths he chose.

The Four Brothers

Baba, Anna, Dada and Tatya—the four brothers had conducted their family affairs as a traditional joint family. The brothers were very close and looked out for each other over the years.

However, several years after the eldest brother Baba died in 1903, the three remaining brothers decided that it would be better not to conduct their financial affairs as a joint family anymore. All three brothers had growing families, and retaining the joint family must have started to become an extremely bulky and unwieldy enterprise, particularly since Tatya was settled in Bombay and his brothers in Baroda. Accordingly, on 26 September 1920, an agreement was drawn up on 5-rupee stamp paper. In it, headed by two brown profiles of King George V, the three brothers acknowledged that they were 'till lately … living together in food, worship and estate as members of a joint and undivided Hindu family' and together owned moveable and immoveable property in Sitaram Buwa's Wada in Raopura, Baroda. The agreement stated that none of the brothers had any ancestral property, and that all their present assets had been acquired by their own efforts. They agreed, now, to divide the assets between themselves, with the exception of Sitaram Buwa's Wada which, they said, should 'be kept joint and should be allowed to remain as the only joint property in which all the members of the respective families whether male or female … should be entitled to reside'. The agreement was signed in the presence of solicitor Shri Purshottamrai, who ran a firm called Messrs Purshottamrai & Co, Attorneys-at-Law.

Within less than a decade of this agreement, Anna and Dada had passed away—just as Tatya, their youngest brother, was at the peak of his success in the textile industry and in film production.

Anna's teaching career had been abruptly cut short when he lost his job at his Baroda school in 1916 at the age of forty-five, caught in the retrenchments being carried out by the ruler of Baroda, Sayajirao Maharaj. For the next seven or eight years he travelled between Bombay and Baroda, involved in some share market ventures and also in some of Tatya's business dealings. Tragically, he died in Nasik in 1924 where the entire family had travelled for the wedding of Tatya's son Bhausaheb. The wedding was very likely held at Houdacha Bangla, which housed the residences and film studio of the Hindustan Film Company, and was celebrated with great pomp. Bhausaheb was twenty and his bride, Manorama, was eleven years old. After the wedding some family members stayed behind for a few days in Nasik. During this time Anna, his two sons and Dada's son all fell ill with typhoid. The three young men recovered, but Anna died in Nasik itself, on 1 July 1924, a terrible end to the wedding festivities. Just two weeks later, his son Raghunathrao and Dada's son Balasaheb were obliged to leave Nasik to begin college in Bombay. Anna left behind his wife (Radha), two sons (Baburao and Raghunathrao) and four daughters (Kashi, Banu, Sonu and Lalu).

Just three years later, in 1927, Dada passed away. Dada, who was a talented teacher of English and mathematics, had become the headmaster of a government high school in Baroda and had retired in 1926 at the age of fifty-eight on a monthly salary of 400 rupees. His wife, Anandi, had died in 1916 at the age of forty-one due to double pneumonia. Dada left behind a son, Balasaheb, and two daughters, Ahutai (known as Avdi) and Shanta.[1]

A series of postcards written by Dada to Tatya, between August 1926 and November 1927, survives. Dada was in Baroda and Tatya was in Bombay. The postcards tell a moving story of the closeness between the two remaining brothers, written even as Dada's health was failing him. It is possible that Tatya preserved the postcards because they were part of the final correspondence he received from his brother. It is interesting to note that the brothers corresponded with each other in English rather than Marathi, with Dada addressing his younger brother as 'my dear Tatya'. Dada's postcards cover all manner of family matters, including concern about his son's studies, some domestic strife relating to a son-in-law of their late brother Anna, anxiety about his pension due to bureaucratic bungling and instructions for Tatya to send beedis, hapus mangoes and litchis to Baroda.

But through it all, the postcards unfailingly refer to Dada's poor health, with a growing sense of doom.

In August 1926, Dada writes, 'I was down with fever for three days. It is partly malarial fever. My present health has become so delicate that a rise of 1 degree upsets me altogether … The rains which have not subsided tho' all ask for a break, brings on these fevers and dysentery from which also I am suffering. It may take about a week or two to have my normal strength and health. There is nothing to be anxious for.'

The next postcard, in January 1927, is even more cheerless. 'Time has begun to hang heavily on me,' writes Dada. 'I don't know how I can engage myself.' Just five days later, he continues on another postcard: 'Nowadays I suffer from acute pain in the belly … yesterday it was unbearable. In fact, I am afraid of taking a meal on account of this pain. This prevents me from going to Bombay as I fear I shall be a source of trouble to you all.'

A month later, in February 1927, Dada strikes a more upbeat note, asking for beedis: 'Ask Purshottam or Rama to send for me 100 beedis (not cigarettes or their boxes).' In March 1927 he writes, 'Please send … 250 beedis; I have received 250 sent with Radha; two cigarette boxes "555" may be sent; beedis may be positively sent; it does not matter if cigarette boxes are not sent.' A passion for beedis was clearly something shared by Dada and Tatya.

But April 1927 sees a return to Dada writing about his health: 'I am sorry to say that my strength is failing me day by day. I myself cannot understand the reason. I get good sleep. Constipation is the usual complaint but I believe asthma is the chief cause of my growing weakness.' Then, too late, he realises that he may be causing Tatya worry, and adds, rather unconvincingly, 'There is nothing particular to be anxious for.'

A postcard written in May 1927 further shows the closeness of the two brothers when Dada writes, anxiously, that Tatya should avoid taking long car journeys: 'To tell you the truth I do not like you to move long distances in a motor, as I always read up about accidents in newspapers.'

Thereafter, his health swings from better to worse and back again, but there is no mistaking the downward slide. In May 1927 he writes, 'I have no fever but weakness is terrible. I am unable to move in the house.' In June he writes, 'From yesterday I find that there is vast improvement in my health. I can now walk some distances with normal easiness.' In July: 'I am constantly improving though progress is slow. I feel that I can undertake the journey to Bombay. However, I don't wish to leave for Bombay for a week or two.' But the very next day he writes, 'I feel so much exhausted that I find it even now a great exertion to go to … my room; and I feel doubtful whether I shall be ever so far recovered as to have free movements in the house only.'

The last postcard from Dada is dated 18 November 1927. The trip to Bombay, anticipated in the postcards for almost a year, never took place. He passed away shortly afterwards in the final weeks of 1927.

Tatya's two older brothers had died within a few short years—Anna in 1924 and Dada in 1927—and Tatya was now the head of the family. He felt a deep sense of responsibility for the well-being of his brothers' children—nine in all—as well as Anna's wife, his only surviving sister-in-law. Tatya took it upon himself to look after the interests of all his nieces and nephews, including arranging their marriages. He took as his role model his eldest brother Baba, who had looked after him so well. His enduring respect for his eldest brother was evident in a life-sized oil painting of Baba, commissioned by Tatya around 1950 and placed in a prominent spot at his home in Woodlands.

In addition of course, Tatya had his own son and daughter, Bhausaheb and Durga, and his wife Kaku, to look after.

Of Tatya's three nephews, the eldest, Baburao, born in 1898, was already twenty-six years old when his father Anna died, and was settled in Baroda as a lawyer. But at this time, the other two youngsters, along with Tatya's son Bhausaheb, were still at various stages of their college education. Tatya inducted his son into the textile business, with Bhausaheb working daily at the pedhi at MJ Market and at Kohinoor Mills. Tatya advised Anna's younger son Raghunathrao to leave college after a year of education. In 1925, a year after Anna's death, he began training Raghunathrao at his own pedhi at MJ Market, and arranged for him to work at cloth merchant Tansukhrai Karundia's pedhi as well. Within two years Raghunathrao had acquired a selling agency for Dharamsee Morarji Woollen Mills in partnership with his mentor Karundia. He went on to a successful career as a selling agent and later also served on the board of directors of the Phaltan Sugar Works.[2] Dada's son, Balasaheb, a chemistry graduate, was initially sent by Tatya to work with a railway contractor, and then sent to Calcutta to work in Tatya's textile shop there; later Tatya appointed him as the general manager of Phaltan Sugar Works. Tatya and Kaku treated their three nephews as their own sons, and treated their wives on par with their own daughter-in-law; no special favours were shown to Manorama, their son Bhausaheb's wife. For instance, when jewellery was made for Kaku and Manorama, identical jewellery was also made for the wives of Tatya's nephews.

Bayotai, who was the only child of Tatya's eldest brother Baba, was also treated like a daughter by Tatya. She was almost the same age as Tatya's wife, Kaku, and Bayotai and Kaku got on very well together. Bayotai's son, Anna Divekar, was appointed to a post at the Phaltan Sugar Works.

In later years, Tatya also helped his daughter-in-law Manorama's brothers by recommending them to various posts—her brother Balu was given a job in Arvind Oil Mills, Bhaskar became a merchant for Kohinoor Mills, while Anant was given a job at the Sangli oil mill for a short time. Tatya saw himself as the head of a very wide and extended family, and tried to help whichever family members he could.

Tatya and Kaku's grandchildren were born during the late 1920s and early 1930s. Their son, Bhausaheb, had four children within a period of six years: Manju was born in 1929, Kuma in 1931, Madhav in 1932 and Arvind in 1934. Their daughter, Durga, had five children: Kamla in 1921, Indu in 1924, Kushi sometime between 1925 and 1929, Nalli in 1930, and Khandu in 1932.

Tatya's Children: Durga and Laxman

Durga

Durga was born in 1900. She was very close to her brother, Laxman, who was four years younger than her. She called him 'Bhau' ('brother'). The name stuck. Tatya also called him Bhau, and Laxman became known to all as Bhausaheb. Like Tatya, Bhausaheb was a soft-spoken, reticent person. Durga would joke that if she did not make the effort to seek him out for conversation, they wouldn't have spoken for days. Bhausaheb was very fond of his sister. He knew her fondness for mangoes, and especially aamras, and for years sent her the first mango crate of the season. Durga was a merry personality. When she found something funny, she laughed long and hard and could not stop. She loved reading, and was a regular reader of the newspapers *Navakaal* and *Kesari*. Surprisingly, she even subscribed to a Hindi magazine called *Kalyan*, published in Gorakhpur. In the mornings she read religious texts.

Durga was a good-looking girl, and had long hair which fell thick and black up to her knees. It was her misfortune that she had been born with a deformed arm, and suffered from epileptic fits. Initially, when she was a newborn baby, nobody realised that something was wrong, but it soon became clear that she had infantile paralysis, a condition caused by the polio virus. The child was unable to move one arm and one leg. Kaku's mother, known as Rahtyachi Aai, was a formidable woman, who arrived at their home and declared that Tatya and Kaku were foolish to look after this girl child who was simply going to be a burden on them. But Tatya and Kaku refused to countenance such an attitude. Durga was very dear to her parents, and as she grew up it became apparent that though she could not fully use one arm and leg, she could walk quite easily by dragging one foot along the ground. She could feel no sensation in her paralysed right arm, which she always held close to her body, but she could use it to help with some tasks around the house—she could use it, for instance, to help her lift a cooking pot. She could even cook, though she never really needed to do so.

In 1913, when she was about twelve years old, Tatya found the perfect groom for her. Balwant Shankar Dabke, known as Baburao Dabke, was seventeen years old, a Chitpavan Brahmin from a poor family from Rajkot, Gujarat. His mother had died when he was young. His father had recently passed away too, and he was studying and living with his uncle. He was intelligent, tall, fair and extremely good looking. Since he had no real family of his own, after marrying Durga he moved into the apartments at Peerbhoy Mansion with Tatya's family. He completed his BCom. degree at Sydenham College after the marriage. He then worked at Imperial Bank, followed by working for Tatya at the Hindustan Film Company's Bombay office. Since Tatya had the selling agency of Morarjee Gokuldas Mills in Parel, Baburao Dabke was given a job in the Morarjee Mills store purchase department, and later worked for the Phaltan Sugar Works. Eventually he became the manager of Morarjee Mills.

Baburao Dabke opened up a new world for Durga. She found that like her, he was an avid reader. In an orthodox household where men and women barely spoke face to face, he was of a different nature altogether, speaking openly to his wife about his work and experiences. Through her husband, she had a wider exposure to the world than what had been available to her before. Though she had been keen to study, Tatya and Kaku had removed her from school when she reached the fourth standard. Her teacher at her Marathi-medium school on Lamington Road was a woman called Shantabai Nadkarni, who sent a message to Kaku with an appeal that Durga should be allowed to continue her studies since she was a good student. But the orthodoxy of the times won the day. Tatya did not think it desirable for a girl to study any further than the fourth standard. The young Durga was a favourite of the Leles who lived next door to the Aptes in Khatryachi Chawl. Tatya's cousin, Nana Lele, had two sons, Moru and Baghu. When Baghu started learning English from Tadkhadkar's standard text book of the time, Durga would use the textbook to write down words in English with Baghu's help. Then she would memorise the words while sweeping the floor or doing other chores. With this love of learning, she must have relished the opportunity to vicariously experience wider horizons through Baburao Dabke, who proved to be an open-minded and loving husband.

Durga and Baburao Dabke's first child was a son called Mukund, born in Baroda. When Kaku arrived there to see her new grandson, she found that Durga's cousin was helping to pick up the child and clean him, due to Durga's bad arm. Kaku put a stop to this immediately. She ordered the cousin to do no more, and told Durga, 'He is your child, and it is your responsibility to look after him.' Durga was very hurt at her mother's harshness and wondered, miserably, how she was going to manage with her paralysed arm. But she taught herself to do everything for the child, and in later years acknowledged that her mother had been right—it meant that Durga was not dependent on anyone and became confident in her ability to look after her own children.

Mukund was followed by a daughter called Kamla, born in 1921. Mukund died when he was two or three years old. As a result, Kamla and the next daughter, Indu, wore his boyish clothes in their early childhood. Then came two more daughters, Kushi and Nalli. Kaku's anxiety was growing, for there seemed to be no prospect of a grandson. A son was finally born to Durga in 1932, after Kaku's prayers to the god Khandoba of Jezuri, and so the child was named Khandu. Happy and relieved, Kaku smeared her palm red with kunku and put an imprint of her palm on Nalli's back: a son had been born straight after, or 'on the back of' Nalli, and so Nalli was considered a lucky child.

In 1938, when Tatya moved from the apartments at Peerbhoy Mansion to the Woodlands bungalow, Baburao Dabke and Durga decided that it was time to set up their own home. They moved into apartments in Sikka Nagar in Girgaon. Their eldest daughter Kamla had recently married. So when they moved it was with their younger children Indu, Kushi, Nalli and Khandu. While in Sikka Nagar, their second daughter, Indu, married in 1940 and moved to Nagpur. Tatya continued keeping an eye on Durga's family, and provided her with a car and driver with instructions to take her children out every evening.

Within a year of Tatya moving into Woodlands, the Second World War began. In 1942, at the height of the war, Tatya insisted that Durga's family move in to Woodlands. It was a time of night-time blackouts in Bombay when window panes and car headlights had to be covered with black or brown paper. There were air-raid sirens, and sand bag barriers appeared around the city. Next to Woodlands was Govind Nivas, a three-storey building with the top floor occupied by British Navy officers who practised signalling to ships at sea. Royal Air Force planes conducted practice flights in twin-engine propeller planes, flying low over the city.[3] Fearful of the possibility of bombs falling on Bombay, Tatya had a bomb shelter built at Woodlands, and he wanted his daughter to be close to him. So Durga, her husband and three children came to live at Woodlands.

Just a few years after moving into Woodlands began a difficult phase of Durga's life, for she lost one of her daughters, her mother, and then her husband. For Tatya and Kaku, the only real jolt to their long years of happiness together was the tragedy of their granddaughter Kushi, who burnt to death.

Kushi, the third of Durga's daughters, had married into a family called Kolatkar in 1945, after Durga's family had moved to Woodlands. She lived in Poona after her marriage. Within a few months of her marriage she was gone. On 1 January 1946, Kushi attended a wedding in Poona. In the midst of the wedding festivities, she hurried home to cook, probably thinking that she would finish her work quickly and go back to the wedding. She was cooking on a kerosene stove outside her house, and when she was done she picked it up with the padar of her sari to take it inside. Fatally, she held the stove with the lower opening facing her. The door of the opening accidentally flew open and her clothes caught fire. She died of her burns at the Sassoon Hospital sixteen days later, on 16 January 1946, in agony. Durga, through her terrible grief, felt for her daughter's in-laws too. Kushi's mother-in-law had been away on a pilgrimage when the tragedy occurred, and Durga later told her, 'It is fortunate that you were away, otherwise people might have said you did this to your daughter-in-law.'

Later in the same year Durga's mother, Kaku, died of tuberculosis, and five years later her husband Baburao Dabke passed away too, suffering from diabetes, high blood pressure and loss of sight in both his eyes. He was fifty-seven when he died. By this time, all of Durga's daughters were married. So when Durga's husband died in 1951, only she and her son Khandu remained at Woodlands. When Tatya himself died barely a year later, mother and son left Woodlands and moved into their own apartment.

Tatya had protected his daughter from her infancy. He protected her from Kaku's mother, who was of the harsh opinion that a handicapped daughter was not worth looking after. No doubt there were others at the time who held a similar opinion; Kaku's mother's views were very much of her times. As Durga grew up, Tatya must have felt keenly the difference between her and other girls of her age, in terms of her limited mobility, her epileptic fits, as well as the appearance of her partially paralysed hand and leg, though she was a good-looking girl. He must have worried about her marriage prospects. Would he have to give her away to a groom who was not her equal, not worthy of her, due to lack of options? In this matter too Tatya managed to protect his daughter. The wealth he had earned meant that he could choose a worthy, intelligent groom who would also be glad of Tatya's support. They all lived together at Peerbhoy Mansion after Durga's marriage. Tatya loved Durga so much and considered her so lucky for him that her birthday was celebrated every year even when she was an adult, though customarily only a child's birthday was celebrated. '*Pahili beti dhanachi peti*', he and Kaku would say—'the first daughter is a treasure chest'.

Apart from the brief Sikka Nagar interlude during the early years of the Second World War, Durga had spent her entire life under the loving protection of her father. Tatya protected Durga from her grandmother, from the possibility of an unworthy marriage and even from the possibility of war-time bombs. But in the end he could not protect her from becoming a widow, and it was a terrible grief for Tatya. Durga and Baburao Dabke's was an exceptionally happy marriage that came to an untimely end in 1951, and all that Tatya could do now was to say to his daughter, 'Stay strong, child. Nothing is going to turn back the clock.'

Laxman

Bhausaheb was born in 1904. He studied at Aryan Education High School. He was a keen sportsman and was primarily interested in looking after Tatya's textile business rather than any of the other businesses. He enrolled in National College after matriculating, but left the college at a time when many students were dropping out of college to join the independence movement. He himself, however, was not involved in any political activism. He worked at the MJ Market pedhi and visited the mills daily, developing a deep knowledge of the construction of cloth and its costing. Later he was instrumental in introducing synthetic cloth at Kohinoor Mills.

Bhausaheb got on well with his male cousins, Balasaheb (Dada's son) and Raghunathrao and Baburao (Anna's sons). The four cousins loved playing bridge together—whenever there was a family function the four of them could be seen huddled around a game of cards. Balasaheb and Bhausaheb regularly went to the Hindu Gymkhana in Bombay in their late teens and their twenties, going there directly from college and later from work. At the Hindu Gymkhana, Balasaheb would head towards the table tennis tables while Bhausaheb enjoyed playing tennis, billiards, bridge and cricket. Raghunathrao would also join them at the Hindu Gymkhana. The three cousins spent most of their evenings together, while the eldest, Baburao, lived in Baroda and met them less frequently.

In 1924, when Bhausaheb was twenty years old, he married Kamal Ganu, then eleven. After the marriage her name was changed to Manorama. As was the custom, she stayed with Kaku for four years, till she came of age in 1928. At the time the Ganu family lived in Phanaswadi, Girgaon. Tatya and Kaku had gone there from Peerbhoy Mansion to see a prospective bride called Chiku; but on the way they saw Manorama playing with her friends in Phanaswadi and liked the look of her. On inquiring who she was, they made the proposal to her father, a railway contractor, and never went to see Chiku at all. Initially Manorama's parents hesitated for they felt that their daughter was perhaps a bit too young; but they reconsidered when they found out that Tatya was a well-respected businessman. Ironically, Manorama was a friend of Chiku. While Manorama went on to live a life of prosperity, it was a cruel twist of fate for Chiku: she married an electrician who ill-treated and eventually abandoned her. Many years later in the 1950s, after Tatya had passed away, Chiku came to Woodlands with her three children to seek sanctuary and was given quarters in a small chawl-like building that had been constructed within the grounds for employees and other tenants. She lived thus on a property of which she could have been mistress.

Life in Peerbhoy Mansion

In 1911, Tatya had entered a period of increasing success for his textile selling agency, having acquired the prized sole selling agency of Kohinoor Mills. The financial stability meant that in 1912 he could move from his two-room dwelling in Khatryachi Chawl to an apartment block a stone's throw away, called Peerbhoy Mansion on Sandhurst Road. He rented spacious apartments here from 1912 to 1938, after which the family moved to Woodlands. Starting off with one apartment in Peerbhoy Mansion, at a rent of 60 rupees a month, he later rented two more, and then again an additional one, so that eventually by 1929 the family lived in four spacious apartments on the top two floors of the three-storey building.

An ordinary exercise book of Tatya's has survived from this period in which he has written accounts in a mixture of English and Marathi, with the earliest notes from the year 1898. Most wonderfully, belying the success that was to come his way, there is a small, insignificant noting about the opening of his pedhi at MJ Market, awkwardly squeezed into an upper margin of a page: 'Shop was started 1 July 1898, Friday'. The notebook also establishes the date of moving into Peerbhoy Mansion along with the attendant expenses: for the year 1912 he notes (in Marathi), 'This year there have been no savings in the household account at all. There has been Anna's operation; the expense of the whole family going to Borivali. A silver cigarette box for Sou. Kashi.* We moved into the new home, the expenses for that. There has been a lot of expenditure.'

The jottings in this book give a wonderful insight into Tatya's thinking and organisation. For one thing, though it is an ordinary exercise book with several scattered notes, he has numbered all the pages in pencil and created an index page at the beginning of the book. Second, there are many notes to himself in English, and the nature of these notes shows his fluency and comfort in the language, as well as revealing him to be a person who paid attention to details and was capable of having a dialogue with himself—because he writes to himself in complete sentences, with a clear intent to avoid ambiguity.

The account book also shows that his daughter Durga got married in 1913, shortly after the move to Peerbhoy Mansion, as a noting for that year shows the 'cash cost of Sou. Durgi's wedding' as 1082-8-0 rupees, and the sum of 170 rupees as a 'present given in cash to shop's men for marriage'. A noting shortly after that, but without a date, makes a mention of his son 'Bhau's thread ceremony'.

It is also clear from this exercise book that during these years at Peerbhoy Mansion, Tatya was maintaining, or helping to maintain, the accounts of his brothers Baba (who died in 1903,

---

* Kashi (Anna's daughter) had married in 1909 as per the noting of her wedding expenses in this exercise book, so this was presumably a gift for her husband. 'Sou' is short for Soubhagyavati, used to refer to a married woman.

so these are among the earliest pages), Dada, Anna, and Tatya's wife Kaku; there is a page for Govind Charity Fund (Baba's real name was Govind, so this fund was no doubt established in his memory), and twenty-four pages for Tatya's own accounts, all neatly written out. There are also a few pages, more roughly written, for Baba's daughter Bayotai, and for Tatya's sister Sakhu. He even seems to have been helping with the accounting of his old benefactor, Seth Vallabhdas Jairam, who had taken him on as an unpaid trainee in 1892 in his cloth shop in MJ Market. Vallabhdas appears to have fallen on bad days by the year 1904, for Tatya has accounted for the jewellery that his wife had to sell, followed by this note in English: 'The above items are in fact Valli bai's, wife of Vallabhdas Jairam. The credit side are the proceeds of the sale of her ornaments and debits are the sums she spent for the family and court expenses of her husband Vallabhdas during his insolvency suits.'

It was in Peerbhoy Mansion that Tatya acquired his first car, a Fiat, around 1923. He could have bought one much earlier, but being of a prudent nature he bought his first car only when he felt that he could afford to buy two or three cars. His reasoning was that having bought a car, he should not ever have to slide back to using a tram, and therefore waited till he was on a sound financial footing before getting used to this luxury. After that he went on to buy a Buick with a car radio and a five-seater Ford.

On the first floor of Peerbhoy Mansion was a Chinese dentist patronised by Tatya and Kaku. It is most likely that they continued going to him even after moving to Woodlands (incidentally, both used the traditional masheri, or burnt tobacco, for cleaning their teeth; both eventually wore dentures). Behind Peerbhoy Mansion was a residential wadi called Haji Kasam chi Wadi. Haji Kasam was the owner of the New Islam Mills, the selling agency of which Tatya had acquired in 1902. Opposite Peerbhoy Mansion was a typing institute, with its constant 'tuk-

tuk' sounds of the typewriters; below the typing institute was an eating house called Kelkar Jevan Graha; in a nearby lane was a vegetable market where the family bought its vegetables, and behind Peerbhoy Mansion was Khatryachi Chawl with their old friends still nearby. Trams rattled up and down Sandhurst Road, the tram drivers dressed in khaki uniforms and turbans, noisily ringing the foot-operated bell. Horse-drawn victorias frequently trotted by, with Muslim drivers wearing red, tasselled fez caps and carrying a long whip.

Sandhurst Road was one of the main roads leading to Chowpatty beach, and a key route for political and festive processions such as Ganesh Chaturthi. At Gokulashtami, groups of men sang and danced down the road, and made human pyramids to climb up and break the dahi handis, while the residents drenched them in water from their balconies and windows. At Nag Panchami, snake charmers visited the homes on Sandhurst Road with cobras in their cane baskets. When the basket was opened, the cobra would emerge and housewives would worship it with offerings of milk. During the monsoon, Tatya's grandchildren sailed paper boats on the street which often flooded.[4]

Though Peerbhoy Mansion was in a busy area with trams running nearby and had inconveniences like the tap water stopping at 11 a.m. in the summers, by today's standards it was idyllic: from the terrace one could see the slopes of the Hanging Gardens, for there were no tall buildings in the vicinity, while cross-ventilation filled the apartments with cool air. In the summer, on the terrace, the women and children would put unripe mangoes, kairis, in a pot of water to heat on a stove, and would then pat the warmed water on their skin to keep away heat rashes.

It was a large joint family: eventually, over the years, the family members living in Peerbhoy Mansion were Tatya and Kaku, their son Bhausaheb and his wife Manorama (with their four children), their daughter Durga and her husband (with their five children),

Tatya's nephew Raghunathrao (with his wife and four children), Tatya's niece Bayotai Divekar (with her daughter and grandson) and other young relatives of Tatya and Kaku who studied in Bombay at different points of time.

Around 1912, when Tatya moved to Peerbhoy Mansion, he started having a large annual family gathering for about six weeks in April and May during the children's summer holidays. The venue was Borivali, a place that was truly a far-flung, out of the way place at the time. The owner of Islam Mills, Haji Kasam, had two bungalows in Borivali in a village that had been given to him as an inaam, or reward, by a former ruler. Every summer vacation Tatya rented the two bungalows as a holiday home. The two bungalows were next to each other along with a Konkan-style mandav, a large open space with a roof, which was used as a kitchen, a puja room as well as a dining room. Everyone sat on the floor and ate off banana leaves. At night the women slept in the bungalows while the men slept outside on cots in the mandav. Around the bungalows was fruit in abundance, on mango trees, chikoo trees and bushes on which grew wild karvanda, a small, black, sour berry. There were also taadgole, fruit of the fan palm tree. From Monday to Friday Tatya commuted by train to Bombay from Borivali train station, leaving at 9 a.m. and returning at 7 p.m. On Saturday, Tatya's friends would arrive from Bombay, and till Monday morning they would all be busy playing cards, usually bezique.

At this time, Durga was twelve years old, Bhausaheb was eight, and their cousins (Tatya's brothers' children) were a similar age as well. It was a large gathering: Tatya and his wife Kaku; Anna and his wife Radha; Dada and his wife Anandi; Tatya's two children, Anna's six children, Dada's three children and several other relations. Family members living in Baroda travelled to Borivali especially for the gathering. In all about twenty-five to thirty people gathered for the summer, including house help from Bombay. Around this time, several of Tatya's nieces would have been married since it was common for girls to marry around the age of twelve. It appears, though, that even those who were married made a point of coming to spend at least a few days in Borivali for the family gathering. Anna's married daughter Kashi Date, for instance, would come to spend fifteen or twenty days every year in Borivali.

The tradition of spending summer holidays in Borivali carried on for about six years and came to a halt shortly after Dada's wife, Anandi, passed away in 1916. Her son, Balasaheb, who was in school at the time, remembered the family summer holidays in Borivali in his memoirs as among his finest memories: 'We children would go berserk every day. After picking karvanda we would munch them and wander about all day. Every two or three days we would get taadgole—we saw these trees only in Borivali. The joy and fun of three families living together for one and a half months was something great. It brought us all together and we developed deep affection for each other.'

Life in Woodlands

Tatya moved his family from Peerbhoy Mansion to Woodlands in 1938, when the Phaltan Sugar Works was riding a wave of success. Woodlands was a world away from busy Sandhurst Road. It was a two-and-a-half-acre property on a small hillock, with an enormous sea-facing bungalow which was more than a hundred years old. There were hard tennis courts, garages, staff quarters and stables. There were also two independent cottages on the property, called Ashmore House and The Cottage. Pedder Road, named after W.G. Pedder who had been Bombay municipal commissioner in 1879, was a quiet, tree-lined road with bungalows on either side, owned mainly by Parsi and British families. The previous occupants of Woodlands had also been British and Parsi. It was a peaceful area, and no buses or trams ran on this road.

The Woodlands garden was filled with trees: peepul and babool trees, coconut trees, fruit trees like jackfruit, chickoo, cashew nut, ber, bhokra, tamarind, drumstick and banana, and an enormous banyan tree (which stood for decades before a storm brought it down in 2021). The Bombay Gazette reported that there was a legend that a 'bearded, human-faced snake' lived in the roots of the banyan tree.[5] Tatya's family was also aware of it, with a couple of people mentioning during interviews that there was a 'hairy snake' in the grounds, though nobody claimed to have seen it. There were, however, cobras at Woodlands that emerged from time to time. Some of the domestic staff objected to killing them because they believed that a cobra was a Brahmin; so if it became necessary to kill one, the snake was cremated with religious rites.[6] There were mango trees by the tennis courts too. Vegetable patches dotted the grounds, planted wherever there was space. In the cattle shed behind the bungalow were cows and buffaloes to provide fresh milk. Tatya often sat on a bench nearby and had a glass of warm milk, freshly milked from one of the cows.

Behind the house, in a courtyard where clothes were hung out to dry, there were trees with flowers used for the daily puja, such as sonchafa and madhumati, along with a tulsi vrindavan. Behind the banyan tree was a small hut where a woman called Bayabai lived with her mute son. In the morning she would light a stove in front of her hut and prepare hot, delicious-smelling chapattis. She grew magnolias near her hut to sell. Tatya did not interfere with this arrangement, and let her continue living there on the understanding that she did not own the place.

The staff quarters were in a chawl-like structure comprising six or seven rooms all on the ground floor. A large driveway swept up from Pedder Road towards the bungalow, looping around a small oval lawn. Adjacent to this lawn was the large garden, in front of the main entrance to the bungalow.*

Inside the Bungalow

Upon entering the bungalow through the main entrance, one could see a marble staircase that went up past a small circular fountain. Next to the staircase was a Schindler elevator that went up to the first and second floors. To the right was an independent, self-contained apartment comprising four or five large rooms and a kitchen, with a private entrance from the driveway. To the left was a large hall.

The first floor had a sweeping view of the open sea. One could see as far as Marine Drive and Ballard Pier at one end of the view, and up to the Mahalaxmi Temple at the other end.† There were no tall buildings nearby to obstruct the view and, moreover, Woodlands stood on a hillock at about 90 feet above sea level. Across the road, directly opposite Woodlands, were the elegant

* The layout of the property was very different from the present layout of Woodlands. Currently, the twenty-five-storey building, built in 1969, has a garden in front and parking spaces at the back. In 1938, at the site of the current garden, one would have seen the bungalow. Where the current building is, were the tennis courts. The multi-storey garages were formerly the site of the staff quarters, and behind the staff quarters, completely cut off from the Woodlands bungalow, was Ashmore House on a lower level of the slope. The current exit to the property is where the Cottage was located. The hut behind the banyan tree was located at the spot overlooking Pedder Road where cars are currently parked.

† In his autobiography Madhav Apte, Tatya's grandson, gives a vivid description of the sweeping view from Woodlands in 1944, when there was an explosion in the Bombay Docks: 'One of the ships carrying heavy explosives to Singapore was docked in port ... Inexplicably, the ship with ammunition caught fire and it exploded. So did two other ships. The explosion was so huge it rocked the entire island city ... The entire Ballard Pier dock area looked like a string of fire ... [From] Woodlands, though only two storeys, we could get a clear view of the dockland on fire. Even at that distance the view, though frightening, was stunning' (Apte 2015, p. 63).

onion-shaped domes of the palatial mansion formerly owned by Sir Harkisandas;* it was now being used as a primary co-ed school run by the Franciscan Missionaries of Mary, founded in 1932 and named 'Villa Theresa'. The sound of waves breaking against the shore at Breach Candy was the only thing that broke through the sheer, dead silence. It was so quiet that often the conversation from the neighbouring property, Mafatlal House, could be heard in Woodlands.

Woodlands had huge rooms, which were more like halls, and very long corridors. When the family moved in, the bungalow had wooden flooring and a gabled roof, and two rooms had fireplaces. Strangely, though, the kitchen was a bit smaller than the one in Peerbhoy Mansion. It was an old-fashioned, rather unwieldy house, too big for the family. Tatya began considering plans to demolish it and build a modern house. But the Second World War started barely a year later, leading to a shortage of materials. This was followed by the discovery that the roof had begun leaking. The repairs to the leaky roof eventually turned into a major renovation of the house, and plans to demolish it were scrapped. Instead, the noisy wooden floor was replaced with tiling; the gabled roof was removed, and six or seven open air terraces were constructed in its place. A small section of gabled roof remained for a while, a dark place with a low roof where Tatya's grandchildren played hide and seek. The first floor, including Tatya's enormous bathroom, got marble flooring. While the cost of buying the Woodlands property was about 3.5 lakh rupees, the renovations cost a further 2 lakhs.[7]

Since the house was too big for the family, the independent apartment on the ground floor was rented to Dadasaheb

---

* The mansion was previously known as Narottamdas Mansion, named after Sir Harkisandas' father. As per Sir Harkisandas' will, the mansion was sold and the money went towards building the Sir H.N. Hospital in Girgaon, now known as the Sir H.N. Reliance Foundation Hospital (pers. comm., Anand Desai).

Merchant, Bhausaheb's friend from the Hindu Gymkhana, who was the manager of Crown Mills. Crown Mills was owned by the cricketer Vijay Merchant (not a relation of Dadasaheb Merchant). Vijay Merchant was therefore a frequent visitor to Woodlands in the early 1940s, often staying to play a bit of tennis ball cricket with Tatya's grandsons, Arvind and Madhav, or tennis with the adults. Bhausaheb was a regular tennis player, often playing in the mornings with his friends and his son-in-law Kamlakar Modak, who had married Bhausaheb's daughter Manju in 1946.

The kitchen was on the first floor, and had piped gas from the Bombay Gas Company. A fridge was installed there after the war. Also on the first floor were a pregnancy room, a dev ghar, a table tennis room, a guest room for women, two or three rooms known as kothi chi kholi, used for cleaning and storing the annual stock of grain, and a store room which was filled with firecrackers at Diwali, and mangoes in the summer. There were large pictorial encyclopaedias on the bookshelves. There was also a gramophone, though it was not used much by the family. The house had been bought unfurnished, so the wooden furniture from Peerbhoy Mansion was taken along and installed in the house.

Tatya and Kaku's bedroom was at the far end of a long sea-facing corridor of about 150 feet, with the kitchen at the other end. Their bedroom was like a large hall which could have held 300 people, so a partition was installed to separate it into a bedroom and a dressing room. Its ensuite bathroom was almost 400 square feet. On a carpeted balcony attached to the bedroom, Tatya set up his armchair where he would sit every evening, puffing at his beedis. It was a good vantage point to keep an eye on things: from this position he could see the garden, he could enjoy the sea breeze and he could also look straight down the long passageway to the kitchen and dining table.

The pregnancy room on the first floor, known as the balanteen kholi, was used for a month or two by a new mother when she returned home from the hospital after the birth of her baby. As per the traditional customs, the room was kept darkened or dimly lit, to be as much like a womb as possible for the comfort of both mother and baby. In this room a woman called Subhadra would come to oil and massage the mother. She was then given a sheyk or heat treatment: the mattress of the bed was removed and a large pot, called a ghamela, was filled with burning coals and some dhoop and placed under the bed. When the new mother lay on the bed, the smoke provided heat for her back, while the dhoop may have acted as a disinfectant for the room. Subhadra would then bathe and dry the new mother, and make up a clean mattress for her to sleep on.

Also on the first floor was a large hall with a seating capacity of 300; two open air terraces; and two large rooms occasionally used as office rooms by Gotu Mule, which housed some old steel cupboards from the Hindustan Film Company.

On the second floor was a small sitting room with sofas where the family often gathered, opposite the staircase and elevator. Bhausaheb and Manorama's bedroom was on this floor, with their four small children sleeping in their parents' room on floor mattresses. About ten years later, in 1948–49, more bedrooms with attached bathrooms were added for the older children. There were two large terraces on the second floor—the children often played cricket here, and the bowling was done while sitting on a stool.

The third floor was made up simply of three big open terraces and some storerooms.

The interior of the house was very comfortable, but also purely functional, for neither Tatya and Kaku nor their two children had any interest in what, today, would be called interior decoration. There were just a few paintings in the house, and hardly any curtains.

The bomb shelter, which Tatya had built at the height of the Second World War, was next to the main bungalow, and held a huge Godrej safe into which all the jewellery and stocks and shares were moved. Unexpectedly, the roof of the bomb shelter also served as a pleasant open-air terrace for the family.

The garages housed three or four cars at any given time. Over the years, Tatya bought mainly American cars like Ford, Buick and Dodge as they were more suited to Indian roads, large families, and the regular cross-country trips to Poona and Phaltan. A new Chevrolet was bought every year—a Bombay Garage salesman would make an annual visit to Woodlands with a new Chevrolet which would be switched with the old one. In the 1940s there was a lone English car, a Sunbeam Talbot. Tatya also appears to have retained his first car, the old Fiat, for several years. When the Phaltan Sugar Works was started, the three partners, Tatya, Mafatlal and Nahalchand, had all ordered Buicks: with his large family, Tatya opted for a seven-seater with a glass between the driver and the passenger seats; Seth Nahalchand had a five-seater; and Seth Mafatlal chose a convertible. Petrol rationing during the Second World War meant that Tatya's Buick, which regularly made the trip to Poona and Sakharwadi, was converted to a coal-powered car, with coal being topped up in Lonavala.

There were two or three Rolls-Royce models brought to Woodlands for Tatya to consider; he went for a spin in them out of curiosity or admiration, but there was no question of buying one. The reason was that his old Hindustan Film Company partner, Mayashankar Bhatt, had fallen on bad times shortly after buying a Rolls. Tatya developed a superstition about Rolls-Royce cars after this episode, considering them to be bad luck.

Woodlands came with two tenants already in place in the two small houses on the property. In the Cottage was a British man called Chadwick, followed by a British solicitor called Martins who was a partner in a solicitors' firm called Little & Co.; and in

Ashmore Cottage, which had a separate entrance from Pedder Road onto the property, was the Bhatia family. The Cottage, which was on the slope facing Pedder Road, had its own independent little garden, and the Martins kept it neat and well-tended. When the couple had a son and daughter, Tatya expanded the cottage by building an annexe with a kitchen on the ground floor and a bedroom upstairs. The Martins also kept a kitchen garden, raised turkeys for Christmas and employed a Nepali cook and a chauffeur to drive their Daimler. After India became independent in 1947, the Martins family returned to England; later the Cottage was rented out to a British man called Henderson. Despite the close proximity of the Martins to the Woodlands bungalow, there was no interaction between the families at all, apart from a few rare occasions when the children of the two families played together.

Next door to Woodlands was Mafatlal House, the mansion bought by Tatya's friend and colleague Mafatlal Gagalbhai, at around the same time as Woodlands was bought. Another neighbour was Sir Narayan Mandlik at the Hermitage & Green Gables, who had sold Woodlands to Tatya through a broker called Baburao Jhakaas. Sir Mandlik's father, a well-known lawyer, had been famous for always being on time; people set their watches when they saw him drive by in his victoria every morning, and Tatya's grandson Arvind even had a chapter in his school Marathi textbook on his punctuality. Sir Mandlik had the eccentric habit of travelling with two cars—the second car followed in case the first one broke down. Like the Aptes, he too kept cows and buffaloes but, much to Kaku's chagrin, he believed that the colostrum, or 'first milk', of cows after giving birth to a calf, was not fit for human consumption and had it destroyed, even though it was traditionally used to make a sweet delicacy called kharvas.[8]

Every Diwali, Tatya's grandsons Madhav and Arvind would visit the Hermitage to pay their respects to Sir Mandlik and return home with a box of chocolates each. Relations with Sir Mandlik were very cordial, but as per the times, there was a certain old-fashioned formality to the interaction: when the children's games at Woodlands sent a ball sailing into Sir Mandlik's garden, he wrote a polite letter to Tatya requesting that more care be taken by the children to prevent it happening again. Diwali was also a day for the children to visit Mafatlal House to pay their respects, along with a stream of cloth merchants and other visitors.

Tatya employed about twenty people at Woodlands, including three or four drivers, staff to look after the cattle, three or four Nepali Gurkhas as watchmen and two or three gardeners. The domestic help comprised three cooks (they were shaven-headed widows called Uma bai, Shanta bai and Anandi bai) and six or seven male staff. Of the male helpers, Sadu was employed solely for making and serving tea, while Sadashiv, Raghav and Digambar were in charge of serving food. Another was called Bhaskar. They all ate their meals and slept within the bungalow. The rest of the staff lived in the chawl-like quarters on the property. One of the drivers, Keshav, regularly applied leeches on his body to relieve his high blood pressure. Another driver was an acquaintance of the actor Prithviraj Kapoor, who stopped by now and then to talk to him, though he had no interaction with the family members in the bungalow. Joglekar driver often took children and family members out, for example to the vegetable market.

In 1938, only eight people had moved into the massive property: Tatya, Kaku, their son Bhausaheb, daughter-in-law Manorama and four grandchildren, Manju, Kuma, Madhav and Arvind. In 1942, when Durga moved in with her family, the number went up to thirteen: Durga and Baburao Dabke, along with their children Kushi, Nalli and Khandu. Durga also brought along two of her own domestic staff. In addition, there was a constant coming and going of relations, particularly during the school holidays, when family members from Baroda would come and spend a couple of months at Woodlands. Some relations stayed for months and even years, such as the Kelkars from Rajapur. There were also two Brahmin students, Pavle and Joshi, who stayed at Woodlands, and another Brahmin student who would come for meals. It was common at the time for well-to-do families to support poor students in this manner. On average, there were about twenty people served at lunch every day, not counting the staff. At dinner the number reduced, as only family members were present. It was not the custom for friends or outsiders to be invited to dinner. Despite the number of people who lived in and visited the property every day, it was a quiet environment. The sheer size of the house and the grounds meant that people were scattered over a large area and there was never any sense of a hustle and bustle about the place. In addition to that, nobody in the family had the tendency to shout or create a fuss even when upset. Tatya himself never raised his voice and, following his lead, nobody else did either. Peace reigned.

Festivals were celebrated with gusto, however, and Kaku loved filling her house with relations and friends. In later years, there were musical performances too, most memorably an evening where the celebrated natya sangeet artiste Bal Gandharva (who was a close friend of Dr Bhadkamkar) performed for a large audience.

A colourful addition to the family party was Kaku's mother, Rahtyachi Aai ('mother from Rahte'). She was called this because she lived with one of her two sons, Chintu, in a village called Rahte in Nagar district, where he worked as a civil engineer in the irrigation department., 'Chintu, who will look after me if you get married?' she would lament. And so the loyal son remained a bachelor till his mother died around 1945, and married very late in life. Rahtyachi Aai visited Woodlands occasionally, staying for a month or six weeks, and, despite all her initial antipathy towards Durga, received a warm welcome. Tatya's grandchildren looked forward to her visits for she was an eccentric and affectionate old character, a quick and excellent cook, fond of preparing phodnicha bhaat (spiced rice) for the children as a mid-morning snack. Driving down from Rahte, she would appear at Woodlands in her large Chevrolet, which was filled to bursting with pumpkins, oranges, sweet limes, fresh harbare (chick peas), peanuts, all kinds of seasonal fruits and vegetables, and the occasional additional gift like a paata varvantaa (grinding stone and pestle) or, once, a dolaara (swing) made of six kilos of silver for Kaku's Chaitra Gaur pooja. In the midst of this cornucopia was visible the diminutive figure of Rahtyachi Aai, driven by her loyal major-domo, a Kannadiga driver called Ramchandra.

Rahtyachi Aai was a short, dark woman, a shaven-headed widow in the widow's garb of a white sari, with her padar tightly wrapped twice around her head.* She wore spectacles and artificial teeth. She suffered from body ache and would often need to have her body massaged and pressed. She was a hot-tempered woman with a strong streak of independence in her, who felt that women should not be hemmed in and subdued. When her daughter Kaku was a newly married girl and had recently started living in Khatryachi Chawl, Rahtyachi Aai had created a sensation by sending her two books in the post. In the late nineteenth century, when most women remained illiterate, for something to arrive in the post for a girl, and for that something to be books, had created a flurry in the chawl. A woman, said Rahtyachi Aai, must be like a snake, a nagin—she must not be lethargic—she must be aware of everything around her and slither forward quickly. She freely told her daughter that her method of birth control had been to lock herself into her bedroom to prevent her husband coming in.

---

* The traditional garb of a widow was a red or maroon sari, as explained later in this chapter. In the sole surviving photo of Rahtyachi Aai, however, she wears a white sari. She was already an old woman when the photo was taken, and it may be that times had changed by then to allow for widows to wear white as well as the prescribed red colour.

She was not in favour of women having too many children—after Manorama's fourth child, she wryly commented that it was time to stop. When her husband had died, Rahtyachi Aai did not want her head to be shaved but had been compelled to submit to it; but though a widow was supposed to renounce worldly pleasures, she did not allow her independent personality to be entirely repressed. She loved perfume. She knew she could never wear it—but nevertheless had a collection of perfumes in little bottles that her driver Ramchandra procured for her, nobody knew from where. She spoke to Ramchandra in Kannada, making extravagant hand gestures all the while; since nobody else understood the language, their communications remained confidential. She liked to bicycle around the grounds of Woodlands, and she had even learnt from Ramchandra how to drive the Chevrolet in her compound in Rahte. She enjoyed listening to music and would often go to the theatre to watch musical dramas. She loved tasty food and enthusiastically supervised the making of hand-churned ice-cream to be served on occasions like Haldi Kunku. She would round up the children and even their mothers, Manorama and Durga, to play catch-catch in the garden or to play cards. Tatya was rather disapproving of this state of affairs, but was powerless to say anything to his mother-in-law. Indeed, as per the custom of the time, he hardly ever spoke to her directly, but whenever she arrived at Woodlands, and when she was leaving Woodlands, he would come to receive her or see her off, wearing his pagdi as a mark of respect.

No doubt Rahtyachi Aai's son, Chintu, supported his mother in all she did, and his own views on the cruel treatment of widows were apparent in his eventual choice of wife: after his mother died, he married a woman who had been a child-widow. The guruji who normally came to Woodlands to conduct pujas refused to conduct the marriage because of his disapproval of widow remarriage. Manorama had harsh words for him, reminding him that he himself was a widower who had remarried, and if remarriage was acceptable for a widower, it ought to be the same for a widow; the guruji's opinion remained unchanged though, and another guruji had to be found to conduct the marriage ceremony.

For Rahtyachi Aai, the British could do no wrong. She was a wholehearted supporter of the British, particularly during the Second World War. This was in sharp contrast to the family doctor, Dr Bhadkamkar, who disliked the British, was a staunch supporter of the Germans, and liked to teach Tatya's grandchildren how to do the Nazi salute and say 'Heil Hitler'. Dr Bhadkamkar, who had been instrumental in setting up the Phaltan Sugar Works, was greatly respected by all the family. In 1944, he saved Tatya's youngest grandchild, Arvind, from an attack of diphtheria that almost proved to be fatal. He was, therefore, a regular visitor to the household, and a discussion about who was better, the British or the Germans, was sure to surface when he visited.

Meals and Daily Routines

The day started early in Woodlands. Tatya woke up at 3.30 a.m. and had a cup of tea at 4.30 a.m. Kaku woke up at 5 a.m. and had her tea with her children, Durga and Bhausaheb, at 5.30 a.m. At 7.30 a.m. Ganu, one of the manservants, went shopping for fresh vegetables armed with a few cloth bags. There was a market nearby, close to Burnham Lane. When he returned, the three women who worked in the kitchen, Uma bai, Shanta bai and Anandi bai, cleaned and cut the vegetables. Kaku had bathed by this time and every morning, without fail, she took great pleasure in sitting down with the three women and cutting the vegetables very even and fine, though she had ample help and did not need to do so. Afterwards she sat down to her puja for about 45 minutes, which included reading pothya and doing jup with her beads, her hand held under her sari's padar. She would also sing gopalya in the mornings.

Nobody ever ate any breakfast, but lunch was very early: by the time Kaku's prayers were finished, it was time for the first pangat, or first group of people, to eat lunch at around 10.30 a.m. with Manorama helping to serve the food. Meanwhile, Bhausaheb would have gone to Kohinoor Mills early in the morning, and returned around 11 a.m. (In earlier years, Tatya would have done so.) On returning from the mills, he ate his lunch at 11.30 a.m., along with any others who had not eaten in the first pangat. After a short nap, he would head out to the MJ Market pedhi for the afternoon, returning home only after his evening visit to the Cricket Club of India to play sports and socialise. By 2 p.m. the staff had finished eating, and dinner was at 7 p.m. Tatya always wanted his family to finish eating early because he was concerned that the staff meal would be delayed.

In later years, Tatya ate on his own; he had developed diabetes, and believed that it was paramount to take his meal immediately after his injection. So, having taken his injection in his bedroom, he would rush, almost at a fast trot, from his bedroom to the dining table at the other end of the long corridor to eat his meal. He was also the only one to eat at the dining table. Everyone else ate sitting cross-legged on paats, low wooden seats, on the floor. The men ate before the women, though Bhausaheb often ate with his mother and sister. Menstruating women and girls sat for their meals separately. Tatya and Kaku, of course, never ate together.

A regular part of the morning routine at home was the visit of Gotu Mule. Gotu Mule was the indispensable, loyal, right-hand man of Tatya and Bhausaheb at the pedhi in MJ Market. Every morning he would arrive at Woodlands to write down the household expenses of the previous day. Kaku and Manorama sat with him at the dining table with their individual little thailis, cloth purses of money, while Mule jotted down the expenses. If even one paisa was not accounted for, both Kaku and Manorama would be restless till it had been tracked down; the one paisa clearly did not matter in terms of its value, but what mattered to them was the discipline of accurate accounting. On the rare occasions when additional money was needed, Manorama or Kaku would ask Gotu Mule for it and he would bring it home. Otherwise, every month money for household expenses was sent home from VS Apte & Son, Tatya's company. The other go-to man at the pedhi was Keshav, who would also do all kinds of odd jobs for the family, from buying medicine to delivering papers and documents.

In the afternoons, Kaku and the other women in the house took a nap and afterwards they all changed from their saris of zari, worn in the mornings, into a fresh sari, a simple cotton nine-yard one, to feel refreshed for the approaching evening. When going out of the house at any time it was the custom for women to wear a 'shela', which was like a stole made of four and a half yards of heavy embroidered silk. Draped over a sari, it was used to entirely cover a woman's shoulders and torso.

Afternoon snacks along with tea or coffee consisted of traditional dishes like saboodanyachi khichdi (spiced sago), sweet sheera, spicy sheera (semolina) and pohe (savoury rice flakes). Occasionally, there were exotic fruit sent as gifts by Tatya's business associates, such as big boxes of black, seedless grapes from Kabul, which were considered a great delicacy. For lunch and dinner too the menu rarely deviated from the traditional vegetarian fare of rice, two kinds of bhaaji, poli, aamti, chutneys and two or three kinds of pickle, all prepared as per Kokanastha Brahmin conventions. There was, however, some amount of Gujarati influence on the food—for example, undhiyu was often prepared—since the family had its roots in Baroda, and because Tatya's business associates were almost exclusively Gujarati. But apart from the slight Gujarati influence there was not much openness to other kinds of food—for the most part this was simply because there was no exposure to any other kind of food. Eating outside the house was unheard of; food could never be brought in from outside; and the people who were invited to eat at home were also Brahmin. Non-Brahmins, even close business associates, were not invited to eat at home. Even if one of the children's school friends of another caste came home and had a glass of water to drink, Kaku would order the domestic staff, 'Put that glass outside the house to be washed.'

With such orthodoxy comes limited exposure. Therefore, even something as commonplace as batatawada was initially unknown in the Apte kitchen; batatawadas, for example, were introduced to Kaku while the family was living at Peerbhoy Mansion, when a neighbour, Dr Vaadh's wife, showed her how to make them. Kaku made dhirdi, which is very much like a soft dosa; she made saandan, which uses the same ingredients as idlis, but is soaked in mango juice before being steamed; but neither idlis nor dosas were known in the household. The 1940s, however, brought about quite a few changes in Kaku's kitchen. With the Merchant family living as tenants in Woodlands came exposure to different kinds of food, including macaroni, which Mrs Nirmala Merchant used to make at home; Durga tried her hand at making it and most of the family enjoyed eating it, though it is highly unlikely that either Tatya or Kaku had any. By this time, though, the three cooks, particularly Uma bai, had learnt to make idlis and dosas, while bread was often bought for Tatya to eat toast. Apart from the children, who occasionally ate bread too, nobody else ate it, and it was the only 'outside' food permitted in the house. Even so, the bread was not allowed in the kitchen and had to be left outside on the dining table. So strict were the conventions of not eating food prepared outside the house that Kaku and her mother, Rahtyachi Aai, would not even eat pohe, because the rice had been roasted and flattened outside the house, even though it was to be cooked at home; they only tolerated pohe which had been bought from one particular shopkeeper, presumably a Brahmin who prepared the pohe himself. But there was one secret in this strictly orthodox, vegetarian household: Manorama, worried at the weak growth of two of her children, Madhav and Manju, regularly took them aside at Peerbhoy Mansion and quietly cracked open eggs which they then had to swallow raw. It is impossible that Kaku ever knew about it—but far more likely that Tatya was aware of it and had decided to turn a blind eye to it.

Many of these conventions slowly began breaking down by the mid-1940s, particularly after Kaku passed away in 1946. It was only in 1945, for example, that Tatya's grandson Arvind had his first taste of an egg (an omelette which he did not like), at the Lucky restaurant in Pune, en route to Sangli where Tatya and others were going to discuss the new industrial complex. As Arvind and Madhav grew up, they became more involved in sporting activities, occasionally eating out after matches, while Bhausaheb, of course, regularly socialised at the Cricket Club of India and very likely ate there on occasion.

Tatya's all-time favourite dish was aamras, for which of course he had to wait for the summer months. All the women in the house would sit together to juice the mangoes. A big silver bowl was set aside for serving aamras. Tatya also took great pleasure in eating vegetables that had been grown at home in Woodlands, including pickles made from the small, round fruit of the bhokar tree that stood on the grounds, and drinking the milk from the cows in the Woodlands stables.

A custom in Brahmin households, and integral to the preparation and serving of meals, was 'sohle'. Based on caste distinction, this revolved around an exaggerated notion of hygiene and purity. A woman in sohle essentially meant a Brahmin woman who had bathed and worn a clean sari, which she had washed herself. The washed sari, and indeed the person who was in sohle, could not be touched by anyone who was not in sohle. In practical terms this meant that the woman would have washed her own sari and choli the previous day, hung it out to dry, and then removed it from the drying line herself the next day after she had bathed.

Only persons who were Brahmins, and in sohle, were allowed into the kitchen and were allowed to cook. Till they had finished cooking, nobody, apart from others who were already in sohle, was allowed to touch them. Uma bai, Shanta bai and Anandi bai, the three women who cooked, were therefore all in sohle before they entered the kitchen.

So, for example, Uma bai would have her bath, and wear her clean sari without drying herself (it was not common to use towels at the time). She would then be allowed to touch Shanta bai's clean sari to put it in the bathroom, so that Shanta bai could go and have her bath. Though Kaku did not wash her own clothes, they were washed by Uma bai, Shanta bai or Anandi bai; since they were all Brahmins, the clothes they washed would be considered as sohle. A male Brahmin servant could not wash Kaku's clothes, though—women's clothes had to be washed by women.

At meal-times, the food was served by Brahmin staff, helped by female family members, though the people serving the food did not need to be in sohle. Those who were already eating were forbidden from serving themselves, even using their clean left hand, as is common today—this would have rendered the food kharkat or ushta, meaning it would be considered unclean.

The notion of sohle extended to the washing of utensils. The male helper who washed the utensils was not in sohle. Therefore, he would wash the utensils outside the kitchen and deposit the washed utensils at the door of the kitchen. Then one of the women in sohle, either Kaku or one of the three bais, would take the utensils and once more rinse them out in the kitchen before using them.

While Manorama and Durga were less concerned about the custom of sohle, Kaku was very strict about it. Kaku also needed to be in sohle for her daily morning puja, as it was considered to bring sanctity to the prayers. When the guruji came home to do the puja on special occasions, he too would be in sohle for the puja as well as for his meal, and nobody was allowed to touch him till he had finished.

A widow was in sohle only if she was shaven-headed and wore a nine-yard sari of a particular red or maroon colour. They were called 'laal baaya' or red women, because of the colour of their saris. They would use their saris to keep their heads covered at all times. Uma bai, Shanta bai and Anandi bai, who worked for many years for the Apte family, were all shaven-headed widows. The primary reason behind the cruel practice of shaving a widow's head was to make her look unattractive, so that no man would look at her with any kind of desire, and so that she would remain 'pure'. When a woman became a widow people would describe her, in Sanskrit terminology, either as 'sakesha' (with hair) or 'vikesha' (without hair). If she was 'vikesha' she was allowed to live in the house, and a barber would regularly visit the house to shave her head; but if she was 'sakesha', she was shunned entirely by society. A barber visited Woodlands regularly to shave the heads of Uma bai, Anandi bai and Shanta bai, and the place for doing so was on the first floor, outside the kothi chi kholi, the room where grains were stored for the year.

Clothes and Jewellery

It was customary for the women in the household to wear gold jewellery every day; by today's standards it would be considered very heavy jewellery. Silver was not worn at all. The only precious stones worn were diamonds set in rings or earrings. On festival days, women did not change out of their everyday jewellery, but simply added extra jewellery such as a chandrahaar, for example, which is a long necklace made of multiple strings of gold. Interestingly, the saris that the women wore at night were kept in the same room as the safe where the women's jewellery was stored. The men's clothes were put elsewhere, as the clothes of men and women were never kept together.

In the old days, when living in Girgaon, Kaku used to frequent a sari shop run by the Laghate family, who also happened to be Tatya and Kaku's neighbours in Khatryachi Chawl. When Tatya and Kaku moved to Woodlands, the owner, Yashwant Laghate, would send a man over with a pile of saris for the women to choose from. The families were close friends, and Kaku used to call him 'Yashwanta'. The need for clothes shopping arose primarily when there was a wedding. The wedding of Kamla, Durga's daughter, in 1938 was the first big wedding in the family after a long time, as she was the first of Tatya's grandchildren to get married. That was the time when piles of fancy saris, such as Banarasi silks, were sent home by various merchants like Laghate as well as Athavale & Shahade. The selection of saris was done by Kaku, Manorama and Durga, as well as the wives of Tatya's nephews. When buying saris for their children, it was not the custom to ask them about their preferences. When new jewellery needed to be made, say for a wedding, a man from the Pethe's shop in Girgaon would come home for the women to select the designs they wanted, which were then custom-made.

This style of shopping at home meant that Kaku hardly ever needed to leave the grounds of Woodlands, and slowly lost the habit of going out into crowds. There was an incident when Kaku and Manorama, along with the young girls Manju, Kamla and Indu, went to a market to buy steel utensils. So unused was Kaku to the clamour of the market and the clanging of the utensils that she could not continue shopping and had to be escorted back to the car.

The younger children's clothes were usually stitched at home by the women of the house. Sometimes Manorama did the cutting of clothes, while Kaku stitched them, and did a little bit of knitting too. Cloth sometimes arrived home from Kohinoor Mills in pieces or even bundles; at this time, Kohinoor's long cloth, soft cotton cloth used to make shirts and underclothes, was famous and of a high quality.

When small girls outgrew frocks, they wore parkar-polkas, comprising a short blouse and an ankle-length skirt. When they outgrew those, they began wearing saris, starting with a smaller eight-yard sari and then progressing to a nine-yard one. Durga's eldest daughter Kamla, though, never wore a frock—she wore her deceased baby brother's shirts and pants, and moved on directly to wearing parkar-polkas. Her sister Indu also wore shirts and pants for several months. It seems strange now that the young daughters of a prosperous family would use hand-me-downs of a brother who had died; but it seems to be a reflection of the times. People appear to have been prudent and practical as a matter of course, making do with what they had, even if they could afford to buy new things.

During the Second World War, around 1942, cloth became relatively expensive and nine-yard saris became expensive too. Five-yard saris were cheaper and known as 'gol' saris because they were wrapped around the waist creating a round shape, as compared to the nine-yard saris that were worn tied between the legs. Several women began wearing 'gol' saris during this time, also taking a lead from the many women in the nationalist Congress movement who wore five-yard saris. Tatya did not approve of this style of wearing the sari, but fashions were steadily changing; his granddaughter Kuma never wore a nine-yard sari, graduating from parkar-polkas directly to the 'gol' sari.

Festivals and Weddings

Tatya and Kaku were both fond of celebrating festive occasions with their family members and close friends. They often hosted about fifty or sixty people at Woodlands for the whole day with the children running around the large grounds for games and merrymaking. Those who came from far away stayed the night. The festive menu always included shrikhand, made by Manorama and a helper called Ranade, who placed the chakka on a large wooden frame for the water to drain away. It was made in such abundance that the shrikhand was served not with a spoon, but was poured onto everyone's plates. In mango season, aamras made from hapus as well as pairi mangoes was a must. Kaku would personally go around the pangat (meal settings laid out in rows on the floor) and enquire after each person and check that everyone had enough to eat. Kaku, Manorama, Durga, and all the women and girls in the house would sit together to prepare snacks like chakli, chivda and chirote, as well as karanji made with coconuts from the Woodlands garden. Ice cream was made at least once a year in a large ten-litre hand-churned ice-cream maker. The milk was heated well, cream and spices added to it, and then poured into the ice-cream maker, which had been placed on the terrace. Manorama, Balasaheb and a driver called Keshav took turns at spinning the handle.

At Diwali, the abhyang snaan was at 4 a.m. when everyone applied ground sesame, poppy seeds and perfumed oil on themselves before bathing. The men did this on Narka Chaturthi, while the women did it the previous day; since it is a time-consuming ritual, the idea was to avoid a rush with everyone doing it on the same day. Around 8 a.m., there was a Diwali morning pharaal (a light, festive meal) with snacks like chakli and karanji, and lunch was at 1 p.m. There were no outsiders for lunch on this day; since it was a family affair, everyone was busy celebrating in their own homes. Business associates of Tatya and Bhausaheb sent gifts of large boxes of fireworks, including extremely long strings of firecrackers, as well as boxes of fruit: oranges, sweet limes and red-skinned bananas.

During the Diwali festival, Tatya invited home two or three of his English business associates from Killick Nixon, including the chairman of Killick Nixon, Duncan Shepherd. Tatya invited all his merchants at the same time, and this became an opportunity for the merchants to meet the Englishmen who ran Killick Nixon and Kohinoor Mills. On such occasions, the guests were served sweets and fruit juices. It was essentially a business gathering, and neither the women and children, nor other male family members, were present. Diwali was also an occasion for Tatya's grandchildren to visit the pedhi at MJ Market, particularly for the Laxmi puja. Women, however, never visited the pedhi.

Bhaubeej was a major event and the house filled up with at least sixty relatives, including family members from Baroda, members of Kaku's family and Manorama's five or six brothers. All the women and girls formed a long line, waiting their turn to perform an ovalni* for their brothers, including first cousins and second cousins. Each brother or cousin would give his sister one or two rupees—the amount was fixed in advance, and it was not done to give extra money to a favourite. Some brothers gifted satin pieces to make frocks or blouses instead of gifting money. A couple of extra hands were hired that day just to serve tea.

Haldi Kunku was the other large event in the Woodlands garden, celebrated every year on a grand scale. This was exclusively for women. Invitations were sent on a printed card to relations and friends, including to the wives of some of Tatya's Gujarati business associates. An invitation was never to a single person—it meant that the person it was addressed to could bring along

* This is a ritual where the sister circles her brother's face with a small platter arranged with a lamp, turmeric, vermillion, grains of rice, a ring and a betel nut.

the other women in her family, as well as any houseguests she might have. On average, about 150 women attended the Haldi Kunku at Woodlands every year. Though Kaku had been hosting a Haldi Kunku since the Peerbhoy Mansion days, after moving to Woodlands the day was celebrated on a much larger scale.

The Haldi Kunku was held in the month of Chaitra, the first month of the Hindu calendar. The menu was fixed: hand-churned ice cream, aambyachi daal (sour and spicy chana daal with grated green mango), harbaryachi usal (fresh or dried Bengal gram cooked in coconut) and panha (a cooling drink made of green mango). The children in the house prepared some kind of pretty model to display at the Haldi Kunku, such as a village scene on a mountain made of mud; one year Tatya's grandchildren created a miniature wheat plantation. Kaku, Durga, Manorama and some of the older girls like Durga's daughter Kamla dressed up in heavy saris and jewellery. At 4 p.m., the guests would start arriving and be served ambyachi daal in a dron, a bowl made of sal leaves, along with panha to drink. The ice-cream was flavoured with saffron and cardamom—the concept of fruit ice cream was unknown at the time. Cloth bale handlers from Tatya's pedhi were asked to come and hand-churn the vast quantity of ice cream,[9] no doubt a job that required some muscle. For the Haldi Kunku ceremony, a silver platter was arranged with a lit lamp, haldi (turmeric), kunku (vermillion) and a supari. Each guest had the haldi-kunku applied to her forehead. The ceremony included gifting all the guests with harbare, a small golden variety of banana called a son-kela, haldi-kunku, attar (perfume), a rose, ambyachi daal, and a batasha (flat sugar candy) or saakhar phutane (sweetened whole chana daal).

The goddess Gauri, who is worshipped on the day of the Haldi Kunku, sat in a dolaara (a swing) made of 6 kilos of silver, gifted by Rahtyachi Aai to Kaku. Despite the religious aspect to the day, the ritual of Haldi Kunku had more of a social significance rather than a religious one. During this era, it was not common for women to go outside the house much, and so Haldi Kunku served as an invaluable occasion to invite each other home to meet and socialise.

Other festivals were celebrated on a relatively low-key level by Tatya and Kaku. Tatya's brothers, Anna and Dada, who had lived in Baroda with their families, tended to put more emphasis on celebrating religious festivals than Tatya.

At Gudi Padwa, the gudi was worshipped in Woodlands and a special sweet prepared for family members. At Holi, while nobody in the family was fond of playing with colour on Rang Panchami, a Holi fire was lit under a large tamarind tree at Woodlands into which the children threw a coconut or one anna or a paisa; there was no shortage of wood for making a fire since fallen branches were easily found on the tree-filled property.

On Gokul Ashtami, it was mainly the domestic staff who celebrated by putting up a handi filled with yoghurt and pohe, and breaking it.

On Shraavani Somvaar, every Monday during the season of Shraavan, all the male relatives of the Aptes would come to Woodlands for a meal. They sat in the pangat and recited shravanya or mantras.

On Kaande Navami, Kaku's family, the Leles, regularly came home for a meal. Kaande Navami was in the month of Ashaad. On this day all the dishes were made using onions, such as onion rice, onion bhaaji and kaanda-batata rassa (onion-potato curry)—it was an onion feast because for the next four months, known as the Chaturmaas period, nobody was supposed to eat onion or garlic.

There were no new year celebrations on 31 December or 1 January, as only the Hindu calendar was followed by the family at this time—though it is likely that by the late 1940s, Bhausaheb may have participated in some new year celebrations at the Cricket Club of India.

Kaku began celebrating the Ganesh Chaturthi festival only after Bhausaheb and Manorama's first son, Madhav, was born. Even then, it was a relatively low-key affair that lasted only five days, with Kaku herself doing the puja rather than a guruji coming home to conduct the religious rituals. In the evenings, a sweet dish like kheer was prepared as a prasad, and after five days, all the children would accompany the Ganpati for the visarjan ceremony at the sea shore. The women and older girls did not go for this, but several domestic staff went to look after the children among the crowds at the beach; Tukaram, a trusted hand, was deputed especially to look after Tatya's youngest grandchild, Arvind.

Weddings were occasions for celebrations on a grand scale. Tatya and Kaku, of course, had married in modest circumstances, while Tatya was living in a chawl. There is no information about the marriage of his daughter Durga with Baburao Dabke in 1913, but it must have been a large wedding since Tatya's textile selling agencies had made him prosperous by this time. When his son Bhausaheb married in 1924, Tatya was even wealthier, and was at the peak of his success with the Hindustan Film Company, with the wedding taking place at the film studio in Nasik. By the time Durga's eldest daughter Kamla married in 1938, Tatya was a very wealthy and respected man indeed—though little information survives about her wedding, it is safe to say that it must have been a grand affair. During Kamla's sister Indu's wedding, though it was during the austerities of the Second World War, Tatya bought a cooking set with enormous vessels that could be used to cook for a thousand people. It was not the custom to employ a caterer—rather Brahmin achaaris, or cooks, were employed to cook at home for the event.

Bhausaheb's eldest daughter Manju's wedding took place in 1946. When the Modak family came to Woodlands to see Manju for the first time, custom dictated that her mother, Manorama, could not be present; but, eager to see her prospective son-in-law, she positioned herself by a crack in the door to peep in. It is most likely that Tatya, Kaku and Bhausaheb were present to receive the prospective groom's family, along with a few other male relations or close friends. The marriage was held in the Woodlands garden on 9 March at 6 p.m. About 1,500–2,000 people were present for the wedding dinner. The war had ended only a year earlier, in 1945, and in 1946 there was still rationing of food; the rule was that in every household one could not feed more than twenty-five people at a time in one pangat. So to save time, some of the pangats took place simultaneously at the house of the Aptes' neighbour, Vasantrao Vaidya. The aaher, or return gift, was given to a selected number of people: for men the aaher was a silver pot, which was available for about 10 or 12 rupees at the time, and for women it was a sari or a khun (blouse piece).

Manju's wedding shopping was fairly meagre—she remembered not more than one or two new saris being bought for her, while new jewellery, as per the custom, was to be presented to her by her in-laws. But there was clearly no shortage of saris, as seen in an interesting document that has survived: a partial list of the wedding gifts received, which gives an insight into the kinds of wedding gifts people gave in 1946. Cash gifts range from 21 rupees to 355 rupees. There are several cooking pots, silver trays and silver boxes listed, while the standard gift appears to have been saris. With over a thousand guests at the wedding, the number of saris received must have been overwhelming.

Tatya's Grandchildren

The orthodoxy of the day meant that Tatya never spoke directly to any of the women in the house unless necessary.

It was also the norm that women hesitated to speak in front of men; they felt shy or embarrassed to do so, particularly because they tended to remain uneducated or under-educated. Durga, for example, was withdrawn from school in the fourth standard despite being a good student, as Tatya and Kaku did not think it correct for a girl to be educated too much. But their daughter, Durga, and their daughter-in-law, Manorama, were the last generation in the family where women remained under-educated. Things changed very rapidly during the 1940s. Manorama's daughters, Manju and Kuma, both went to college, though Manju did not complete her degree, withdrawing when she got married (she earned her degree a few years later after her second daughter was born). Kuma played sports very much like her brothers, participating in college tournaments. There was no opposition from the older generation to any of this; her father, Bhausaheb, in fact, actively encouraged his daughter's enthusiasm for sports, though her mother, Manorama, insisted that Kuma wear a sari while playing cricket and other games. Manorama herself completed her education along with her children; she enrolled as an external student at Karve University, studied with the teacher who came home to tutor her children, and sat for her matriculation exam in 1948 at the same time as Madhav and Kuma. Later, she graduated with an arts degree from SNDT Women's University.

Just as women hesitated to speak in front of men, children hesitated to speak in front of elders, and particularly male elders. Corporal punishment was common, and no distinction was made between boys and girls as far as punishment was concerned. Kaku kept a coir rope to beat disobedient children, while Manorama bought a leather hunter. Children were meant to be seen and not heard. Overly noisy games were not tolerated at Woodlands, as it would disturb the elders. It was considered unseemly for parents to praise their own children; a mother would never tell her daughter, for example, that she looked nice in a particular sari. It was thought that praising children would make them arrogant and overconfident. Therefore, appreciation was never shown with direct words, but in indirect ways, such as making a child's favourite dish if he or she had done well at school.

Tatya's grandchildren received pocket money only when they began going to college. Thirty rupees a month was supposed to cover their bus fares as well as food. The calculation was 4 annas a day for the bus, which worked out to 7 rupees and 8 annas per month. The balance of 22 rupees and 8 annas was for lunch: about 4 annas for a plate of potato bhaaji with puris, and 8 annas for some extra puris; an omelette cost about 12 annas or a rupee. If more money was needed, Manorama would give it to her children, but an accounting of the 30 rupees had to be given to her, along with the reasons as to why more money was needed. There was no stinginess, and the children had whatever they needed; on the other hand, there was no question of spending money liberally on fancies like sweets or particular kinds of clothes. In fact, clothes were not chosen by the children at all—Manorama would purchase all her children's clothes and shoes.

This way of life seems rather restrictive in today's context, but there is no evidence that Tatya's grandchildren perceived it to be so. On the contrary, life was idyllic for the children. With so many children in the house—Manju, Kuma, Madhav, Arvind, Indu, Nalli and Khandu, not to mention Raghunathrao's children from Sikka Nagar, Surendra, Mali, Shashi and Ravi, there was never any shortage of playmates. They rarely travelled, since during the school holidays the house was packed with relatives from Baroda, Kalyan and Poona who would come to Woodlands for the holidays along with their children. The children played sports to their hearts content in the large grounds of Woodlands: tennis, cricket, badminton, laghori, viti-danda. In the summer, they ate the unripe mangoes that had fallen scattered across the tennis court. There were tamarinds from the tamarind tree too. In the winter, there were trips to the farms near the Phaltan Sugar Works for hoorda parties. It got cold in those days in Bombay, so they would often light a stove, or shegdi, to keep warm. Sometimes the children would ask Kaku for permission to eat dinner on the bomb-shelter terrace, and she would indulge them by arranging for the food to be served there so that they could all eat in the moonlight, sitting on paats. At other times, they would ask Tatya to organise bhel puri on the terrace, or hand-churned ice cream. After Kamla married and moved away, there were regular trips to visit her in Thane to eat batatawadas and ice cream (let alone far-off Thane, but even a trip to Dadar to visit Manju's marital home was considered a major excursion and a long way away from Pedder Road). For those who liked to read, Marathi books and novels were available from the Marathi Granth Sanghralay library in Girgaon, and magazines from the Petit Library. Manorama enjoyed dressing up small girls in satin parkar-polkas, making a crown of flowers and taking photos of them. At Sankranti, she enjoyed making halwa jewellery, or spiky sugar jewellery, for the children. One summer she enrolled the children in swimming classes at a pool in Vile Parle, where her own parents lived at the time. In the early 1940s, she took her children on bus and tram rides around the city on sightseeing excursions to places like the Rajabai Tower or even the Sonapur cremation ground[10] (an odd pick, but chosen as an educational experience).

There was discipline too: Manorama woke her four children every morning at 5 a.m. while singing a rupali—'*Ghanshyam sundara, shridhara*'—after which they were expected to bathe and sit to study in their bedrooms before going to school; in the evening before dinner, they sat on the bomb-shelter terrace to recite and memorise the Ram Raksha, Ganpati stotra, various shlokas, and the fifteenth and eighteenth adhyay of the Gita; they also had to memorise mathematical tables up to 30 in multiples from 1¼ to 3½; while their father, Bhausaheb, was fond of giving his children long, complicated sums in the evenings to see who could solve them the fastest using mental arithmetic. He also insisted that they learn important literary passages by heart, such as Mark Antony's speech in Shakespeare's *Julius Caesar*. Before dinner they washed their hands and feet, did namaskar to the elders, and after dinner at 6.30 p.m. there was no idling—the children went upstairs to study some more before sleeping. A singing teacher was engaged for Manju and Kuma. While Manju enjoyed it (and went on to become an accomplished classical singer, singing well into her seventies), Kuma would try to run away to play sports. Fed up with this, Kaku threatened to stop the music lessons, but their father Bhausaheb insisted they continue learning as he was very fond of music himself and could play the harmonium. Occasionally the children had the opportunity to travel a bit farther afield—in 1944, for example, Kaku, Manorama, Manorama's four children and her brother Anant (known as Antamama) went to Bangalore and Ooty for a holiday by train.

It was a protective environment—the children were not encouraged to go to their friends' houses, rather their friends were invited to Woodlands to play. The local boys from neighbouring families used to jump over the wall to come and play in Woodlands—indeed, when there were so many sporting facilities at Woodlands, it was not necessary for the children to go elsewhere. It was also unusual to invite the children's friends to stay for a meal, unless it was a special occasion. If the children did go out, especially when they were older and in college, the rule was that they must be home by sunset.

The sporting facilities offered by Woodlands, with its cricket pitch, tennis court and badminton court, turned out to have a significant impact on the sporting careers of three of Tatya's grandchildren: Madhav, Arvind and Kuma. Madhav Apte writes in his autobiography, 'Woodlands was to influence our lives, especially Arvind's and mine, in ways we could not have imagined. Our future careers and success in sports, particularly cricket, was undoubtedly due to Woodlands.' In addition, a big influence was their father Bhausaheb's passion for playing cricket and tennis. He introduced the boys to club life at a young age, and they began learning to play cricket at the Hindu Gymkhana around 1939, where Bhausaheb captained the gymkhana's 'B' team, which played cricket on Saturday afternoons.[11] Both Madhav and Arvind had successful cricket careers, playing university-level and first-class cricket, and both went on to play test cricket for India. They also played competitive badminton and squash respectively. Their sister Kuma represented her college and played tennis, table tennis and badminton in tournaments.

Tatya's grandchildren went to various schools at different points of time: when they were at Peerbhoy Mansion, the children who were old enough walked to Aryan Education in Girgaon. Later there was the Children's Academy on Matthew Road at Chowpatty, which mainly had Gujarati students, with separate Marathi language classes for Marathi children. In 1943, the Children's Academy was taken over by the government for use during the Second World War (the seafront gymkhanas along Marine Drive were also taken over, with ack-ack guns lined up there as defence against the possibility of a Japanese air attack across the sea). With the Children's Academy closed down, the children were enrolled in different schools: St Theresa High School in Kelewadi, Girgaon, St Columbus High School, Chandaramji and Sharada Sadan. Arvind and Madhav went to Wilson High School till the SSC exams, taking the B route bus from Kemps Corner or a tram from Gowalia Tank, particularly during war-time petrol rationing, which went on till 1947. The children each carried a 'phirki cha tambya', a tambya with a screw-top lid, filled with water, while somebody from home would bring a lunch box to the children in school. At Wilson High School, there was a real cross-section of children from differing backgrounds—while some came to school in cars, others came without chappals on their feet. Boys who were very disobedient were caned, while others got knocked on their knuckles with a wooden blackboard duster or had the duster thrown at their heads.

In 1942, many families left Bombay temporarily as it was feared that the Axis Powers would bomb the city. Since there was no threat to the interiors of the country, for a few months the women and children of the Apte family went to Sakharwadi, where the sugar factory was in full swing. There they stayed in a newly constructed building that was meant to be a small clinic and hospital but that wasn't yet operational. The children swam in a nearby tank and played cricket in front of their living quarters, also battling flies that were so large that they had to be swatted with brooms. By May it was too hot to stay in Sakharwadi, so Tatya rented a bungalow in the hill station of Mahabaleshwar, where it was much cooler and they could all go horse-riding. Tatya and Bhausaheb stayed behind in Bombay and visited Mahabaleshwar on weekends. Around June of that year, the threat to Bombay was considered to be over, so the family returned to the city at the end of the summer holidays, in time for school.

A few months later, on 8 August 1942, Tatya took his grandchildren to Gowalia Tank, just around the corner from Woodlands, to witness the All India Congress Session and to see the leaders of the independence movement from a distance—Gandhi, Nehru and Abul Kalam Azad. Around 1944, Arvind, probably with his siblings, went with his mother to a prayer meeting conducted by Gandhi at Parnakuti in Poona. All the children present who went up to meet Gandhi, including Arvind, each received a mango from him. This was also a period of war-time rationing. Tatya's daughter-in-law, Manorama, was very particular about not using the black market. She felt strongly that the family should not benefit from the black market simply because they were wealthy and could afford it. She ensured that they only bought food that was available in the open market—which meant that a lot of nachni (millet) was eaten at home during these years. She also ensured that all the domestic staff received the rations taken in their names.

Birthdays were celebrated till a child was ten or eleven years old. (An exception was Durga, whose birthday Tatya liked to celebrate every single year.) On the birthday, the child would do a puja of the ghusal khamb, the churning stick to make buttermilk, using haldi, kunku and flowers. The idea was to worship and pay respect to something that was used every day. The child's favourite sweet was made that day for the whole family, though there were no presents and no concept of inviting the child's friends home.

While all of Tatya's grandchildren travelled to school or college by bus and tram, an exception was made for Manju when her marriage was arranged in 1946: her husband-to-be was Kamlakar Modak, son of the prominent civil engineer Narayan Vinayak Modak,* a family that was far more liberal than the Aptes. Tatya feared that Kamlakar would go to meet Manju directly at her college in the run up to the wedding, and so, every morning before Manju left for Elphinstone College, Tatya asked her what time her classes would finish. At the correct time, a chauffeur-driven car would arrive at the college to escort her back to Woodlands, safe from any possible romantic meetings. Meanwhile, no such luxury was extended to her brothers and sister; they continued using public transport. In fact, Kamlakar did manage to get a message to Manju with an invitation to go see a movie with him. Manju, who was seventeen years old, consulted her fifteen-year-old sister Kuma, who was convinced that the marriage would break off if Manju did not accept the invitation. So Manju went to the movies with him, keeping only Kuma in confidence. Neither dared to tell their mother. The plan to keep it a secret failed, however. Manju was very late getting

* N.V. Modak is best known for building a dam on the Vaitarna river. The reservoir created provides the second largest supply of water to Mumbai and was named Modak Sagar after him.

home in the evening, and when Tatya began asking where Manju was, Kuma had to confess the plan to her mother. Manorama was furious, but fortunately managed to keep the news from Tatya and Kaku. Times had truly changed by now.

Chapter 8

Tatya and Kaku

Kaku

KAKU, OR YAMUNA, CAME INTO TATYA'S LIFE AS A TWELVE-YEAR-old bride in 1894. Tatya was nineteen years old.

They lived in Khatryachi Chawl, next door to her mother-in-law's family, the Leles. Since Tatya's mother had already passed away, no doubt she was taken under the wing of the female members of the Lele family. At the wedding, as per custom, she pressed her foot into some wheat flour and an astrologer looked carefully at it to tell her fortune. This girl, he declared, had Laxmi in her feet; she would bring great prosperity to her husband. So it proved to be. Though the couple started married life in two rooms of the chawl, economising wherever they could, four years later, in 1898, Tatya had opened his own pedhi in MJ Market. And only two years after that, the year their daughter Durga was born in 1900, Tatya had his first taste of great success when he made a profit of 11,000 rupees, a very large sum indeed at that time. Despite the financial success, though, the first few years of married life were emotionally difficult for Kaku, as her first-born son Shankar died when he was just a year old, and then Durga was born with infantile paralysis.

Just over a decade later, in 1912, the family moved out of the chawl into spacious apartments, and eventually to the grand Woodlands bungalow. Through it all, there is no evidence that Kaku changed her basic way of life at all. She carried her traditions with her from the cramped rooms of the Girgaon chawl to the apartment block on Sandhurst Road, and from there to the cosmopolitan environs of Pedder Road, where she and Tatya had a big bedroom and hall for their own use, in addition to an extra room where she took her afternoon nap. Despite the luxury offered by Woodlands, she had initially not been in favour of moving to Pedder Road, feeling that it was much too far away from 'the city' and too different from the hustle and bustle of Girgaon.

But having moved to Pedder Road, she loved the place and rarely left Woodlands and its gardens to go out. Like Tatya, though, she never lost touch with her old friends and enjoyed visiting the chawl to participate in group activities of the women there, such as making papads together. Likewise, her chawl friends would visit her at Woodlands with gifts of kharvas or fresh vegetables. She was far more talkative than Tatya was, and enjoyed laughing and chatting with friends and family, and even with her grandchildren; her mother, Rahtyachi Aai, was similarly chatty. A great joy for Kaku was to see the house filled with family members, all well-dressed, amply fed and celebrating festivals. She kept an open house, especially for her nephews, who found the environment at Peerbhoy Mansion and Woodlands far more open and fun-loving than the family home in Baroda, which was run by Anna's son Baburao and his wife, both rather serious personalities. Kaku liked inviting people for special occasions and doing things for the family—in this her views matched perfectly with Tatya's, for both felt that everybody in the family should always be together, do things together and look out for each other.

She was fond of dressing well, and loved pearl and diamond jewellery. She played chess with her brothers, Chintu and Dattatreya, when they visited her, and with her daughter, Durga, all of them good players. She would cane any grandchild who had been disobedient, and pull the ears of the girls who wouldn't sit still while she plaited their hair. But she was loving too, and also told them stories from the Puranas as they lay with their heads on her lap; and was fond of composing ovya, little poems, to lull the grandchildren to sleep. She liked using the large halls of Woodlands to play badminton—or, as she called it, 'shotty-shotty'—with her grandchildren. She liked reading, and regularly read the *Kesari* newspaper as well as religious texts like pothya and Puranas. She was also fond of learning English, and had the basic books to learn the language. Having read the *Kesari*, she would then enjoy discussing politics with her son and nephews. She was hot-tempered, but calm even when angry, and there was never any ill-tempered shouting to be heard in the house.

With her daughter-in-law, Manorama, Kaku enjoyed a close bond, for Manorama had lived with her since she had arrived as an eleven-year-old child bride. But, as per convention, the desire for a grandson was paramount, far more important than her bond with Manorama. Manorama's first two children were girls, Manju and Kuma. In fact, so great was the disappointment when Kuma, the second child, was born that nobody from the Apte family visited Manorama for a whole week.[1] She had given birth in her parents' home in Bombay, and no doubt spent the week dejectedly wondering when someone from Peerbhoy Mansion would come to see her. Had the third child also been a girl, Kaku had made up her mind that her son would take a second wife, though she was also determined that Manorama would always have precedence in the house as the senior wife. Fortunately for

Manorama, this scenario did not take place as her third child was a boy, Madhav, and so relieved was everyone that the driver bearing the news from the hospital jubilantly honked all the way home. The fourth child was also a boy, named Arvind, and Kaku was more than satisfied. Similarly, she was in great anxiety when her daughter, Durga, delivered four girls in succession (though she had previously had a son who died in infancy). When the fifth child proved to be a boy, Kaku was so elated that she removed the gold chain from her neck and gave it to the person who brought her the news.

The orthodoxy of the time meant that husband and wife could never be seen demonstrating any affection or closeness towards each other. When Kaku spoke to Tatya, she stood in the doorway of the room to do so. She would not have dreamt of sitting down in his presence and was very uncomfortable when she was obliged to do so on some rare social occasions. Even if Tatya was ill she would not tend to him herself, but would stand nearby and give instructions to Ramu, Tatya's manservant, to lay strips of cloth soaked in cologne water on Tatya's forehead. Nor did she serve Tatya his meals, but instead would stand behind the door of the room while Tatya ate, usually by himself, and direct the servers as to what they should offer him next.

No doubt the closeness of the couple would have decreased along with prosperity. In the days of Khatryachi Chawl, living in two rooms together, and even in the early years at Peerbhoy Mansion, Kaku would have done such tasks herself. But as wealth grew, and the family grew, a certain orthodoxy would have set in, such as the need for the elder couple to be dignified, which involved remaining aloof from one another in public, even if 'public' simply meant close family members or domestic staff.

Kaku never visited Tatya's pedhi at MJ Market in her entire lifetime, though it was the source of their prosperity; it was simply not done for an orthodox woman to be seen at MJ Market. She found it unbearable that her son Bhausaheb frequented the Cricket Club of India (CCI), going there directly from work every day to play cricket and meet his friends. She knew that men and women mixed freely at the CCI, and that there was alcohol and meat served there. Though she never forbade him from going, she was deeply disapproving. During the Second World War she would irritably declare, 'If only the Germans would bomb CCI!'

Tatya and Kaku had a harmonious married life—Kaku had an open, innocent nature, and she was like his shadow, devoted to him. Perhaps her sole act of selfishness, if one can call it that, was that she was obsessed with the idea of not becoming a widow. She wanted to die before Tatya. And so, when she was diagnosed with tuberculosis, she neglected herself, even insisting on bathing when she was not supposed to. She was determined to die a married woman, with the red colour of kunku on her forehead. During her illness, she was despondent and worried, and would often sit in the long sea-facing corridor outside her bedroom in Woodlands, looking out with a sad, troubled expression on her face. Eventually she also suffered from paralysis. She was ill for six to eight months before she died. Her daughter-in-law, Manorama, slaved to look after the mother-in-law she loved so much; till Tatya, alarmed that Manorama would fall ill herself, hired additional help to look after Kaku. Kaku died in 1946, leaving behind Tatya and a household changed by her departure. She had lived the last eight years of her life in the idyllic environs of Woodlands. When she died, Bhausaheb was at the CCI. He had the strong sensation that his mother was calling him; when he arrived home it was too late. On the thirteenth day after her death, for the meal when the deceased person's favourite food is eaten, Tatya filled the house with mangoes.

Tatya

Hard-working, determined, quiet, honest, reticent, modest, soft-spoken, a sharp nose for business and a head for numbers: this is how Tatya was described by my many interviewees. He was also described as a shrewd judge of character, but neither distrustful nor suspicious of people.

A wonderful portrait of Tatya relaxing at home emerges from the *Kirloskar* magazine interview, written by journalist Parvate around 1947, when Tatya was about seventy-two years old:

> I have met one man whose achievements among Maharashtrians, and whose status in Bombay business and industry, is truly uncommon. And despite that, there isn't the slightest egoism or arrogance in him … In Woodlands, the palatial bungalow … Shri Apte and I sat in an open porch on the second floor, drinking tea at a small table. As he lit his cigarettes, he spoke rapidly in his soft voice. Dark skinned, all his teeth fallen out, much of his hair turned white, he was wearing a half-sleeved mulmul sadra with stitched cotton buttons and a dhoti. Sitting on his chair with his legs pulled up, he looked to me like a pensioned government or customs officer. I had gone to meet him assuming that he would be an overpowering man with a stern look in his eyes, pot-bellied, of few words, a person with a tendency to be cantankerous, full of pride at his own glory. But when the reality turned out to be so different, I was bewildered.

Parvate goes on to describe the contrast between the modest, affable persona of Tatya and the vastness of his business interests:

> He is a partner and director in five or six mills in Bombay. Morarjee Gokuldas Mills and Kohinoor Mills function on the basis of his directions. He is the principal selling agent of several mills. Every year he handles business worth crores—not lakhs—of rupees. Today he is counted among the big 'lakhpatis' of Bombay. In Malabar Hill and Cumballa Hill, the premier address

> of Bombay's big names whose worth is counted in lakhs, one would be hard put to find houses belonging to Maharashtrians. One would struggle to count them on the fingers of one hand. Even among those, Apte is the only one who can be described as a businessman and industrialist … During our two meetings of 4–5 hours in total, I got a good idea of how vast Shri Apte's business interests are. In that time, there were 10–15 important telephone calls concerning transactions of thousands of rupees, and 5–10 men met him briefly to deal with various points of business. Despite the interruptions, however, he did not allow the flow of his narrative to break, and kept me occupied with chatty anecdotes. I never felt as if there was any gap or that he had trouble recollecting anything … I saw, too, that he speaks Gujarati as casually and naturally as Marathi.

The interview ends with Tatya's ire at the lack of ambition among Maharashtrian youth, recounting how he had been giving money towards scholarships for bright students, and how he had been particularly 'inclined to help competent and ambitious youths who are prepared to work in the manner of Gujaratis and Marwaris who traditionally focus entirely on their business, and work for twenty-four hours a day till they achieve success'. Having sharpened his business acumen as the sole Maharashtrian among the businessmen of MJ Market, Tatya had great respect for the Gujarati business community and felt frustrated that Maharashtrians did not work as hard or have the same high ambitions. Writes Parvate, 'He feels extremely angry with young men who waste their time on mischief and idleness, and had only harsh words for them. "Only if Maharashtrian youth take an interest in business and industry will future generations find a good direction. Otherwise their future will be very difficult." He repeated this sentiment, with great agitation, several times during our discussion.' Indeed, to emphasise Tatya's strong views on this, Parvate titled the published interview, as if it were a clarion call, '*Maharashtrian Youth, Become Businessmen!*'

There is no question that Tatya was exceptionally ambitious for a Maharashtrian Kokanastha Brahmin, with a highly unusual appetite for the risks that are inherent in business. In contrast, his brothers were far more representative of the Kokanastha Brahmin community, in being very learned and becoming salaried teachers and administrators. Ironically, Tatya, with the least education among his siblings, became the wealthiest. Despite that, he had a great respect for education, as evidenced by his donations towards scholarships, as well as his appreciation of the academic achievements of some of his grandchildren.

Unlike his son Bhausaheb, and Bhausaheb's children, Tatya did not have much interest in sports or much understanding of it. He told his grandson, Arvind, that he did not like it when Arvind kept wickets, and that he should bat instead—the crouching figure of the wicket-keeper probably seemed to him to be a lowly job compared to the flamboyance of the batsman standing straight and tall; when his other grandson, Madhav, took ten wickets in ten balls at a school match and was featured in the papers, Tatya was extremely pleased—but, not realising how unusual it was, berated him when in the next match he did not repeat the feat. His granddaughter Kuma, who was a keen squash player, remembers an incident when she returned home from playing a match. Tatya asked her what the result of the match was. I lost the match, she said; to which the irritable response was, 'Why do you go to play then, if you are going to lose?' Tatya did not look kindly upon losing, whether it was in sports or in business.

Nevertheless, he occasionally liked to listen to the English language cricket commentary on radio by the famous commentator Talyarkhan, particularly when the Pentangular matches* were on.

---

* The hugely popular Pentangular matches had their origin in the annual Parsi–European fixture in Bombay beginning in 1892. This became a Triangular match when a Hindu team was included in 1907, and a Quadrangular match with the addition of a Muslim team in 1912. The tournament finally became

In an amusing incident in Peerbhoy Mansion, the radio at home had gone for repairs while a match was on, so his grandchildren were made to sit in the Buick parked on the road to listen to the commentary on the car radio. In sign language, they conveyed the latest score to Tatya's manservant, Raghav, who stood leaning over the railings, and who in turn conveyed it to Tatya in his room.

In later years, Tatya's grandchildren would sometimes joke amongst themselves about his addiction to smoking. The chimney has started, they would say to each other in the mornings. Indeed, by 4.30 a.m. Tatya had started on his quota of about fifty cigarettes a day. He went through one tin of 555 or 777 cigarettes daily. He also tried smoking cigars and a pipe. But his first love remained beedis. His manservant at home would wrap pieces of damp muslin around the end of his beedis to act as a kind of filter.

Though the journalist Parvate's account describes Tatya as rather modestly dressed at home, when Tatya went out he was a very well-dressed man, extremely particular about being smartly turned out. He always wore a dhoti, a long coat and on his head a maroon or crimson Puneri pagdi, while on his feet he wore the Puneri joda, with its distinctive red colour and upturned toe. In the morning he would go to Kohinoor Mills, come home for lunch, and in the afternoon would go to the pedhi at MJ Market. In later years, when his son Bhausaheb took over this routine, Tatya went only occasionally to the pedhi, sometimes only to sit there and chat with his old associates.

Long after the Hindustan Film Company had closed down, and when mention of it had ceased in the house, a lone foot-operated harmonium belonging to the film company had survived, and stood mostly unused in the Woodlands bungalow. Sometimes

---

known as the Pentangular matches when 'the Rest', meaning Christians and others, were included as a team in 1937. The Pentangular matches were discontinued in 1946 (Astill 2013, p.18 and Majumdar 2002, p.157).

Tatya would sit idly at the harmonium and try out a few notes of a song. He held season tickets to watch natya sangeet performances, where a sofa would be reserved for him. He liked reading and had an excellent command of the English language. One of his favourite books was *The Pickwick Papers* by Charles Dickens.

He was happy in his own company, and not fond of lounging about aimlessly with friends. Often he quietly played a game of patience on the vast bed in his room. But he had a few select friends with whom he liked to spend time and, even after moving to the palatial Woodlands bungalow, he never lost touch with his old friends like Joshi and Bhide from Girgaon, who would regularly visit him to drink tea and play cards, mainly bezique or ganjifa. Some friends stuck to a rigid visiting schedule, such as two gentlemen of the same surname, affectionately dubbed by the family as Daily Kanhere and Weekly Kanhere. Mafatlal Gagalbhai often visited Tatya too, for they were good friends as well as neighbours. Apart from visits from friends, there were several Gujarati and Marwari business associates who visited Tatya regularly in Woodlands.

Though Tatya was reticent and soft-spoken, with his friends he retained an earthy spoken Marathi. Kaku, too, could come out with an earthy, rustic manner of speaking which could be as blunt as a cudgel, particularly when irritated. Bhausaheb's children, in particular, could raise her ire because they were more interested in sports than in studies and were constantly to be seen carrying bats, balls and racquets; whereas their cousins, her nephew Raghunathrao's children, did very well at school. Once she burst out in irritation, telling Bhausaheb's children, 'Try eating your cousins' crap, your minds might improve!' In short, Tatya's and Kaku's language could be very sophisticated, but also very colourful on occasion.

Tatya's quiet nature extended to the public sphere. Despite being a prominent and well-known businessman, he did not wish to be feted and have streets named after him, though given his position it would have been easy to do so. When he made charitable donations, he disliked it being publicised. He was a trustee of the Brahman Sabha in Girgaon for six years and later an advisor for twenty-seven years. He regularly made donations to the Brahman Sabha's social causes such as contributing towards the expenses of students who went abroad to study. The Brahman Sabha's records state that 'he benefited the maternity home and the education wing of the Sabha by giving liberal donations. He also helped other institutions in a similar way'. Though he did not usually wish his name to be publicised, he wasn't always successful at keeping himself in the background. On 29 April 1951, the Brahman Sabha put up an oil portrait of Tatya in their hall. The painting was inaugurated by Vaikunth Mehta, the finance minister of Bombay State. Tatya's older brother, Anna, had been an active supporter of the Brahman Sabha too, and his oil portrait was also put up in the same hall. The portraits were taken down only sixty-seven years later, in 2018. While the interview for *Kirloskar* magazine was itself a rarity in terms of Tatya speaking publicly, during the interview he expressed his displeasure at one of his donations being made public. Parvate writes:

> Recently his name had appeared in the newspaper because he had given 5,000 rupees to the Hindu Sangathan Fund. I asked him about this to get an idea of his views on charitable donations. He said, 'I gave the money on the condition that they would not publicise my name; but in the end it was made public. The only other condition I have put is that the money should not be used to incite dispute among political parties.'

Tatya also gave scholarships to several arts, medical and engineering college students, as well as naval and aviation students.[2]

Tatya's reticence, particularly about his wealth, meant that sometimes his communications were almost cryptic. For example, around 1944–45 Kaku's niece, Kashi tai, in wonder at her aunt's and uncle's wealth, asked innocently, 'Kaku, how much money do you really have? Do you have one crore of rupees?' To which Kaku replied, 'I don't really know. But if I do have one crore of rupees, I will give you a gold chain.' Thereafter Kaku narrated this conversation to Tatya. Tatya did not respond. A few months later, no doubt after a steady run of good business, he said to Kaku, 'Give Kashi the gold chain.' Of course, apart from an insight into Tatya's manner of speaking, the incident also gives an insight into his wealth towards the end of the Second World War—for those days, a crore of rupees was a colossal sum.

Tatya was not particular about food, and had a habit of not finding fault with it even if, for example, the cook had forgotten to put salt in a dish. As a snack he enjoyed sweet shira with lemon pickle, or a couple of Marie biscuits with his tea. He also enjoyed drinking Vimto, a bottled soft drink. But his one passion was mangoes. Every season, when his business associates, traders and merchants sent crates of mangoes as gifts to Woodlands, many of the crates would be stored under Tatya's bed—perhaps he loved the smell pervading his room. He also took a childish enjoyment in noting that the mangoes had been sent for him. 'The mangoes have all been sent especially for me,' he would remind Kaku, mischievously and proudly. 'So are you going to sit and eat them all by yourself?' she would chide him in annoyance, rising to the bait. During mango season, he made it a point to cut one mango to eat every morning. At meals there were unlimited mangoes and freshly squeezed aamras for everyone to eat their fill.

Tatya's other weakness was for his grandchildren. He could not bear to hear a child crying and would be restless till the crying had stopped. While his wife and daughter-in-law did not hesitate to cane children who had been disobedient, he never did so himself. He enjoyed taking the children out with him, whether it was occasions such as Diwali celebrations at the pedhi or low-key outings such as strolls on the Worli Sea Face, where they would all go piled into two cars, with two manservants to mind the children. At the Sea Face, he was often joined by his business partners Seth Mafatlal and Seth Nahalchand, who drove there directly in their own cars. Mafatlal Gagalbhai would come in his Mercedes which had a radio inside, and Tatya's grandson Arvind was fascinated by this car, urging Tatya to buy one too. On rare occasions, he took his grandchildren to watch a religious-themed film, such as the 1947 film *Meera*, the lead role played by MS Subbulakshmi. His nephew Raghunathrao's daughter Mali was very fond of singing and dancing when she was a schoolgirl, much to the disapproval of her father, but Tatya often amused himself by asking her to sing two famous film songs of the time, *Chal chal re naujawan* and *Ghar ghar mein Diwali*, to which she would dance as well. Then, to her delight, he would teasingly start speculating about what kind of husband he would find for her when she grew up, insisting that her husband would have to be someone very intelligent.*

While Kaku had no particular favourites among her grandchildren, Tatya's favourite grandchildren were the eldest and the youngest of the lot. The eldest was Kamla, his daughter Durga's child, while the youngest was Arvind, his son's youngest child. Both children could take liberties with Tatya that others could not. While there was no dearth of love and affection for the grandchildren, the conventions of the era were such that children were not supposed to voice their opinions, or even sit in the presence of elders, let alone engage in any kind of chit-chat with them. Affection was demonstrated not by hugging a

* The husband found for Mali was the writer Sharatchandra Gokhale, and her father-in-law was the chief editor of the *Kesari* and *Maratha* newspapers. Sharatchandra Gokhale himself later served as editor of the *Kesari*.

child or praising him, but in a way that would seem very indirect nowadays, such as Tatya taking the children for outings, or asking a child to press his feet—this was a task that Arvind and Kuma particularly enjoyed doing.

For all the reticence and deference in the house towards elders, and particularly towards Tatya, Kamla managed to get away with talking quite directly with Tatya. Meanwhile the baby of the family, Arvind, was favoured in other ways—when Tatya wanted to sell his Buick Roadmaster in 1947, the thirteen-year-old Arvind, who was extremely fond of it, began to cry so dreadfully that the car was not sold, and Arvind happily went on to use it for many years, including driving it through his college days. On another occasion, Tatya bought a Mercedes because Arvind was obsessed with Mercedes cars—in fact since he had been a small child he would determinedly say that he was going to buy a Mercedes. At wedding meals there was a custom to put a 1-paisa coin next to the plate of each child who was eating—on such occasions Kaku would enjoy asking Arvind, 'So Aru, what are you going to buy with your 1 paisa?' He would always reply, to everyone's amusement, 'I'm going to buy a Mershaydeej Benj.' His aunt, Durga, called him 'Benja' till the end of her days. However, there were limits to how much Tatya would indulge even Arvind. The Mercedes that he bought on Arvind's insistence happened to be a convertible with a low roof. It was difficult for Tatya to get in and out of the car since he wore a pagdi on his head. When, one day, his pagdi fell off while getting out of the car, the car was promptly sold.

The overly formal atmosphere in the family relaxed to a large extent when Tatya's granddaughters started getting married from around 1940 onwards. Not all Kokanastha Brahmin families were as orthodox as the Aptes, and the new sons-in-law often came from far less conservative backgrounds. In particular, Kamla's husband Pandurang Dandekar, who worked at United India

Insurance, and her sister Indu's lawyer husband, Diwakar Chitale, who worked at All India Reporter (his own family's company), often sat and chatted with Tatya in a way that would have been unthinkable for anyone from the younger generation to do in earlier days.

Tatya was not an overly religious person. A priest came home every day to conduct the daily puja, but it was Kaku who was the more religious of the two. Tatya wore sohle only on Shravani Somvaar, and in later years mildly urged Kaku not to observe sohle so rigidly. 'Let go of these rituals of sohle, for the world is changing rapidly,' he would tell her. She, of course, would have none of it. Unlike Tatya, who had had a chance to broaden his views by interacting with people from all walks of life, her world was small, centred on family and tradition; she could not be expected to share his views on this matter. Tatya did, however, have one 'mystical' experience. There was a Bhagirathi bai from Bavdhan, near Wai, who was a Hanuman devotee. There is no information about how he met her, but he confided to her that he never had dreams at night, and this was something that troubled him. She gave him some uncooked rice to put under his pillow, and that night he did dream. It is not clear when this incident took place, or why it troubled him that he did not dream at night. On the other hand, he had no time for superstition or mumbo-jumbo. After Kaku had passed away in 1946, a sadhu appeared at Woodlands and asked to speak to Tatya. When Tatya met him, the sadhu told him, 'Your wife appeared to me in my dream, and said that you should give me money.' To which Tatya's curt response was, 'I will wait for her to appear in my dream, and tell me the same thing.'

Around this time, Ganu, Tatya's manservant who had been with Tatya since the age of twelve and who had left his service shortly after Kaku passed away, reappeared at Woodlands and wanted to work for Tatya again. When asked why he had returned, he said that Kaku had appeared to him in a dream and said, 'Ganu, what are you doing here? Seth is over there, why are you not looking after him?' Following these dream instructions Ganu returned, and left only after Tatya himself had passed away.

Three days before Tatya died, his old dog, Tommy, mysteriously ran away. Perhaps the animal sensed an impending calamity. The first serious incident of poor health had occurred when Tatya was in Sakharwadi, Phaltan, in August 1952—it was a minor heart attack. About six cars filled with people from Bombay rushed to Sakharwadi to bring him back. He recovered from this and was able to move about again fairly soon. But old age had caught up with him and his heart was weak. While he was recuperating back in Woodlands his granddaughter, Manju, sang for him. She chose '*Aamhi zaato aamchya gaavi*' ('I am returning home to my village'), made famous by the Bhakti poet-saint Sant Tukaram, a song which reminded everyone that the end was near. Two months later, he had another heart attack. There was an oxygen cylinder in the house, bought especially in advance, but the only person who knew how to operate it, Durga's son, Khandu, was not in the house at the time. When the doctors arrived, as a last resort one of them gave Tatya an injection in his heart to revive him. But it was too late. Tatya died peacefully in his armchair. It was 30 October 1952, and he had lived to be seventy-seven years old. Balasaheb wrote in his history of the Phaltan Sugar Works: 'Persistence and integrity were his life's virtues … His nature was simple and without any ego … His death is an irreparable loss to the company. The colony's workers and staff were emotionally very much moved.'[3]

With Tatya's death came the end of an era, and the end of a certain way of life. The family would never be quite the same again. Tatya must have often felt that he had been fortunate beyond his wildest dreams. Perhaps it perplexed him at times, for, as he said, there were others who were as hardworking and intelligent as he was, and who had not been so favoured by fortune. He had started life in Bombay sharing a room in a chawl; he had avoided taking the tram and walked, in order to save some money for beedis; on occasion he had done manual work lifting bales of cloth; when he married, one oil lamp was all he could afford to light up two rooms. Yet, he ended his life like a prince, amid vast wealth, in a mansion overlooking the sea. Except that unlike a prince, he had earned it all himself.

A Note on This Biography

I BEGAN DELVING INTO TATYA'S LIFE IN 2008. I DID NOT REALISE then that it would turn into a decade-long, intensely personal project that was never far from my mind; it was 2019 by the time I finished it. I became progressively excited about the project as time went on and as I began conducting interviews that uncovered compelling information. I started digging through old photographs in the houses of relatives, trawled through the library of the National Film Archive of India in Pune, and spent hours at the British Library and the School of Oriental and African Studies library in London. I even found myself hunting for an old, forgotten location in Rangoon. But I never envisaged that it would take so many years to complete this biography. I could have finished it sooner had I been content with simply narrating the events of Tatya's life. That approach, however, seemed an incomplete one to me. I wanted to build up a living landscape around him in order to picture him moving through it. It became imperative for me to dig deeper into the wider familial, social and business contexts, and present as complete a picture of his life and times as possible. This is not the wisest approach—for the question arises as to where one should draw the boundaries of a history.

Theoretically I could go on forever, uncovering more and more information in the pursuit of 'completeness'. The thing that stopped me from doing so was the sheer impracticality of it (the logistics were daunting since I live outside India), along with a fear of the project turning into a never-ending, Casaubon-like 'Key to All Mythologies'. I also had a feeling that such a project—any historical biography, in fact—would necessarily retain a sense of the impossible and the unfinished. I could not articulate this in so many words at the time, but later recognised it instantly on reading the British historian Richard Holmes' eloquent words: a biography is the pursuit of a 'fleeting figure', a 'tracking of the physical trail of someone's path through the past, a following of footsteps'. But, he wrote, 'You would never catch them; no, you would never quite catch them.'[1]

Apart from the large scale of the research, the many years that passed were simply due to the project being overtaken by life events, long stretches of time when I had to set it aside entirely. Between 2008 and 2019 my family and I moved countries six times, living in Cambodia, Thailand, Myanmar, Bangladesh, Azerbaijan and Fiji; we had a baby daughter during these years; I was working on two books, a short story collection and an environmental education book, both published in this period. And an event that broke my heart: my father, Arvind Apte, passed away in 2014.

As Tatya's favourite grandchild, my father would have been fascinated to read the narrative that I uncovered, many of the facts being unknown to him. By the time I started writing an early draft, it was too late—he only managed to read the first few pages and was too ill to read any further or discuss it with me. It will be my lasting regret that he never got to read this biography, because he was so excited and enthusiastic about it. He launched me on this project, starting me off by providing a great deal of information over lengthy interviews and accompanying me to Sakharwadi and old locations in Bombay like Kohinoor

Mills, Khatryachi Chawl, Peerbhoy Mansion, St Theresa's High School and Wilson High School. He willingly translated Marathi documents into English for me, spending hours typing them out on his laptop so that I could refer to them quickly and easily. The invaluable translations he did were of Tatya's autobiographical information which Tatya had narrated to his nephew, Baburao Apte, who had acted as scribe; and two very lengthy documents written in Marathi by another of Tatya's nephews, Balasaheb Apte, who wrote a personal memoir as well as a detailed history of the Phaltan Sugar Works. This biography would not have been written without my father's help and enthusiasm.

After my father died, I realised that to a large extent the project had lost its purpose, lost its urgency. For many, many months the project fell by the wayside. I had been writing it as something interesting that he and I could share and discuss. Who, now, was I writing it for? What was the point of completing it? Should I finish writing it for myself? It was a weary question. At the very least, it appeared that I ought to complete writing it on the principle that one should finish what one has started. Though initially I pushed myself forward on this principle alone, soon the necessity of writing it began emerging once more. This is Tatya's biography, but it is my history, my story too. It follows that if it is my story, it is also my daughter's story. And so I wrote it for her, and for myself, because I think that if we don't know where we came from, we don't really know ourselves. I wrote it as an act of self-awareness for me and for her, and I think it would be hard for this biography to find a better purpose than that.

Inspired by Tatya's story, I embarked on a new project: I began writing *The Secret of More*, a novel set in early twentieth-century Bombay. Loosely based on his life and times, it takes many fictional leaps in building the plot and characters. To my delight, the novel won the Tata Literature Live! Award for Book of the Year (Fiction) in 2023. It feels wonderful, now, to present through this biography the 'real-life' story behind *The Secret of More*. My sincere thanks to Mita Kapur of Siyahi, and Karthika V.K. and Aurodeep Mukherjee of Westland Books for their enthusiasm and support in publishing this biography.

There are many family members who passed away before I could complete this book, who would have loved to read it: Manju Modak, Dutta Rajwade, Indu Chitale, Madhav Apte, Anant Ganu, Kamla Dandekar, Usha Karandikar, Sharatchandra Gokhale, Brahma (Mukund) Mendhale and Nana Apte, who was like a family member. Once again, I regret being too late. They all made an immense contribution to this biography by answering my numerous questions and sharing their memories.

I also thank the following people who answered my questions, many of whom also let me look through old photo albums and documents in their homes: Anand Apte, Anand Desai, Anita Bapat, Anjali Ganu, Anjali Joshi, Anju Apte, Arun Apte, Ian Buchanan, Janhavi Apte, Jyotsna Kale, Kuma Rajwade, Madhushree Ghatage, Mali Gokhale, Meena Apte, Nalli Paranjape, P.K. Nair, Sada Gokhale, Sandeep Apte, Satish Apte, Shambhu Kumar Kasliwal, Sharada Dwivedi, Sheela Apte, Shree Rajwade, Shreekant Apte, Sunita Rajwade, Surendra Apte, Tanay Paranjape, Vaman Apte, Vasanti Vaidya, Veena Singhal and Yashodhan Kale.

It would be remiss of me to not thank Tatyasaheb himself—he has been such an interesting and supportive companion over the last fifteen years that he seems as alive and present in my life as current-day folk. (It may just be that I need to get out more, but I think fellow-biographers and historians will know what I mean.)

My heartfelt thanks to my husband, Björn Rahm, for meticulously editing and commenting on this biography, and for his unfailing support over the years for all my marathon research and writing projects. And to Sukanya Andrea, our daughter, for inspiring me in every way.

Appendix 1

Annual Information about Kohinoor Mills 1933–51

Compiled from *Millowners' Association of Bombay Annual Reports*.[1]

NA = Not available

1933–39

	1933	*1936*	*1937*	*1938*	*1939*
Name of mills	Kohinoor Mills Co. Ltd	Kohinoor Mills Co. Ltd		Kohinoor Mills Co. Ltd	Kohinoor Mills Co. Ltd
Names of agents or owners and office addresses	Messrs Killick Nixon and Co.	Messrs Killick Nixon and Co., Agents, Killick Building, Home Street, Fort, Bombay		Messrs Killick Nixon and Co.	Messrs Killick Nixon and Co.
Situation of mills	Naigaum Cross Road, Dadar	Naigaum Cross Road, Dadar		Naigaum Cross Road, Dadar	Naigaum Cross Road, Dadar
Capital					
No. of shares	20,000	20,000	20,000	NA	NA
Nominal value of each share	100	100	100	100	100
Amount paid on each share	NA	..	..	NA	NA
Total amount of capital paid up	20,00,000	20,00,000	20,00,000	29,99,750	25,00,000

	1933	**1936**	**1937**	**1938**	**1939**
Number of spindles					
Mule	988	988	..	..	..
Ring	58,896	68,872	74,448	87,384	87,384
Total	59,884	69,860	74,448	87,384	87,384
Average no. of spindles at work daily	59,433	68,186	68,746	78,377	84,703
No. of looms installed	1,431	1,495	1,495	1,552	1,552
Average no. of looms at work daily	1,338	1,464	1,456	1,498	1,549
Approx. quantity of cotton consumed during the year in candies of 784 lbs.	9,163	15,668	16,316	17,138	18,793
Average no. of hands employed daily	3,162	3,745	3,896	4,032	4,144

1940–44

	1940	*1941*	*1942*	*1943*	*1944*
Name of mills	Kohinoor Mills Co. Ltd	Kohinoor Mills Co. Ltd	Kohinoor Mills Co. Ltd	Kohinoor Mills Co. Ltd	Kohinoor Mills Co. Ltd (Nos. 1, 2, 3)
Names of agents or owners and office addresses	Messrs Killick Nixon and Co.	Messrs Killick Nixon and Co.	Messrs Killick Nixon and Co.	Messrs Killick Nixon and Co.	Messrs Killick Nixon and Co.
Situation of mills	Naigaum Cross Road, Dadar	Naigaum Cross Road, Dadar	Naigaum Cross Road, Dadar	Naigaum Cross Road, Dadar	Naigaum Cross Road, Dadar
Capital					
No. of shares	NA	NA	NA	NA	NA
Nominal value of each share	100	100	100	100	100
Amount paid on each share	NA	NA	NA	NA	NA
Total amount of capital paid up	25,00,000	30,00,000	30,00,000	30,00,000	45,00,000

	1940	**1941**	**1942**	**1943**	**1944**
Number of spindles					
Mule	..	..	..	..	..
Ring	87,384	94,368	95,072	97,184	97,184
Total	87,384	94,368	95,072	97,184	97,184
Average no. of spindles at work daily	83,317	87,258	92,500	94,569	95,541
No. of looms installed	1,552	1,552	1,552	1,552	1,834
Average no. of looms at work daily	1,513	1,552	1,535	1,552	1,834
Approx. quantity of cotton consumed during the year in candies of 784 lbs.	17,436	22,710	25,197	26,265	24,868
Average no. of hands employed daily	3,874	3,995	4,094	4,187	5,365

1945–49

	1945	***1946***	***1947***	***1948***	***1949***
Name of mills	Kohinoor Mills Co. Ltd (Nos. 1, 2, 3)	Kohinoor Mills Co. Ltd (Nos. 1, 2, 3)	Kohinoor Mills Co. Ltd (Nos.1, 2, 3)	Kohinoor Mills Co. Ltd (Nos. 1, 2, 3)	Kohinoor Mills Co. Ltd (Nos. 1, 2, 3)
Names of agents or owners and office addresses	Messrs Killick Nixon and Co.	Messrs Killick Nixon and Co.	Messrs Killick Nixon and Co.	Messrs Killick Industries Ltd	Messrs Killick Industries Ltd
Situation of mills	Naigaum Cross Road, Dadar	Naigaum Cross Road, Dadar	Naigaum Cross Road, Dadar	Naigaum Cross Road, Dadar	Naigaum Cross Road, Dadar
Capital					
No. of shares	NA	NA	NA	NA	NA
Nominal value of each share	100	100	100	100	100
Amount paid on each share	NA	NA	NA	NA	NA
Total amount of capital paid up	45,00,000	45,00,000	50,00,000	1,00,00,000	1,00,00,000

	1945	1946	1947	1948	1949
Number of spindles					
Mule	..	..	..	..	..
Ring	97,184	97,184	97,184	1,02,312	1,07,240
Total	97,184	97,184	97,184	1,02,312	1,07,240
Average no. of spindles at work daily	95,414	95,665	96,302	96,994	1,00,174
No. of looms installed	1,834	1,834	1,846	1,846	1,846
Average no. of looms at work daily	1,822	1,797	1,812	1,812	1,811
Approx. quantity of cotton consumed during the year in candies of 784 lbs.	25,294	21,120	17,776	18,730	20,150
Average no. of hands employed daily	5,444	5,238	5,172	5,146	5,149

1950–51

	1950	***1951 (Nos. 1, 2)***	***1951 (No. 3 mill)***
Name of mills	Kohinoor Mills Co. Ltd	Kohinoor Mills Co. Ltd	Kohinoor Mills Co. Ltd
Names of agents or owners and office addresses	Messrs Killick Industries Ltd	Messrs Killick Industries Ltd	Messrs Killick Industries Ltd
Location of mills	Naigaum Cross Road, Dadar	Naigaum Cross Road, Dadar	Lady Jamshedji Road, Dadar
Capital			
No. of shares	NA	NA	NA
Nominal value of each share	100	100	..
Amount paid on each share	NA	NA	NA
Total amount of capital paid up	1,00,00,000	1,00,00,000	..

	1950	**1951 (Nos. 1, 2)**	**1951 (No. 3 mill)**
Number of spindles			
Mule	..	..	..
Ring	1,10,056	1,11,464	..
Total	1,10,056	1,11,464	..
Average no. of spindles at work daily	1,06,158	1,06,531	..
No. of looms installed	1,846	1,552	294
Average no. of looms at work daily	1,822	1,532	285
Approx. quantity of cotton consumed during the year in candies of 784 lbs.	21,778	20,767	..
Average no. of hands employed daily	5,399	4,545	894

Appendix 2

Filmography of the Hindustan Film Company

THE FILMOGRAPHIES OF THE HINDUSTAN FILM COMPANY AND the Bharat Film Company in Appendix 2 and 3 are based on the filmography compiled by Virchand Dharamsey in 1994, subsequently updated in 2013, and appearing in the book *Light of Asia: Indian Silent Cinema 1912-1934*, edited by film historian Suresh Chabria. While Dharamsey's filmography includes the entire silent film era during which 1,338 silent films (1,290 full length films and 48 short features[1]) were produced in India, I have extracted from it only the information pertaining to the Hindustan Film Company and the Bharat Film Company.*

Dharamsey's information is based on exhaustive archival research, including the records of the Indian Censor Board, which began keeping records of the titles, footage and dates of films only in 1920, eight years after the first Indian feature film had been produced. The Censor Board records were by no means accurate and had to be cross-checked by Dharamsey because in several cases they included films that were

* Previous filmographies of note include: *Silent Filmography* by B.V. Dharap (National Film Archive of India, unpublished), *Indian Filmography: Silent and Hindi Films* by Firoze Rangoonwala (1970), *Indian Motion Picture Almanac* by B. Jha (1986) and *Filmography: Silent Cinema 1913-1934* by R.K. Verma (2000).

re-released with a different title (and therefore were recorded as two separate films), and foreign films released with an Indian title.

With regard to the credits of a film, well into the 1920s films only carried the names of the producer and the scenarist. This often led to filmographers filling in the gaps in information by making generalisations: for instance, all of the films of the Hindustan Film Company were assumed to be directed by Dadasaheb Phalke. This discrepancy has been corrected in Dharamsey's filmography by cross-checking censor records and previously existing filmographies with other contemporary sources such as news reports that announced film titles, as well as film advertising in a number of journals of the time such as *Bombay Samachar*, *Bombay Chronicle*, *Times of India*, *Mouj Majah*, *Photoplay*, *Filmland*, *Chitrapat*, *Vismi Sadi* and *Moving Picture Monthly*.[2]

Dharamsey's methodology in compiling his filmography also includes what he calls the 'plausibility factor', which involved verifying information by cross-checking, for instance, which cinematographers, directors or actors were employed by a studio when a particular film was released.[3]

The Hindustan Film Company and the Bharat Film Company both specialised in mythological films. Therefore, all of the films in the following lists are in that genre, except where the genre has specifically been mentioned differently, such as 'devotional' or 'costume'. Apart from mythological films, the other main genre of both film companies was the devotional film. While mythological films were based on themes from the Puranas, Mahabharata or Ramayana, devotional films were about specific saint-poets or local deities.[4]

Of the Hindustan Film Company's ninety-seven titles, ninety-one are feature films and six are short films. (Film historian B.V. Dharap gives a slightly different figure, writing that the Hindustan Film Company made ninety-seven feature films, as well as twenty-six short documentary films that are not listed here.) Intriguingly, Dharamsey's filmography notes that the 1924 film *Draupathi Bhagya* was produced by the Hindustan Film Company for the Indian Art Craft Co. of Madras; and the 1924 historical film, *Shivaji the Social Reformer*, failed to get a censor certificate as the censors felt it would 'promote ill-feeling'. Further details about these films are unfortunately not available.

Abbreviations:

D: Director
C: Camera
St: Story
Sc: Script
Lp: Leading players (actors)
Ft: Length of the film measured in feet.

1918

Shri Krishna Janma (also known as: ***The Birth of Shri Krishna***)
5,500 ft, **D/C/St/Sc**: D.G. Phalke, **Lp**: D.D. Dabke, Purshottam Vaidya, Mandakini Phalke, Bhagirathibai, Neelkanth, Gajanan Sane

1919

Kaliya Mardan
6,000 ft, **D/C/St/Sc:** D.G. Phalke, **Lp:** Mandakini Phalke, Anna Salunke, Neelkanth, Sahadev, Sahadevrao Tapkire, Baburao Patil

*Ahilya Uddh*ar
5,000 ft, **D:** Gajanan V. Sane

1920

Jalandhar Vrinda
6,000 ft, **D:** Gajanan V. Sane

Ram Janma
6,000 ft, **D:** Gajanan V. Sane

Shani Prabhav
5,169 ft, **D:** Gajanan V. Sane

1921

Govardhandhari
5,940 ft, **D:** Gajanan V. Sane

Kansa Vadha (also known as: ***End of the Tyrant King***)
6,157 ft, **D:** Gajanan V. Sane

Pundalik
6,875 ft, **D:** Ganpat Shinde

Sati Sulochana
5,927 ft, **D:** Gajanan V. Sane, **Lp:** Shanta Nalgunde, D.B. Sukte

Shree Krishna Leela
5,344 ft, **D:** Gajanan V. Sane

Tukaram **(**Genre: Devotional)
6,000 ft, **D:** Ganpat Shinde

Valmiki
5,608 ft, **D:** Gajanan V. Sane

Vikram Satva Pariksha
5,469 ft, **D:** Gajanan V. Sane

1922

Ahiravan Mahiravan Vadha (also known as: ***Ahi-Mahi Vadha***) 6,950 ft, **D:** Gajanan V. Sane, **C:** Anna Salunke, **Lp:** Bhaurao Datar, Sane, Bachu Pawar, Shanta Nalgunde, Ghanshyam Singh

Gadhaganjravancha Swapna Vihar (also known as: ***Mr Sleepy's Good Luck***) (Genre: Comedy)
1,978 ft, **D/St/Sc:** D.G. Phalke

Ganesh Avatar (also known as: ***Shri Ganesh Janma***)
5,560 ft, **D:** Gajanan V. Sane, **C:** Anna Salunke, **Lp:** Bhaurao Datar, Madhav Malusare

Haritalika
2,295 ft, **D:** Gajanan V. Sane, **C:** Anna Salunke, **Lp:** Bhaurao Datar

Pandav Vanvas (also known as: ***Pandav in Exile***)
6,123 ft, **D:** Gajanan V. Sane, **C:** Anna Salunke, **Lp:** Bhaurao Datar, Bachu Pawar, Sakharam Jadhav

Rajarshi Ambarish
5,780 ft

Sant Namdev (Genre: Devotional)
6,655 ft, **D/St/Sc:** D.G. Phalke

Sant Sakhubai (Genre: Devotional)
5,987 ft, **D:** Gajanan V. Sane, **C:** Trymbak V. Telang, **St:** H.N. Apte, **Lp:** Shanta Nalgunde, V.S. Nirantar

Satyanarayan
5,962 ft, **D:** V.S. Nirantar, **Lp:** Anna Salunke, Ganpat Shinde

Shishupal Vadha (also known as: ***Rajasooya Yagna***)
6,642 ft, **D:** Gajanan V. Sane, **C:** Anna Salunke, **Lp:** Bhaurao Datar, Sane, Bachu Pawar, Sonubai

1923

Aswathama
5,953 ft, **D/St/Sc:** D.G. Phalke, **C:** Anna Salunke/P.B. Chavan, **Lp:** Bhaurao Datar, Gotiram, Dada Pendse, Madhav Malusare

Babruwahan
6,207 ft, **D/St/Sc:** D.G. Phalke, **C:** Anna Salunke/P.B. Chavan, **Lp:** Bhaurao Datar, Sakharam Jadhav, Dada Pendse

Buddha Dev
6,973 ft, **D/St/Sc:** D.G. Phalke, **C:** Anna Salunke, **Lp:** Anna Salunke, Bhaurao Datar

Gora Kumbhar (Genre: Devotional)
6,013 ft, **D:** Gajanan V. Sane, **C:** Anna Salunke/P.B. Chavan, **Lp:** Bhaurao Datar, Bhonsle

Guru Dronacharya
6,282 ft, **D/St/Sc:** D.G. Phalke, **C:** Anna Salunke, **Lp:** Bhaurao Datar, Dada Pendse, Charubai

Jarasandha Vadha
5,496 ft, **D/St/Sc:** D.G. Phalke, **C:** Anna Salunke/P.B. Chavan, **Lp:** Bhaurao Datar, Bachu Pawar, Ghanshyam Singh

Kalicha Narad (also known as: ***Ram Maruti Yuddha***, ***Quarrel Game of Narada***)
5,848 ft, **D:** Ganpat Shinde, **Lp:** Bhaurao Datar, Sakharam Jadhav

Kanyavikraya (also known as: ***Sharada***) (Genre: Social)
6,056 ft, **D:** V.S. Nirantar, **C:** Anna Salunke/P.B. Chavan, **Lp:** Bhaurao Datar, Krishna Chavan

Mahananda (Genre: Devotional)
6,786 ft, **D/St/Sc:** D.G. Phalke, **C:** Anna Salunke, **Lp:** Bachu Pawar, Dada Pendse, Bhaurao Datar

1924

Datta Janma (also known as: ***Sati Anasuya***)
6,495 ft, **D:** Gajanan V. Sane, **C:** Anna Salunke/P.B. Chavan, **Lp:** Bhaurao Datar, Bachu Pawar, Motiram, Ashrabai

Draupathi Bhagya (also known as: ***Draupadi's Fate***, ***A Game of Krishna***)
5,435 ft. (This film was produced by Hindustan Film Company for Indian Art Craft Co., Madras.)

Jayadratha Vadha
6,313 ft, **D:** Gajanan V. Sane, **C:** Anna Salunke/P.B. Chavan, **Lp:** Bhaurao Datar, Bachu Pawar

Municipal Nivadnuk (also known as: ***Municipal Election***) (Genre: Social)
2,892 ft, **D:** D.G. Phalke, **Lp:** Bachu Pawar, Sakharam Jadhav (female role), Ganpat Shinde, Bhaurao Datar

Ram Ravan Yuddh (also known as: ***Sita Shuddhi***)
5,145 ft, **D:** Gajanan V. Sane, **C:** Anna Salunke, **Lp:** Vasant Shinde, Krishna Chavan

Shivaji the Social Reformer (Genre: Historical)
6,320 ft. (The censor board refused to give a censor certificate to this film because it was 'likely to promote ill-feeling'.)

Shivajichi Agryahun Sutaka (also known as: ***Shivaji's Escape from Moghul Court at Agra***) (Genre: Historical)
7,567 ft, **D/Sc:** D.G. Phalke, **C:** Anna Salunke, **Lp:** Bhaurao Datar, Jardos, Laxman Malusare

Sita Vanvas (also known as: ***Uttar Ram Charita***)
6,582 ft, **D:** V.S. Nirantar, Vasant Shinde (Maruti)

Sundopasunda
6,013 ft, **D:** Gajanan V. Sane, **C:** Trymbak B. Telang/Anna Salunke/ P.B. Chavan, **Lp:** Bhaurao Datar, Bachu Pawar, Sane, Krishna Chavan

Vinchucha Dansh (also known as: ***Scorpion Bite***) (Genre: Social)
2,633 ft, **D:** D.G. Phalke

1925

Anant Vrata
6,987 ft, **D:** Gajanan V. Sane, **C:** Anna Salunke, **Lp:** Bhaurao Datar, Krishna Chavan

Chaturthicha Chandra (also known as: ***Moon Cursed By Ganpati***)
4,029 ft, **D/St/Sc:** D.G. Phalke, **C:** Trymbak B. Telang, **Lp:** Bhaurao Datar, Vasant Shinde

Hedimb Bakasur Vadh
5,280 ft, **D/St/Sc:** D.G. Phalke, **C:** Trymbak B. Telang, **Lp:** Bhaurao Datar, Bachu Pawar, Yamuna Gole, Baba Nachan

Kakasahebanchya Dolyat Jhanjhanit Anjan (also known as: ***Kakasaheb Outwitted***) (Genre: Social)
7,982 ft, **D:** D.G. Phalke, **C:** Trymbak B. Telang/Anna Salunke, **Lp:** Bachu Pawar, Sahadeva, Krishna Kumbhar

Khod Modali (also known as: ***Habit Crushed***) (Genre: Comedy)
2,967 ft, **D:** D.G. Phalke (Probably based on the same subject as Phalke's early pre-Hindustan Film Company film, titled *Pithache Panje* of 1913.)

Mahashivratra (also known as: ***Shankar Leela***)
6,327 ft, **D/St/Sc:** V.S. Nirantar, **Lp:** Vasant Shinde

Pandav Shodh (also known as: ***Jimut Vadha, Search for Pandavas***)
4,667 ft, **D:** Gajanan V. Sane

Sant Janabai (Genre: Devotional)
6,798 ft, **D:** Gajanan V. Sane, **Lp:** Vasant Shinde, Madhav Khaire, Bhaurao Datar

Sati Tara (also known as: ***War between Vali and Sugriv***)
6,982 ft, **D:** Shinde, **C:** Trymbak V. Telang, **Lp:** Bhaurao Datar, Shelar, Krishna Chavan

Satyabhama
6,892 ft, **D/St/Sc:** D.G. Phalke, **C:** Anna Salunke, **Lp:** Bhaurao Datar, Krishna Chavan

Shatmukh Ravan Vadha (also known as: ***Birth of Kalika***)
6,392 ft, **D:** Kashinath Bharadi, **C:** Trymbak V. Telang, **Lp:** Bhaurao Datar, Kashinath Bharadi, Vasant Shinde, Gangaram Nhavi

Syamantaka Mani (also known as: ***Krishna Under Charge of Theft***)
6,848 ft, **D/St/Sc:** D.G. Phalke, **C:** Anna Salunke, **Lp:** Bhaurao Datar, Krishna Chavan, Vasant Shinde

Vachan Bhang (also known as: ***Broken Promise***) (Genre: Social)
1,927 ft, **D:** D.G. Phalke

1926

Balaji Nimbalkar (Genre: Historical)
5,560 ft, **D:** D.G. Phalke, **C:** Trymbak B. Telang, **St/Sc:** Saralkar, **Lp:** Bhaurao Datar, Vasant Shinde, D.B. Sukte, Krishna Chavan

Bhakta Prahlad
7,447 ft, **D/Sc:** D.G. Phalke, **C:** Anna Salunke, **St:** V.H. Palnitkar, **Lp:** Gangaram Nhavi, Bhaurao Datar, Bachu Pawar, Yamuna Gole

Bhim Sanjivan (also known as: ***How Bhim Was Brought Back to Life***)
6,495 ft, **D:** Gajanan V. Sane, **C:** Anna Salunke, **Lp:** Bhaurao Datar, Anasuya

Janki Swayamwar (also known as: ***Dhanurbhang***)
7,150 ft, **D/St/Sc:** D.G. Phalke

Keechak Vadh
6,475 ft, **D/Sc/St:** D.G. Phalke, **C:** Anna Salunke, **Lp:** Bhaurao Datar, Bachu Pawar, Yamuna Gole

Rama Rajya Viyog
8,071 ft, **D:** Gajanan V. Sane

Sant Eknath (also known as: ***Saint of Paithan***) (Genre: Devotional)
6,233 ft, **D/Sc/St:** D.G. Phalke, **C:** Anna Salunke, **Lp:** Bhaurao Datar, Gotiram

1927

Bhakta Sudama (also known as: ***Sudamache Pohe***)
6,159 ft, **D/Sc/St:** D.G. Phalke, **C:** Anna Salunke, **Lp:** Bhaurao Datar, Dattatray Kshirsagar

Daksha Yagna
5,904 ft, **D:** Gajanan V. Sane, **Lp:** Bhaurao Datar, Bachu Pawar, Gangubai Mohite

Draupadi Vastra Haran
6,759 ft, **D/Sc/St:** D.G. Phalke, **C:** Anna Salunke, **Lp:** Bhaurao Datar, Gangubai Mohite, Bachu Pawar

Hanuman Janma (also known as: ***Birth of Maruti***)
5,650 ft, **D/Sc/St:** D.G. Phalke, **C:** Anna Salunke, **Lp:** Bhaurao Datar, Laxman Malusare, Yamuna Gole

Madalasa
6,313 ft, **D:** Gajanan V. Sane, **C:** Anna Salunke, **Lp:** Bhaurao Datar, Anasuya

Nala Damayanti
8,123 ft, **D:** D.G. Phalke, **C:** Trymbak B. Telang, **Lp:** Anna Salunke, Gotiram, Bachu Pawar, Joshi, Dattatray Kshirsagar, Bhaurao Datar, Gangubai Mohite

Rukmangad Mohini (also known as: ***Ekadashi Mahatmya***)
8,291 ft, **D/Sc/St:** D.G. Phalke, **Lp:** Ganpat Shinde, Gangubai Mohite

Rukmini Haran

7,265 ft, **D/Sc/St:** D.G. Phalke, **Lp:** Bhaurao Datar, Anasuya

1928

Bhakta Damaji (Genre: Devotional)
7,281 ft, **D/Sc/St:** D.G. Phalke, **C:** Ganpat Shinde, **Lp:** Gotiram, Bhaurao Datar

Ghosh Yatra
5,969 ft, **D:** Gajanan V. Sane, **C:** Ganpat Shinde, **Lp:** Bhaurao Datar

Malhari Martand
6,654 ft, **D:** Ganpat Shinde, **C:** Trymbak B. Telang, **Lp:** Bhaurao Datar, Kashibai Phatak, Shelar, Joshi

Narad Sansar (also known as: ***Narada's Worldly Life***)
5,122 ft, **D/C:** Ganpat Shinde, **Lp:** Bhaurao Datar, Sakharam Jadhav, Jadhavrao

Parashuram
6,730 ft, **D/Sc/St:** D.G. Phalke, **C:** Ganpat Shinde, **Lp:** Bhaurao Datar, Gotiram, Asarabai

Sati Pingala
6,848 ft, **D:** Gajanan V. Sane, **Lp:** Gangubai Mohite, Bhaurao Datar

Shri Krishna Shishtai
6,097 ft, **D:** D.G. Phalke

Sudarshan
8,870 ft, **D:** Gajanan V. Sane

1929

Bolki Tapeli (also known as: ***Bolti Tapeli, Talking Pot***)
(Genre: Social)
10,708 ft, **D/St/Sc:** D.G. Phalke

Chandrahas
6,631 ft, **D:** D.G. Phalke

Kacha Devayani
8,444 ft, **D/St/Sc:** D.G. Phalke

Malti Madhav (Genre: Adaptation)
8,123 ft, **D:** D.G. Phalke, **C:** Anna Salunke, **St:** Based on Bhavbhuti's play, **Lp:** Anasuya, Krishna Kumbhar

Malvikagnimitra (Genre: Adaptation)
9,717 ft, **D:** D.G. Phalke, **C:** Anna Salunke, **St:** Based on Kalidasa's play, **Lp:** Shakuntala, Kishori Pathak, Krishna Kumbhar

Prabhavati (Genre: Costume)
7,609 ft, **D:** Gajanan V. Sane

Sant Meerabai (Genre: Devotional)
8,810 ft, **D/St/Sc:** D.G. Phalke, **Lp:** Shakuntala Tembe

Vasantsena (Genre: Adaptation)
9,111 ft, **D:** D.G. Phalke, **C:** Anna Salunke, **Lp:** Shakuntala Gotiram

1930

Kabir Kamal (Genre: Devotional)
7,589 ft, **D:** Gajanan V. Sane

Khuda Parashta (Genre: Costume)
9,000 ft, **D:** Ganpat Shinde, **C:** Anna Salunke, **Lp:** Anasuya, Gotiram, Kishori Pathak, Shelar

Sati Sarla (Genre: Devotional)
10,282 ft, **D:** Abhaya Charan Lahiri, **Lp:** Anasuya, Kishori Pathak, Krishna Kumbhar

Savati Matsar (also known as: ***Jealous Co-Wife***)
7,570 ft, **D:** Ganpat Shinde

Shree Subrahamaniyam (also known as: ***Vallikumari's Wedding***)
5,720 ft, **D:** Rao, **C:** Anna Salunke, **Lp:** Kishori Pathak, Madhav Mistry, Brahmadeo

1931

Amirkhan (also known as: ***Chivalrous Adventurer***) (Genre: Costume)
10,325 ft, **D:** Ganpat Shinde, **C:** Anna Salunke, **Lp:** Anasuya, Mathura, Khambete, Sakharam Jadhav

Jail Ke Parinde (also known as: **Gaol Birds**) *(Genre: Social)*
6,000 ft, **D:** Munshi Abbas

Mohabbat Ki Putli (also known as: **Touch of Love**) (Genre: Costume)
9,446 ft, **D:** Ganpat Shinde, **C:** Anna Salunke, **Lp:** Kishori Pathak, Shelar

Shaitan Ka Shikar (also known as: ***Daivache Bhaksh, Victim of Devil***) (Genre: Costume)
8,952 ft, **D:** Ganpat Shinde, **C:** Anna Salunke, **Lp:** Rajkumari, Kishori Pathak, Gotiram

1932*

Setu Bandhan (also known as: ***Bridging of Ocean***)
13,715 ft, **D/St/Sc:** D.G. Phalke, **Lp:** Iqbal, Malti, Gotiram (?) Phalke

* Dharamsey's filmography lists this as a 1933 release, but Watwe writes in his biography of Dadasaheb Phalke that the film was released in 1932. I have noted it as 1932 here, because Tatya closed down the Hindustan Film Company that year.

Appendix 3

Filmography of the Bharat Film Company

Of these twelve titles, ten are feature films and two are short films.

1921

Pradyumna (also known as: ***Krishna Kumar, Burning of Kama***)
5,820 ft, **D:** Vishnupant Divekar, **C:** A.P. Karandikar

Raja Gopichand
5,820 ft, **D:** Vishnupant Divekar , **C:** A.P. Karandikar, **Lp:** Mama Bhatt, Heera Limaye

Thief Entertained (Genre: Comedy)
957 ft.

Tridandi Sanyas
6,447 ft, **D:** Vishnupant Divekar, **C:** A.P. Karandikar, **Lp:** Heera Limaye, Soni, Anand Shinde

Urvashi (also known as: ***Nymph Celestial***)
5,500 ft, **D:** Vishnupant Divekar, **C:** A.P. Karandikar, **St:** Based on Kalidasa's play, **Lp:** Vithabai, Heera Limaye

1922

Draupadi Swayamwar
6,918 ft, **D:** Vishnupant Divekar, **C:** A.P. Karandikar, **Lp:** Kamala

Hairstorm
768 ft

Krishna Tula
6,403 ft, **D:** Vishnupant Divekar, **C:** A.P. Karandikar, **Lp:** V.V. Date, Vithabai

Radha Vilas
5,990 ft, **D:** Vishnupant Divekar, **C:** A.P. Karandikar, **Lp:** Soni, V.V. Date

Sharmishtha Devyani
5,350 ft, **D:** Vishnupant Divekar, **C:** A.P. Karandikar, **Lp:** Vithabai

Veni Bandhan (also known as: ***The Fall of Kauravas***)
5,597 ft, **D:** Vishnupant Divekar, **C:** A.P. Karandikar, **Lp:** Patankar, Soni, Damle

Virat Parva
6,113 ft, **D:** Vishnupant Divekar , **C:** A.P. Karandikar

Notes

Chapter 1. The Early Years in Bombay: 1869–81

1. Dwivedi et al. 2001, p. 138.
2. Ranganathan 2009, p. 131.
3. Dwivedi et al. 2001, p. 127.
4. Information about old Bombay from Dwivedi et al. 2001, pp. 126, 128–31.
5. The title translates as 'A Description of Mumbai', but is published in translation as *Govind Narayan's Mumbai* by M. Ranganathan.
6. Ranganathan 2009, pp. 52–3, 60, 82–3, 85,90, 92, 123–4.
7. Dwivedi 2006, pp. 65–6, 68, 87.
8. Dwivedi et al. 2001, pp. 159, 164.
9. Ranganathan 2009, p. 207.
10. Dwivedi et al. 2001, pp. 164–5.
11. Chandavarkar 2002, p. 175.
12. Chandavarkar 2002, p. 37.
13. Apte, Mahadev (n.d.), p. 1.
14. Apte, Mahadev (n.d.).

Chapter 2. Tatya Returns to Bombay: 1892–1900

1. Dwivedi et al. 2001, p. 164.
2. Chandavarkar 2002, pp. 4, 239.
3. Dwivedi et al. 2001, p. 151.
4. Ranganathan 2009, p. 252.

5. Chandavarkar 2002, p. 41.
6. Information and quotes about the plague from Chandavarkar 2002, pp. 38–9 and 249.

Chapter 3. The Textile Years: 1900 Onwards

1. Bhabha 1950, p. 10.
2. Playne 1920.
3. www.killicknixon.com
4. Kulkarni 1979, pp. 308–9.
5. Parvate, c.1947.
6. Seshan 1950, p. 43.
7. Pers comm.
8. Bhabha 1950, p. 9.
9. Parvate, c.1947.
10. Bhabha 1950, p. 10.
11. Chandavarkar 2002, pp. 251–2.
12. Bhabha 1950, p. 12.
13. Chandavarkar 2002, p. 252.
14. Chandavarkar 2002, p. 26.
15. Chandavarkar 2002, p. 5.
16. Apte 1988.
17. Leadbeater 1992, p. 12.
18. Special correspondent, *The Hindu* 2005.
19. Playne 1920.
20. Pearce 1930, p. 264.
21. The Millowners' Association of Bombay 1925–51.
22. Chandavarkar 2002, pp. 172–3.
23. Chandavarkar 2002, p. 25.
24. Apte 2015, pp. 18–9.
25. Morris 1965, p. 36.
26. D'Monte 2002, p. 199.
27. Karan Grover cited in D'Monte 2002, pp. 202–3.
28. Upadhyay 2004, pp. 83–4.
29. www.morarjee.com/history.
30. Millowners Association of Bombay 1936, p. 13.
31. Joshi 1978, pp. 6–7.
32. S.K. Kasliwal, pers. comm.
33. Bhabha 1950, p. 10.

34. Chandavarkar 2002, p. 41.

Chapter 4. The Film Industry Years: 1917–32

1. Parvate, c. 1947.
2. Dharap 1970, p. 61 and Dharap 1980, p. 29.
3. Dharamsey 2013a.
4. British Film Institute. N.d. Short film.
5. Washikar 1970, pp. 117–9.
6. Chabria 2013a, pp. 3–6.
7. Chabria 2013a, p. 6.
8. Chabria 2013a, p. 7.
9. Dharap 1980.
10. Information from an advertisement for the film reproduced in the Phalke Centenary Souvenir 1970.
11. Rangoonwalla 1964, p. 83.
12. Phalke 1917a, p. 89.
13. Dharap 1970, p. 59 and Wadia 1980, p. 93.
14. Quoted in Dharap 1970, p. 59.
15. Dharap 1970, p. 60.
16. Gangadhar Pathak, quoted in Watwe 2004, p. 124.
17. Watwe 2004, p. 69.
18. Louis, c.1979.
19. Indian Cinematograph Committee 1928d, pp. 874–5, 878.
20. Dharap 1970, p. 60.
21. Watwe 2004, p. 69.
22. Indian Cinematograph Committee 1928a, p. 198.
23. Watwe 2004, p. 70.
24. Chabria 2013b, p. 62.
25. Watwe 2004, p. 71.
26. Dharap 1980, p. 31.
27. Louis, c. 1979.
28. Watwe 2004, p. 73.
29. Quoted in Chabria 2013b, p. 50.
30. Watwe 2004, p. 74.
31. The information about Phalke's relationship with the Hindustan Film Company and its partners is from Watwe 2004, pp. 69–70 and pp. 74–7.
32. Phalke 1970, p. 107.

33. Dharap 1980.
34. Dharap 1980.
35. Louis, c.1979.
36. Watwe 2004, p. 80.
37. Louis, c.1979.
38. Watwe 2004, p. 80.
39. Quoted in Watwe 2004, p. 123.
40. Phalke 1970, p. 107.
41. Watwe 2004, pp. 80–1,
42. Louis, c.1979.
43. Watwe 2004, pp. 82–3, 85, 98.
44. Watwe 2004, pp. 82–3.
45. Dharap 1980, p. 29.
46. Chabria 2013c, pp. 43–80.
47. Watwe 2004, p. 86.
48. Gangadhar Pathak, quoted in Watwe 2004, p. 125.
49. Chabria 2013a, p. 15.
50. Chabria 2013a, p. 19.
51. P.K. Nair, pers. comm.
52. Indian Cinematograph Committee 1928d, p. 881.
53. Barnouw et al. 1963, p.39.
54. Watwe 2004, p. 118.
55. Watwe 2004, p. 127 and Dharap 1970, p. 60.
56. P.K. Nair, pers. comm.
57. Mohan 1980, p. 89.
58. Mohan 1980, p. 89.
59. Indian Cinematograph Committee 1928a, p. 38.
60. Watwe 2004, p. 129.
61. Shinde and Tambat quoted in Watwe 2004, pp. 129 and 131.
62. Dharamsey 2013b, p. 69.
63. P.K. Nair, pers. comm.
64. Bahadur et al. 1980, p. 24.
65. Da Cunha 1980, p. 83.
66. Bhaskaran 1980, p. 64.
67. Phalke 1918a, pp. 96–100.
68. Indian Cinematograph Committee 1928d, pp. 870–3.
69. Rangoonwalla 2003.
70. Indian Cinematograph Committee 1928a, pp. 23, 37.

71. Indian Cinematograph Committee 1928d, pp. 871, 869–85, 883.
72. Nihalani 2003.
73. Da Cunha 1980, p. 82.
74. Nihalani 2003.
75. Chabria 2013a, p. 19.
76. Indian Cinematograph Committee 1928b, p. 178.
77. Bhaskaran 1980, p. 63.
78. Chabria 2013a, pp. 22, 41.
79. P.K. Nair, pers. comm.
80. Chandavarkar 1980, p. 117.
81. DNA correspondent 2014.
82. Chabria 2013a, p. 20.
83. Chandavarkar 1980, p. 118.
84. Chabria 2013a, p. 7, 10; Chabria 2013b, pp. 48–9.
85. Chabria 2013a, p. 19.
86. DNA Correspondent 2014.
87. Da Cunha 1980, p. 83.
88. Indian Cinematograph Committee 1928a, p. 137.
89. Wadia 1980, p. 92.
90. Indian Cinematograph Committee 1928b, p. 1. Written statement of the Bombay Cinema and Theatres Trade Association.
91. Chabria 2013a, p. 20.
92. Indian Cinematograph Committee 1928a, p. 41.
93. Wadia 1980, pp. 91–3.
94. Watwe 2004, pp. 87, 119.
95. Watwe 2004, p. 88.
96. Gvalani 1938, p. 122.
97. Anon 1913a, p. 20.
98. Information on the making of Setu Bandhan from Watwe 2004, pp. 90, 92–3, 95, 131. Gangadhar Pathak quoted on p. 125.
99. Louis, c.1979.
100. Watwe 2004, p. 95.
101. Dharap 1970, p. 61 and Dharap 1980, p. 29.
102. Rangoonwalla 2003.
103. Parvate, c.1947.
104. Phalke n.d., pp. 102–3
105. Anon 1938a, p. 19.
106. Bhaskaran 1980, p. 60.

107. Gvalani 1938, p. 115.
108. Louis, c.1979.

Chapter 5. The Phaltan Sugar Years: 1932–52

1. Apte 1988, p. 42.
2. Attwood 1992, pp. 22–3.
3. Information about the landscape, agriculture, irrigation, sugarcane farming and history of Phaltan and the Deccan is from Attwood 1992, pp. 22–3, 53–5, 59–61, 66, 69.
4. Kansal 1997.
5. Attwood 1992, p. 72.
6. Quoted in Attwood 1992, p. 86.
7. Attwood 1992, pp. 85–7.
8. Kumar 1980, p. 1664.
9. Attwood 1992, pp. 87–8.
10. Information about Tatya's initial foray into the sugar business and interaction with the Phaltan Durbar from Apte 1988, pp. 25–6, 42.
11. Apte 1988, pp. 4, 59.
12. Information on the railway line, irrigation, leasing of land and water works at the Phaltan Sugar Works from Apte 1988, pp. 30–1.
13. Apte 1988, p. 32.
14. Apte 1956, p. 36.
15. Kumar 1980, p. 1664.
16. Chandavarkar 2002, p. 41.
17. Apte 1956, p. 24 and Apte 1988, p. 32.
18. Apte 1956, pp. 39–40.
19. Apte 1956, pp. 11–2.
20. Attwood 1992, p. 193.
21. Apte 1956, pp. 22–4.
22. Apte 1956, p. 21.
23. Apte 1956, pp. 25–6.
24. Tunzelmann 2008, pp. 161–200.
25. Menon 1961, pp. 190–4 and Guha 2007, pp. 40–3.
26. Apte 1988, p. 51.

Chapter 6. Oil, Paper, Cans, Land: Other Business Ventures

1. Apte 1956, pp. 34–5.
2. Apte 1988, pp. 46–7.

Chapter 7. The Family

1. Apte 1988, pp. 1, 14.
2. Joshi 1978, pp. 1, 6, 10, 13.
3. Apte 2015, p. 59.
4. Apte 2015, pp. 48–9.
5. As per research done by Veena Singhal, resident of Woodlands Apartments. The Bombay Gazette date is unknown (Singhal c.1970–80s).
6. Apte 2015, p. 28.
7. Apte 1988, p. 3.
8. Apte 2015, p. 52.
9. Apte 2015, p. 27.
10. Apte 2015, p. 40.
11. Apte 2015, p. 60.

Chapter 8. Tatya and Kaku

1. Apte 2015, p. 45.
2. Parvate, c.1947.
3. Apte 1956, pp. 39–40.

A Note on This Biography

1. Holmes 1986, p. 27.

Appendix 1

1. Millowners Association of Bombay 1925-1951.

Appendix 2

1. Dharamsey 2013b, p. 129.
2. Dharamsey 1994, p. 69.
3. Dharamsey 2013b, p. 128.
4. Dharamsey1994, p. 71.

Bibliography

Anon. 1913a. 'Mr Phalke's moving pictures. Newsletter from Bombay.' News report from *Kesari* (Poona), May 6, 1913. Reproduced in *Phalke Centenary Souvenir*. 1970. Bombay.

Anon. 1913b. Interview with Phalke from *Kesari* (Poona), August 19, 1913. Reproduced in *Phalke Centenary Souvenir*. 1970. Bombay.

Anon. 1914a. News report from *The Bioscope* (London), June 4, 1914. Reproduced in *Phalke Centenary Souvenir*. 1970. Bombay.

Anon. 1914b. News-item from *The Bioscope* (London), May 28, 1914. Reproduced in *Phalke Centenary Souvenir*. 1970. Bombay.

Anon. 1938a. 'The founders.' *The Indian Cinematograph Year Book 1938*. (First Annual Edition). (ed.) Bharucha, B.D. The Motion Picture Society of India. Bombay.

Anon. 1938b. 'The promoters.' *The Indian Cinematograph Year Book 1938*. (First Annual Edition). (ed.) Bharucha, B.D. The Motion Picture Society of India. Bombay.

Anon. 1999. *Girgaon Ganesh: Phadke Shri Ganpati Mandir*. Shrimati Yashodabai G.G. Phadke Charitable Trust. Bombay.

Apte Kulvruttaant Samiti. 1999. *Aapt Apte: Chitpavan Kaushik Gotri Apte, Shevde-Apte, Dixit-Apte Yaancha Kulvruttaant*. Apte Kulvruttaant Samiti. Mumbai.

Apte, K. 1956. *History of the Phaltan Sugar Works, Sakharwadi*. Unpublished. Pune.

Apte, K. 1988. Personal memoirs, narrated to and transcribed by his son Anand Apte. Unpublished. Pune.

Apte, M. 2015. *As Luck Would Have It: Unplugged, Uncut.* Global Cricket School. Mumbai.

Apte, Mahadev. n.d. *Tatyannee Swatah Sangitleli Mahiti.* ('Information narrated by Tatya'). Air Press. Nagpur.

Astill, J. 2013. *The Great Tamasha: Cricket, Corruption and the Turbulent Rise of Modern India.* Bloomsbury. London.

Attwood, D.W. 1992. *Raising Cane: The Political Economy of Sugar in Western India.* Westview Press. Boulder, Colorado.

Bagchi, A.K. 1972. *Private Investment in India 1900-1939.* Cambridge University Press. Cambridge, UK.

Bahadur, S. & Vanarase, S. 1980. 'The personal and professional problems of a woman performer.' *Cinema Vision India: Pioneers of Indian Cinema, the Silent Era.* Vol. 1, No.1, January. The Indian Journal of Cinematic Art. Bombay.

Barnouw, E. & Krishnaswamy, S. 1963. *Indian Film.* Orient Longmans. India.

Basu, S.K. 1958. *The Managing Agency System: In Prospect and Retrospect.* The World Press. Calcutta.

Bhabha, C.H. 1950. 'The Story of the Cotton Textile Industry in India.' *Indian Cotton Textile Industry Centenary Volume 1851- 1950.* (ed.) Gandhi, M.P. Bombay.

Bhaskaran, S.T. 1980. 'Silent cinema in the South.' *Cinema Vision India: Pioneers of Indian Cinema, the Silent Era.* Vol. 1, No.1, January. The Indian Journal of Cinematic Art. Bombay.

Brahman Sabha. 1997. *Brahman Sabha Mumbai: Sanstheche Deepstambh, Kirtistambh, Aadharstambh.* Unpublished. Brahman Sabha. Mumbai.

Buchanan, W. 1960. 'My work and travels abroad: Part 1 - Africa.' Talk given to the Men's Club of Giffnock Congregational Church, 10 February. Unpublished.

Chabria, S. 2013a. 'Before our eyes: A short history of India's silent cinema.' *Light of Asia: Indian Silent Cinema 1912-1934.* (ed.) Chabria, S. Le Giornate Del Cinema Muto. Niyogi Books. National Film Archive of India. New Delhi.

Chabria, S. 2013b. 'Notes on the Indian silent cinema retrospective, Pordenone, 1994.' *Light of Asia: Indian Silent Cinema 1912- 1934*. (ed.) Chabria, S. Le Giornate Del Cinema Muto. Niyogi Books. National Film Archive of India. New Delhi.

Chabria, S. 2013c. 'The Indian Silent Cinema Retrospective, Pordenone, 1994.' *Light of Asia: Indian Silent Cinema 1912- 1934*. (ed.) Chabria, S. Le Giornate Del Cinema Muto. Niyogi Books. National Film Archive of India. New Delhi.

Chandavarkar, B. 1980. 'Sound in a silent era.' *Cinema Vision India: Pioneers of Indian Cinema, the Silent Era*. Vol. 1, No.1, January. The Indian Journal of Cinematic Art. Bombay.

Chandavarkar, R. 2002. *The Origins of Industrial Capitalism in India: Business Strategies and the Working Classes in Bombay, 1900-1940*. Cambridge University Press. Cambridge, UK.

Chaplin, C. 2003. *My Autobiography*. Penguin. London.

Chatterjee, S. 1999. 'The Culture-specific Use of Sound in Indian Cinema'. Paper presented at the International Symposium on Sound in Cinema. London.

D'Monte, D. 2002. *Ripping the Fabric: The Decline of Mumbai and its Mills*. Oxford University Press. New Delhi.

Da Cunha, U. 1980. 'Jairaj.' *Cinema Vision India: Pioneers of Indian Cinema, the Silent Era*. Vol. 1, No.1, January. The Indian Journal of Cinematic Art. Bombay.

Damle, M. 2014. 'When Jinnah represented Tilak for bail: Fiery leader was released on this day 100 years ago.' 15 June. *Sunday Times of India*. Pune.

Desai, C.V. 1938. 'The state and film industry.' *The Indian Cinematograph Year Book 1938*. (First Annual Edition). (ed.) Bharucha, B.D. The Motion Picture Society of India. Bombay.

Dharamsey, V. 1994. 'Introduction.' *Light of Asia: Indian Silent Cinema 1912-1934*. (ed.) Chabria, S. Le Giornate Del Cinema Muto. National Film Archive of India. New Delhi.

Dharamsey, V. 2013a. 'Filmography.' *Light of Asia: Indian Silent Cinema 1912-1934*. (ed.) Chabria, S. Le Giornate Del Cinema Muto. Niyogi Books. National Film Archive of India. New Delhi.

Dharamsey, V. 2013b. 'Introduction to Revised and Expanded Edition' *Light of Asia: Indian Silent Cinema 1912-1934*. (ed.) Chabria, S. Le Giornate Del Cinema Muto. Niyogi Books. National Film Archive of India. New Delhi.

Dharap, B.V. 1970. 'The Phalke Saga.' *Phalke Centenary Souvenir*. 1970. Bombay.

Dharap, B.V. 1980. 'Some important film makers of the silent era.' *Cinema Vision India: Pioneers of Indian Cinema, the Silent Era*. Vol. 1, No.1, January. The Indian Journal of Cinematic Art. Bombay.

DNA Correspondent. 2014. 'It died 30 years ago, will come alive today.' 2nd July. *DNA*. Mumbai.

Dubey, B. 2013. '100 years after first film, Phalke forgotten.' 28 April. *Times of India*. Pune.

Dutta, M. 2013. 'Touring cinemas look back at golden days.' 4 May. *Times of India*. Pune.

Dwivedi, S. & Mehrotra, R. 2001. *Bombay: The Cities Within*. Eminence Designs Pvt. Ltd. Bombay.

Dwivedi, S. 2006. *Premchand Roychand (1831-1906): His Life and Times*. Eminence Designs Pvt. Ltd. Bombay.

Fernandes, N. 2013. *City Adrift: A Short Biography of Bombay*. Aleph Book Company. New Delhi.

Gandhi, J. 2010. *A Tale of Native Towns of Mumbai: Bhuleshwar, Girgaum, Malabar Hill*. Jagdish Gandhi. Mumbai.

Garga, B.D. 1980. 'A new look at an old report.' *Cinema Vision India: Pioneers of Indian Cinema, the Silent Era*. Vol. 1, No.1, January. The Indian Journal of Cinematic Art. Bombay.

Gooptu, S. 2013. 'Silent knights and item songs.' 28 April. *Times of India*. Mumbai.

Guha, R. 2007. *India After Gandhi: The History of the World's Largest Democracy*. Picador. London.

Gvalani, G.R. 1938. 'Motion picture industry in India.' *The Indian Cinematograph Year Book 1938*. (First Annual Edition). (ed.) Bharucha, B.D. The Motion Picture Society of India. Bombay.

Hall, M. 1928. 'Transgressor. The Sailor's Lassie. Talking and Singing. Mr. Chaney. Other Photoplays.' *New York Times*. 22 October. New York.

Herdeck, M. & Piramal, G. 1986. *India's Industrialists, Vol. 1*. Lynne Rienner Publishers. Boulder, Colorado.

Holmes, R. 1986. *Footsteps: Adventures of a Romantic Biographer*. Penguin. London.

Indian Cinematograph Committee. 1928a. *Report of the Indian Cinematograph Committee 1927-1928*. Government of India Central Publication Branch. Calcutta.

Indian Cinematograph Committee. 1928b. *Report of the Indian Cinematograph Committee 1927-1928: Evidence Volume 1*. Government of India Central Publication Branch. Calcutta.

Indian Cinematograph Committee. 1928c. *Report of the Indian Cinematograph Committee 1927-1928: Evidence Volume 2*. Government of India Central Publication Branch. Calcutta.

Indian Cinematograph Committee. 1928d. *Report of the Indian Cinematograph Committee 1927-1928: Evidence Volume 3*. Government of India Central Publication Branch. Calcutta.

Indian Cinematograph Committee. 1928e. *Report of the Indian Cinematograph Committee 1927-1928: Evidence Volume 4*. Government of India Central Publication Branch. Calcutta.

Jasraj, M.P. 2015a. 'My father married the women he loved.' 4 November. *Filmfare* magazine. Mumbai.

Jasraj, M.P. 2015b. *V. Shantaram: The Man Who Changed Indian Cinema*. Hay House. New Delhi.

Joshi, P.P. 1978. *Parichay Aani Gaurav: Raghunathrao Balkrishna Apte*. Publisher unknown. Mumbai.

Kansal, S. 1997. 'Factors Determining Indian Sugar Production and its Comparative Advantage.' Paper prepared for the Sugar and Beverages Group, Commodities and Trade Division, FAO. In: *Proceedings of the Fiji/FAO Asia-Pacific Sugar Conference 1997*. https://www.fao.org/4/x0513e/x0513e16.htm

Karnad, G. 1980. 'Glorious Gohar.' *Cinema Vision India: Pioneers of Indian Cinema, the Silent Era*. Vol. 1, No.1, January. The Indian Journal of Cinematic Art. Bombay.

Kulkarni, V.B. 1979. *History of the Cotton Textile Industry*. Bombay Millowners Association. Bombay.

Kumar, A. 1980. 'Sugar Industry and Government Intervention'. *Economic and Political Weekly*. Vol. 15, No. 40, 4 October. Sameeksha Trust. Mumbai.

Leadbeater, S.R.B. 1992. *The Politics of Textiles: The Indian Cotton-Mill Industry and the Legacy of Swadeshi 1900-1985*. Sage. New Delhi.

Louis, C.A. c.1979. 'Dadasaheb Phalke and his financier Tatyasaheb Apte.' Newspaper unknown.

Majumdar, B. 2002. 'Cricket in Colonial India: The Bombay Pentangular 1892-1946.' *The International Journal of the History of Sport*, Vol. 19, Nos.2-3. Taylor & Francis. UK.

Menon, V.P. 1961. *The Story of the Integration of the Indian States*. Orient Longmans. Bombay.

Millowners Association of Bombay. 1925–51. 'The Millowners Association, Bombay, Cotton Spinning and Weaving Mills Working and in Course of Erection in India on 31st August.' (Foldout). *Millowners Association of Bombay: Annual Reports*. (1925, 1928, 1933, 1936–1951.) Bombay.

Millowners Association of Bombay. 1936. 'Arbitration Rules: Panel of Arbitrators.' *Millowners Association of Bombay: Annual Report 1936*. Bombay.

Mohan, R. 1980. 'The closely guarded secrets of the special effects men.' *Cinema Vision India: Pioneers of Indian Cinema, the Silent Era*. Vol. 1, No. 1, January. The Indian Journal of Cinematic Art. Bombay.

Morris, MD. 1965. *The Emergence of an Industrial Labour Force in India: A Study of the Bombay* Cotton *Mills, 1854-1947*. University of California Press. Berkeley.

Mujawar, I. n.d. *Maharashtra: Birthplace of Indian Film Industry*. Maharashtra Information Centre.

Nair, P.K. 1980a. 'Silent films in the archive.' *Cinema Vision India: Pioneers of Indian Cinema, the Silent Era*. Vol. 1, No. 1, January. The Indian Journal of Cinematic Art. Bombay.

Nair, P.K. 1980b. 'Titling techniques.' *Cinema Vision India: Pioneers of Indian Cinema, the Silent Era*. Vol. 1, No. 1, January. The Indian Journal of Cinematic Art. Bombay.

Nair, P.K. 2017. *Yesterday's Films for Tomorrow.* Film Heritage Foundation. Mumbai.

Nihalani, G. 2003. 'Through the viewfinder.' *Encyclopaedia of Hindi Cinema.* (eds.) Gulzar, Nihalani, G. & Chatterjee, S. Encyclopaedia Britannica (India), New Delhi and Popular Prakashan, Mumbai.

Oberai, B.R. (ed.) 1931. *Cinema* magazine. August. Lahore.

Parvate, T.V. c.1947. 'Maharashtriya Tarunano, Vyaapari Vha!' ('Maharashtrian Youth, Become Businessmen!') *Kirloskar* magazine. Bombay.

Patel, I.B. 1938. 'Motion Picture Theatres in India.' *The Indian Cinematograph Year Book 1938.* (First Annual Edition). (ed.) Bharucha, B.D. The Motion Picture Society of India. Bombay.

Pearce, A.S. 1930. *The Cotton Industry of India: Being the Report of the Journey to India.* Taylor, Garnett, Evans & Co. Manchester.

Pfeiffer, L. 1925. 'The Jazz Singer.' *Encyclopaedia Britannica* online. www.britannica.com/topic/The-Jazz-Singer-film-1927.

Phalke, B. 1970. 'Last days of my father.' *Phalke Centenary Souvenir.* 1970. Bombay.

Phalke, D. 1917a. 'Indian Cinema—I'. Article in *Navyug* (Bombay), November. Reproduced in *Phalke Centenary Souvenir.* 1970. Bombay.

Phalke, D. 1917b. 'Indian Cinema—II'. Article in *Navyug* (Bombay), December. Reproduced in *Phalke Centenary Souvenir.* 1970. Bombay.

Phalke, D. 1918a. 'Indian Cinema—III'. Article in *Navyug* (Bombay), February. Reproduced in *Phalke Centenary Souvenir.* 1970. Bombay.

Phalke, D. 1918b. 'Indian Cinema—IV'. Article in *Navyug* (Bombay), September. Reproduced in *Phalke Centenary Souvenir.* 1970. Bombay.

Phalke, D. 1936. Article in *Kala Bhavan* magazine (Baroda), Diamond Jubilee Number. Reproduced in *Phalke Centenary Souvenir.* 1970. Bombay.

Phalke, D. n.d. 'Ladies from cultured families for acting in films.' Talk by DG Phalke. Reproduced in *Phalke Centenary Souvenir.* 1970. Bombay.

Phalke, S. 1970. 'Remembrances of my father.' *Phalke Centenary Souvenir*. Bombay.

Phalke, Saraswatibai. n.d. 'The Words of Mrs Phalke.' *Phalke Centenary Souvenir*. 1970. Bombay.

Playne, S. 1920. *The Bombay Presidency, the United Provinces, the Punjab, Etc: Their History, People, Commerce and Natural Resources*. Foreign and Colonial Compiling and Publishing Co. London.

Ranganathan, M. (ed. and trans.) 2009. *Govind Narayan's Mumbai: An Urban Biography from 1863*. Anthem Press. London.

Rangoonwalla, F. 1964. 'When Raja Harishchandra was released and how it ran.' *Phalke Centenary Souvenir*. 1970. Bombay.

Rangoonwalla, F. 1980. 'Deities of the days gone by.' *Cinema Vision India: Pioneers of Indian Cinema, the Silent Era*. Vol. 1, No.1, January. The Indian Journal of Cinematic Art. Bombay.

Rangoonwalla, F. 2003. 'The Silent Years.' *Encyclopaedia of Hindi Cinema*. (eds.) Gulzar, Nihalani, G. & Chatterjee, S. Encyclopaedia Britannica (India), New Delhi and Popular Prakashan, Mumbai.

Seshan, P.A. 1950. 'The Financial Structure of the Cotton Textile Industry.' *Indian Cotton Textile Industry Centenary Volume 1851-1950*. (ed.) Gandhi, M.P. Bombay.

Singhal, V. c.1970–1980s. 'Woodlands Building on Cumballa Hill.' Bombay Local History Society. Bombay.

Singhal, V. 2016. 'Cumballa Hill.' Bombay Local History Society. Mumbai.

Singhania, P. et al. (eds.) 1948. *Handbook of Textile Industry 1948*. Bureau of Economic Research. Kanpur.

Special correspondent. 2005. 'Sena leaders buy Kohinoor Mill land.' 22 July. *The Hindu*. Chennai.

Thomas, P. 1935. 'India in the World Depression.' *The Economic Journal*. Vol. 45, no. 179, pp. 469–83. Royal Economic Society. Oxford.

Tunzelmann, A. 2008. *Indian Summer: The Secret History of the End of an Empire*. Pocket Books. London.

Udeshi, J. 1970. 'Phalke… As his children see him.' *Phalke Centenary Souvenir*. 1970. Bombay.

Upadhyay, S.B. 2004. *Existence, Identity and Mobilization: The Cotton Mill Workers of Bombay, 1890-1919*. Manohar. New Delhi.

Verma, R.K. 2000. *Filmography: Silent Cinema 1913-1934*. Dehradun.

Wadia, J.B.H. 1980. 'Those were the days.' *Cinema Vision India: Pioneers of Indian Cinema, the Silent Era*. Vol. 1, No.1, January. The Indian Journal of Cinematic Art. Bombay.

Washikar, R. 1970. 'Shambarik Kharolika.' *Phalke Centenary Souvenir*. 1970. Bombay.

Watwe, B. 2004. *Dadasaheb Phalke: Bharatiya Chitrapatsrushtiche Janak*. National Book Trust. India.

Websites:

Killick Nixon: www.killicknixon.com

NL Group: www.nlpl.com

Morarjee Textiles: www.morarjee.com

Films:

British Film Institute. n.d. *Charles Dickens and the Magic Lantern*. Short film. https://www.youtube.com/@britishfilminstitute.

National Film Archive of India. n.d. *DG Phalke 1870-1944: The First Indian Film Director*. Includes fragments of various Hindustan Film Company films.

Hindustan Film Company. 1932. *Setu Bandhan*. Fragments. National Film Archive of India.

William Buchanan. 1945. *Cane Sugar Manufacture*. 16 mm. Filmed at the Phaltan Sugar Works.